RED HARVESTS

RED HARVESTS

AGRARIAN CAPITALISM AND GENOCIDE IN DEMOCRATIC KAMPUCHEA

JAMES A. TYNER

WEST VIRGINIA UNIVERSITY PRESS / MORGANTOWN

ISBN 978-1-949199-78-9 (cloth) / ISBN 978-1-949199-79-6 (paper) /
ISBN 978-1-949199-80-2 (ebook)

Library of Congress Cataloging-in-Publication Data
Names: Tyner, James A., 1966– author.
Title: Red harvests : agrarian capitalism and genocide in Democratic Kampu-
    chea / James A. Tyner.
Description: First edition. | Morgantown : West Virginia University Press,
    2021. | Includes bibliographical references and index.
Identifiers: LCCN 2020045743 | ISBN 9781949199796 (paperback) | ISBN
    9781949199789 (cloth) | ISBN 9781949199802 (ebook)
Subjects: LCSH: Agriculture and state—Cambodia. | Agriculture and politics—
    Cambodia. | Land reform—Social aspects—Cambodia. | Land
    reform—Political aspects—Cambodia. | Genocide—Economic
    aspects—Cambodia.
Classification: LCC HD2080.3.Z8 T85 2021 | DDC 959.604/2—dc23
LC record available at https://lccn.loc.gov/2020045743

Book and cover design by Than Saffel / WVU Press
Cover image: Khmer Rouge cadre poses in a rice field. Courtesy of Tuol Sleng
Genocide Museum.

To my beloved wife and partner, Belinda

Contents

Preface

Class struggle, Karl Marx and Frederick Engels write in *The Communist Manifesto*, results "either in a revolutionary reconstitution of society at large, or in the common ruin of the contending classes." [1] No statement better captures the tragedy of Cambodia under the Communist Party of Kampuchea (CPK). Between April 1975 and January 1979, the CPK, commonly known as the Khmer Rouge, carried out a class struggle throughout Democratic Kampuchea (as Cambodia was renamed) that led to the death of approximately two million men, women, and children—a death toll that accounted for roughly one-quarter of the country's population. Many victims succumbed to starvation, disease, exposure, and exhaustion associated with forced labor; others were tortured, executed, or outright murdered. [2]

The general history of the Cambodian genocide is well known. [3] On April 17, 1975, after years of subterfuge and armed conflict, the Khmer Rouge forcibly took control of Cambodia and embarked upon a program of sweeping economic, social, and political change. In the immediate aftermath of military victory, Khmer Rouge cadre evacuated Phnom Penh—Cambodia's capital city—and forced the inhabitants onto agricultural collectives. Hospitals, factories, and schools were initially closed, only to be reopened according to party dictates. The Khmer Rouge abolished religion. Throughout the country, Khmer Rouge cadre defrocked Buddhist monks, converted monasteries to warehouses, and targeted the Cham Muslims with genocidal intent. Senior CPK officials abolished currency and introduced food rations, and Khmer Rouge cadre forced the entire populace to clear forests, build dams, canals, and reservoirs, and grow rice in an effort to accumulate rapidly the necessary capital for industrialization.

Beyond these broad observations, minimal scholarship has addressed the inner designs of Democratic Kampuchea's agrarian political economy in a theoretically informed, empirically documented study. This lacuna is significant, in that most interpretations of the Cambodian genocide fail to articulate with any precision why the Khmer Rouge managed agriculture the way it did. Indeed, scholars frequently sidestep this question and assert that CPK policies were irrational, incoherent, or simply nonexistent. Here, I chart a different path, in that *Red Harvests* provides a critical account of the intended transformation of traditional farming into agriculture, for it is my argument that the establishment of state-run agricultural cooperatives is key to understanding the broader structures of the Cambodian genocide. More precisely, I maintain that the dissolution of the traditional Khmer family farm under the aegis of *state capitalism* is central to any understanding of the mass violence unleashed by the Khmer Rouge.[4] Briefly, *state capitalism* refers broadly to a political-economic system of governance whereby a ruling party controls the state apparatus and in turn manages the means of production in order to appropriate surplus value.[5] Such usage traces back to the early writings of Marx and Engels. In *Anti-Dühring*, for example, Engels writes, "the transformation [of capitalist enterprises] . . . into state ownership, does not do away with the capitalistic nature of the productive forces. . . . The workers remain wageworkers—proletarians. The capitalist relation is not done away with."[6] Engels's statement builds upon Marx's earlier observation that state capital exists whenever "governments employ productive wage-labor in mines, railways, etc., and function as industrial capitalists."[7] In other words, as Stephen Resnick and Richard Wolff explain, a "change in ownership of productive assets, from private to state, does not necessarily entail a change in the capitalist, exploitative class structure of production. When it does not, state capital(ism) is just the substitution of state functionaries for private individuals in the roles of capitalist appropriators of surplus labor."[8]

At the outset, a political economy of agrarian-based state capitalism in Democratic Kampuchea rings discordant with the prototypical study of the Cambodian genocide. Prevailing interpretations of Democratic Kampuchea and, by extension, the Cambodian genocide have downplayed the coordinates of the country's *existing political economy* in favor of broader yet unsubstantiated renditions of communism. In other words, scholars too often take as given the communist credentials of the CPK, thereby precluding a more nuanced and grounded assessment of the political economy of Democratic Kampuchea.[9] Studies, consequently, have not positioned Khmer Rouge policies and practices as forms of displacement and dispossession; studies also have not situated the establishment of cooperatives as a form of primitive accumulation.

Most scholars take as given that Democratic Kampuchea was anything other than capitalist.[10] This is no surprise, really, in that many pundits take as given the self-ascription criteria for so-called communist systems: a communist party *by definition* is one that claims to be communist.[11] In tautological fashion, scholars of the Cambodian genocide have simply underscored the apparent Marxist roots of the Khmer Rouge and proceeded apace.[12] Scott Straus, for example, writes, "the Khmer Rouge were Communist. Pol Pot was the secretary of the Central Committee of the Communist Party of Kampuchea (CPK). In official documents the Khmer Rouge referred to itself as The Party; its stated goal was to bring about a 'socialist revolution' in the name of the 'worker-peasant.' Numerous Khmer Rouge idioms and practices directly resonated with other Marxist-Leninist movements, especially Maoism."[13]

Certainly, the CPK was a self-proclaimed Marxist-Leninist party. In many public announcements and internal documents, members of the CPK depicted their revolution as Marxist-Leninist. On September 29, 1977, for example, Party Secretary Pol Pot made public the ideological underpinning of Democratic Kampuchea. "We have solidly laid the foundations of our collectivist socialism," Pol Pot affirmed, "and we are improving them, while consolidating and developing them." He continued: "We promote broad democracy among the people by a correct application of democratic centralism, so that this immense force will mobilize enthusiastically and rapidly for socialist revolution and construction, at great leaps and bounds forward."[14]

Having established the seemingly obviousness of the CPK's Marxist foundations, scholars thus attempt to define the coordinates of Democratic Kampuchea's leftist political economy. Indeed, most scholars debate the type—or degree—of socialism or communism evinced by the CPK rather than questioning whether Democratic Kampuchea was even socialist or communist. To this end, the CPK has variously and uncritically been described as simply "Marxist" or some variation thereof, including "Marxist-Leninist," "Marxist-Leninist-Maoist," and even "ultra-Maoist." Leo Cherne, for example, concludes that the establishment of Democratic Kampuchea constituted "the creation of the first pure Communist society anywhere in the world," a sentiment echoed by Boraden Nhem, who writes that the Khmer Rouge regime was "determined to reorganize society into a pure communist society."[15] For Peter Owens, "The CPK sought to rapidly reshape Cambodia . . . into the purest manifestation of agrarian socialism in the world," and for Werner Draguhn, the aim of the Khmer Rouge of "creating a 'pure' communist society was pursued in an extremely radical way."[16] These exercises in political linguistics provide little interpretive value when analyzing the material practices initiated and carried out by the CPK. Documentary evidence reveals that previous interpretations are sorely lacking in theoretical nuance, thereby providing limited understandings of the intended and actual transformation of agriculture under the CPK. By extension, such narrow readings have distorted our understanding of agrarian transformations and, most directly, our understanding of agrarian capitalism.

It is less helpful to try to pigeonhole a priori Khmer Rouge ideology and material practice into idealized boxes, that is, to presuppose an essentialist Marxist, Marxist-Leninist, Stalinist, or Maoist doctrine and assess the purity with which CPK policies conform or do not conform to these archetypes. Certainly, it is necessary to consider, through empirical documentation, sources of influence on CPK policy and practice, but it is also necessary to position the Marxism evinced by the Khmer Rouge as distinctive. In other words, we should not frame the Khmer Rouge as Cambodian Stalinists or Maoists. We must evaluate the CPK on its own terms, but we must proceed with caution. Fundamentally, this approach requires a robust engagement with the theoretical substance and history of Marxist thought. As Lenin understood, "The categorical requirement of Marxist theory in investigating any social question is that it be examined within definite historical limits, and if it refers to a particular country, that account be taken of the specific features distinguishing that country from others in the same historical epoch." [17]

Marx's theory, Zehra Taşdemir Yaşin writes, is "neither a prediction nor a reflection of historical processes. Rather, it offers at once historical and logical categories, through a dialectical movement from one to another, and a cognitive structure that contextualizes these categories in order to understand and reconstruct history critically. His critical perspective provides a point of departure to understand and contextualize historical processes." [18] Building on this notion, my purpose is to provide a Marxist reconstruction of the CPK's planned agrarian transformation within Democratic Kampuchea while remaining sensitive to the *longue durée*, both of the growth of and opposition to capitalism in decolonizing states. Thus, my approach is not to view the historiography of Democratic Kampuchea as an aberration but instead as firmly embedded in the historical geographies of capitalism, the struggles against capitalism, and the reimposition of capitalism in the Global South. To grasp and to understand Khmer Rouge agricultural policy requires a clear historical sense, theoretically informed and allied to an awareness of the need to view Democratic Kampuchea in relation to other communist movements. [19]

Agrarian (State) Capitalism

In January 1976 senior members of the CPK codified their political stance and fundamental principles when they approved their party statutes. According to the preamble of the statutes, the Communist Party of Kampuchea "is the party of the worker class," and members of the CPK constitute "the most enlightened workers and peasants, walking at the very forefront, the most audacious and determined, and the very best of models." In effect, senior CPK leaders positioned themselves as the true vanguard of the socialist revolution and thus assumed responsibility for the transition of Cambodian society from an epoch of semifeudalism to one of communism. Crucially, the statutes affirm, "the Party holds Marxism-Leninism as the foundation of its views and as the compass for all its activities by lively implementing Marxism-Leninism in accordance with the concrete situation of Kampuchea, in accordance with the principle of connection principle with the concrete, absolutely, along the principles and stances of dialectical materialism and historical materialism."[20]

The CPK's explicit adherence to Marxism-Leninism is noteworthy and provides a key clue toward our unraveling of the Khmer Rouge's attempt to transform rapidly and completely traditional farming practices throughout Democratic Kampuchea. Throughout the unfolding of my argument, I read CPK agricultural policies and programs against the grain of Marx and Marxism in order to document the "actually existing" conditions of the political economy of Democratic Kampuchea. In so doing, my work aligns with prior scholarship that addresses "actually existing socialism," that is, the political economy of so-called socialist states, including the Soviet Union, China, and East Germany.[21] Simply put, to rethink "actually existing socialism" requires us to rethink "actually existing capitalism." We cannot presume to know uncritically what capitalism looks like in practice. As Jairus Banaji writes, "historically, capital accumulation has been characterized by considerable flexibility in the structuring of production and in the forms of labor and organization of labor used in producing surplus-value. The liberal conception of capitalism which sees the sole basis of accumulation in the individual wage-earner conceived as a free laborer obliterates a great deal of capitalist history, erasing the contribution of both enslaved and collective (family) units of labor-power."[22]

Precisely, my interest centers on the agricultural transition resultant from the Khmer communist revolution. Here, *agrarian transition* refers to "those changes in the countryside necessary to the overall development of capitalism or of socialism, and to the ultimate dominance of either of those modes of production in a particular national social formation."[23] In 1975, when the military forces of the CPK achieved military victory, the economic direction of the country remained very much in doubt. To be sure, the stated objective of party leaders was to build a communist society, but they recognized also the need to accumulate rapidly necessary profits to modernize industry. To this end, senior officials of the CPK confronted the "agrarian question."

Initially, the agrarian question had its origins in the concerns of Marx, Engels, and other writers in the late nineteenth century.[24] At first the question was narrow in scope and derived principally from an overtly political concern. Marx premised that socialist revolutions emanate from the proletariat, that is, as waged workers realize that capitalism is the source of their misery and alienated existence, they will rise spontaneously to overthrow the ruling class. Throughout Europe, however, most societies were still predominantly agrarian; capitalism had not yet rooted out and destroyed noncapitalist social relations, thereby attenuating revolutionary movements. Consequently, if—as Marx premised—the proletariat *and not the peasantry* was the dominant revolutionary class, the "agrarian question" was essentially a "peasant question."[25]

For Marxist theoreticians and strategists, the question derived from the political problem of how to capture power in countries composed predominantly of large peasantries.[26] Briefly, the basis for Marxist pessimism about the peasantry as a revolutionary class rests on both the nature of peasant social structure and the nature of peasant values. Marx perceived peasants as occupying two contradictory positions. On the one hand, as small property owners, peasant farmers would align more with the bourgeoisie, but on the other hand, as laborers of the land, peasant farmers might side with the proletariat. Given these opposing roles, orthodox Marxists tended to see the peasantry as unfit for a decisive revolutionary role.[27] Indeed, both Marx and Engels stressed the political apathy of peasants, a lethargy toward revolution born, in part, of their objective material circumstances as both owners and immediate producers of capital.[28]

Throughout the twentieth century, as Marxism underwent substantial revisions associated with the Russian and later Chinese revolutions, the agrarian question broadened in scale and scope. Marxists recognized social differences among the peasantry. They posited, therefore, that some agriculturalists, including small landowners, might exhibit more potential for revolution. Thus, while capitalism had not eliminated the peasantry as a class, capitalism was disruptive in its ability to create new objective conditions, some of which might prove revolutionary. Increasingly, Marxists of the early twentieth century countenanced the idea that peasants as well as the proletariat could populate a socialist revolution. Indeed, it was the peasantry, not the proletariat, that constituted the most decisive base of most, if not all, successful twentieth-century revolutions.[29] Consequently, in the aftermath of the Russian Revolution, Marxists of various stripes reformulated the agrarian question. No longer were debate and discussion limited exclusively or even primarily to agriculture alone but instead plumbed the interconnections between rural and urban economies.

For example, in an economically "backward" social formation dominated by agriculture, Marxist theorists perceived the countryside as an essential source of surplus. Thus, a reformulated agrarian question asked how agriculture could supply the necessary capital for socialist industrialization. The collectivization of agriculture was, in significant measure, a response to this dilemma.[30] This was the dilemma faced by members of the CPK.

An understanding of the agrarian question, the political economy of agrarian transitions, and the differing forms such transitions may assume requires a class analysis.[31] Class, as employed here, refers not simply to a cohort or group of individuals but rather to a relational process in society whereby individuals perform labor beyond (surplus to) that which society deems necessary for their reproduction. A class analysis, consequently, systematizes people according to their relationship to this surplus and asks, who performs the necessary plus surplus labor, how is this socially organized (and enforced), and how does the organization of the surplus impact society as a whole? In other words, the ownership of productive resources does not define a system of production; rather, the key definitional dimension is the organization of production and the distribution and consumption of goods and services produced. A capitalist class structure, for example, consists of a class of producers (wage laborers) who deliver a surplus (usually labeled "profit") to nonproducers (employers of wage laborers). Moreover, as capitalism is a system primarily based on production for exchange, a Marxist class analysis recognizes that different forms of labor, including waged labor, indentured servitude, debt bondage, forced labor, and even slavery may constitute *capital-positing activities*.

Differentiating one class society from another based on the forms in which workers produce, appropriate, and distribute surplus allows a better understanding of the constitutive relations of society.[32] As such, it is important to analyze critically the production and reproduction of agrarian social classes, that is, the political and economic forces that bring them into existence or make them disappear and that facilitate or impede their reproduction.[33] In other words, class struggle is inherently a relational process involving at least two sides: there exist, on the one hand, multifarious forms of resistance to exploitation and oppression, and, on the other, the equally varied means by which ruling groups work to maintain their positions and to contain or suppress such resistance.[34] In so doing, a class analysis brings to the fore questions of class justice, that is, a consideration of the exploitation of workers. However, we must remain mindful that questions of class justice entail both productive and distributive justice. Such questions, for example, ask about justice in production—are workers contributing according to their abilities, are workers alienated from the labor process, from themselves and from each other? In addition, class justice is concerned with the distribution of surplus value—are workers' needs met and are the needs of nonworkers taken into consideration?[35] Together, productive justice and distributive justice must buttress any discussion of agrarian political economy.

Few scholars have analyzed in detail the agrarian transition that occurred during the Cambodian genocide. Yet here is a situation, I argue, whereby a government set out to establish socialism but in the process imposed a variant of (state) capitalism. As revealed in the chapters that follow, despite claims to the contrary, senior CPK officials did not abolish class rule; rather, they embodied class domination. My approach, accordingly, differs but complements other renditions of the Cambodian genocide. To date, scholars such as Meng-Try Ea, Alexander Hinton, Kenneth Quinn, and Huy Vannak have written much on the direct violence unleashed by Khmer Rouge cadre and, in the words of Hinton, ask specifically, "Why did they kill?"[36] The act of killing, however, takes place against the backdrop of structural conditions and transformation. In *Red Harvests* I document and interpret the transformation of agrarian structures as guided by CPK officials.

Charting a Path Forward

Throughout the twentieth century, critics across the political spectrum have attributed all sorts of ills to Marx and Marxism. The genocide scholar Benjamin Valentino, for example, writes that the "communist utopias" of the Soviet Union, China, and Cambodia represent "history's greatest slaughterhouses."[37] However, as Terry Eagleton explains, "to judge socialism [or Marxism] by its results in one desperately isolated country would be like drawing conclusions about the human race from a study of psychopaths in Kalamazoo."[38] It is necessary to work through the fatal histories of so-called Marxist social movements, for as Henning writes, in many instances "Marx provided little more than the odd label, and yet he was made to serve as theoretical cover for what was being done politically."[39] Indeed, as comparative studies of so-called communist parties reveal, a formal commitment to Marxism-Leninism, for example, often may be no more than that—a purely verbal or perhaps opportunistic affirmation of support.[40] However, throughout the twentieth century, most so-called socialist or communist states, such as the Soviet Union, the People's Republic of China, and Democratic Kampuchea, were neither socialist nor communist—certainly not as envisaged by Marx.[41]

Few scholars have viewed the political economy of Democratic Kampuchea as a form of capitalism, primarily because few have chosen to look with unadulterated eyes. Let me be clear: the CPK did not intend to establish a system of agrarian capitalism. I do accept that senior officials and quite possibly many midlevel cadre steadfastly believed both in the revolution and in the purity of the revolution. The accompanying violence is testimony to the desire to maintain, in their view, a clear and unsullied path toward socialism. To this end, CPK officials sought to make a great leap forward, that is, to skip over capitalism altogether. Nevertheless, I argue that in practice the CPK initiated a process that rapidly transformed a society composed overwhelmingly of traditional farming practices into one dominated by the dictates and logics of agrarian capitalism. Effectively, the transformation of Khmer society initiated by the CPK leadership had several unintended consequences, notably the subsumption of precapitalist social relations to capitalism. This, I hasten to add, is not to excuse the Khmer Rouge for genocide and crimes against humanity. The policies introduced—for example, the collectivization of the peasantry, the abolition of currency, and the imposition of forced labor and food rations—were assuredly intentional and so too the famine and purges that followed avoidable. Rather, the unintended consequence, and the paradox of the Cambodian genocide, is that the CPK erected the scaffolding of a capitalist mode of production in its effort to foment a socialist revolution. This paradox, however, is only visible if we take seriously the CPK's stated objective of accumulating capital. In so doing, we derive a radical reinterpretation of the political economy of Democratic Kampuchea, thereby permitting us to evaluate the Cambodian genocide within the framework of state capitalism and not some variant of socialism or communism. Thus, in adopting a Marxist critique of a self-proclaimed Marxist party, we see that the master's tools may indeed dismantle the master's house.

Chapter 1 provides a historical account of the Khmer Rouge revolution. When revolutionary forces captured the capital city of Phnom Penh, on April 17, 1975, the CPK enjoyed neither widespread support nor trust among the citizens of Cambodia. Indeed, while people were all too aware of the Khmer Rouge, most had little or no knowledge of the existence of the CPK. This was to be expected. Secrecy on behalf of the Khmer Rouge during the revolution was deliberate and calculated. Reflecting its Marxist-Leninist foundation, the CPK viewed itself as a vanguard of Khmer society and understood its self-appointed role as one of a revolutionary mentor. Indeed, many if not the majority of Khmer Rouge recruits joined not out of ideological commitment to communism but rather for myriad reasons that centered, on the one hand, on widespread aerial bombing the United States conducted in the course of the war against Vietnam and, on the other hand, the restoration of the former monarch.

Having established the framework of the Cambodian communist revolution, I turn next to the international dimensions of the CPK's state-building efforts. Scholars routinely cast the political economy of Democratic Kampuchea and the Cambodian genocide at the scale of the domestic. Indeed, continued references to "autogenocide," that is, Khmer killing Khmer, solidifies the notion that internal factors largely account for the violence that transpired between 1975 and 1979. To this, there is the added belief that the CPK steadfastly refused to participate in international relations and eschewed any participation in the global economy. Such pronouncements are patently false and obfuscate the decidedly global context of CPK postrevolutionary policy and practice. As such, chapter 2 provides a discussion of CPK government set within the context of the Non-Aligned Movement (NAM).[42] Consider, for example, the following remarks of Nuon Chea, deputy secretary of the CPK. In July 1978 Nuon Chea delivered a speech to representatives of the Communist Workers' Party of Denmark. He explained that the "strategic line" adopted by the CPK was that of independence, sovereignty, and self-reliance. However, he also positioned the struggle of the CPK in solidarity "with all brotherly parties in the world and with all peoples and countries in the world who oppose revisionism, imperialism, neo-colonialism and colonialism of any kind."[43] The remarks of Nuon Chea are telling in that they highlight the strains readily apparent in CPK policy and practice, namely the balance between external alliances and internal autonomy. International treaties and the establishment of foreign relations were not anathema to the CPK. Party members, however, exhibited caution before entering any diplomatic or economic relations. To this end, any analysis of *domestic* agrarian transformations in Democratic Kampuchea must remain sensitive to the importance of the CPK's governance as reflective of its greater, albeit selective, participation in the global economy.

In chapters 3 and 4, I document and interpret those domestic policies that directly led to the transformation of agriculture in Democratic Kampuchea. My guiding thesis is that the agrarian transition initiated by the CPK was incoherent and incomplete. In Democratic Kampuchea we have a nascent agricultural transformation based upon primitive accumulation, that is, the dispossession and displacement of the peasantry and the conversion of traditional farming practices into a system of production for exchange, whereby previously subsistence-based farmers became unfree laborers producing surplus for the ruling party. Specifically, I reconstruct Democratic Kampuchea's efforts to increase rice production to accumulate surplus value. The CPK, as described in its "Four-Year Plan" developed between July 21 and August 2, 1976, premised success on the achievement of two economic goals. The first was to serve the people's livelihood and to raise the people's standard of living quickly, and the second, was to increase capital from agriculture in order to expand industry. More precisely, increases in rice production would constitute a surplus to be sold on foreign markets in exchange for basic commodities and inputs (such as oil, chemical fertilizers, and pesticides), and manufactured goods (such as tractors and ammunition).

To meet these objectives, CPK leadership determined not only that did the amount of land under rice cultivation need to expand but that workers were required to increase rice production to a national average yield of three tons per hectare per year. Senior officials determined that improvements in efficiency realized with mechanical tools, chemical inputs, and scientifically bred seeds and the construction of large-scale irrigation works that could supply water to rice fields during the dry months of the year were necessary to accomplish their desired increases in agricultural productivity. As to the former, industrial workers in Democratic Kampuchea would manufacture tools and chemical inputs, or the CPK would purchase these from abroad using revenues from the sale of surplus rice. Improved varieties of seeds—some developed within the country with foreign assistance, others imported directly—were to be widely disseminated to agricultural collectives. However, a centerpiece of CPK policy was the practice of separating workers from the means of production. To this end, in chapter 3 I trace how the agrarian transformation in Democratic Kampuchea entailed the dispossession and displacement of Cambodia's population onto cooperatives and the subsequent conversion of traditional Khmer farming practices into a market-based agricultural system.

In chapter 4, I introduce and expound upon the concept of the subsumption of labor by capital within the context of CPK policy and practice. More precisely, I question the rationale behind the party's decision to abolish money and thus consider in-depth the consequences of this decision. Money, of course, is merely the representation of value. Accordingly, when senior leaders of the CPK abolished—or, more properly, suspended—currency, they failed to sunder the fundamental class relation between those who control the means of production and the immediate producers. I argue that the Khmer Rouge established a fatal contradiction based on the introduction of food rations (i.e., the literal consumption of rice), the concurrent abolishment of currency, and the export of rice (i.e., the economic consumption, or valorization, of commodities). In so doing I circle back, so to speak, to the fundamental articulation of agrarian capitalism and, more broadly, the degree to which CPK officials commodified agriculture despite the prohibition of private ownership and the lack of a monetary economy. Effectively, in chapter 4 I theorize the dialectics of consumption and production in Democratic Kampuchea, with an emphasis on the promotion of relative as opposed to absolute surplus labor. Crucially, this move enables me to highlight the transformed social organization of production and consumption and to demonstrate how CPK economic policies sutured a nascent commodification of labor power in Democratic Kampuchea.

Overall, *Red Harvests* contributes to the small but vibrant literature on the political economy of genocide, specifically through an understanding of Khmer Rouge agricultural policies. Scholars of genocide have long recognized the importance of state functions. Early on, both Zygmunt Bauman and Irving Horowitz made important contributions toward the statist character of genocide and the technological methods that transformed "nightmares into realities."[44] Recent work has continued to analyze the myriad ways genocide (and mass violence) is functionally useful for state actors.[45] Mark Levene, for example, argues, "States commit genocide because they see it as being in their developmental interests to do so."[46] In other words, there is often an economic "rationality" underlying the seemingly irrationality of misery, suffering, and death. Philip Verwimp explains, rationality in economics is different from rationality in everyday parlance. It does not mean thoughtful, smart or nice thinking but instead means that state actors will use available resources to achieve specific goals.[47] As such, state actors impose particular development policies and programs based on the premise that such efforts will "make the state and nation stronger, more streamlined, more capable of surviving the vicissitudes of a harsh international political economy, even enabling it to compete more effectively within it." Building on this scholarship, I reposition the Cambodian genocide within a political economy of rice production. The CPK leadership believed its socialist revolution to be unique and that they alone were able to foment a "super great leap forward," bypassing capitalism altogether in their establishment of socialism. Specific agricultural policies, party leaders envisioned, would provide a means to catch up—indeed, to surpass—and make good what they perceived as lost ground in a postcolonial global economy.[48] Unexpectedly, though, party policy led Khmer society relentlessly toward a mode of production most appropriately framed as agrarian capitalism.

Acknowledgments

I first visited Cambodia nearly two decades ago. I was struck then and continue to be captivated by the myriad agricultural transformations of the country, of the rice paddies and fishing villages and the complexity of food production. My observations of contemporary practices, however, were always informed by questions more historical in nature, of how agriculture factored into the years of violence during the Cambodian genocide. It is well established, for example, that the export of state-confiscated rice contributed to widespread famine and that the policies of currency abolition and forced collectivization contributed to the suffering endured by the people of Cambodia. Why, I wondered, were these policies pursued, and how did these fit into the longer history of state-led communism? The pursuit of these questions forms the foundation of *Red Harvests*.

I am deeply appreciative to Derek Krissoff for his support and encouragement of this project. We've coordinated on several projects over the years, and as always, he provides the necessary support and key insight to turn a mélange of disparate thoughts into a coherent story. Thanks also are extended to Charlotte Vester and the entire staff at West Virginia University Press who shepherded the manuscript from initial proposal submission through final production. Thanks also are given to the editorial board at West Virginia University Press and the anonymous reviewers who provided critical feedback. At Kent State University I express my appreciation to Jim Blank, Todd Diacon, Marcello Fantoni, Mandy Munro-Stasiuk, and Scott Sheridan for their continued support of my research. In Cambodia I am indebted to Youk Chhang and the staff at the Documentation Center of Cambodia and also to Visoth Chhay and the staff at the Tuol Sleng Genocide Museum for their support and generous provision of materials over the years. I humbly offer my thanks to both institutions. Special thanks are also offered to Sokvisal Kimsroy and Chhunly Chhay for their help; I wish them, and their new daughter, much joy in the years to come.

Over the years I have benefited immeasurably from critical feedback and comments of many students at Kent State: Gabriela Brindis Alvarez, Alex Colucci, Gordon Cromley, Christabel Devadoss, Hanieh Hajj Molana, Kathryn Hannum, Sam Henkin, Josh Inwood, Robert Kruse, Kok-Chhay Ly, Mark Rhodes, Stian Rice, Savina Sirik, Dave Stasiuk, Rachel Will, and Chris Willer. I have also drawn inspiration from and have been challenged in my thinking through conversations, both actual and virtual, with innumerable scholars over the years, including Derek Alderman, Caroline Bennet, Stéphanie Benzaquen-Gautier, Noel Castree, Youk Chhang, Visoth Chhay, Randle DeFalco, Khamboly Dy, Craig Etcheson, Julie Fleischman, Jim Glassman, Steve Heder, Rachel Hughes, Helen Jarvis, Ben Kiernan, Caroline Laurent, Dany Long, Andrew Mertha, Don Mitchell, Anne-Laure Porée, Vicente Sánchez-Biosca, Ian Shaw, Simon Springer, Sarah Williams, and Melissa Wright.

I would not be a geographer were it not for the inspiration of my parents, Dr. Gerald Tyner and Dr. Judith Tyner; I am so grateful for their support and encouragement. My daughters, Jessica and Anica Lyn, continue to provide encouragement, if only as a reminder of the challenges confronting the next generation. Sadly, during the writing of this book, my eighteen-year-old dog and best friend, Bond, passed away. We miss him every day. Two new and energetic companions, though, have moved in: Carter, a three-year-old rescue dog, and Bubba, a three-month-old stray kitten. I look forward to years of their companionship. Lastly, I thank my wife, Belinda. The past year has been challenging both in good and not-so-good ways. Always, however, Belinda remains the beacon in our family, lighting our lives and offering support selflessly. It's been a remarkable journey of three decades, and I look forward to many more. It is to Belinda I dedicate this book.

CHAPTER 1

"Revolution Is the People's War"

Karl Marx, in his voluminous writings, proposed a scientific understanding of the history of humankind. He believed that historical change, that is, revolution, occurs when the relations of production impede the forces of production. In this way, every mode of production, as Marx and Engels memorably write, produces "its own grave diggers." [1] As class antagonisms harden, a revolutionary transformation is initiated that ultimately results in the establishment of a new mode of production—a new society, a new way of life. For Marx history moved according to the dialectics of societal change, notably of the transformation from farming to agriculture to industry and of the variable forms these transitions may assume. For the Khmer Rouge, however, the wheels of history turned only for themselves. A widely spoken slogan of the time goes, "The wheel of history is inexorably turning: he who cannot keep pace with it shall be crushed." [2] According to Henri Locard, this saying captured the sentiment of the CPK leadership that they discovered the "true meaning of the history of mankind," notably the "glorious . . . march towards a Communist society." [3]

In a speech delivered before an assembly of cadres in June 1976, the speaker, most likely Pol Pot, described the role of the vanguard in its liberation of Cambodia from its oppressors. In 1970 the speaker questioned, "Our armed forces were small. . . . The [outside] world said we were weak, small, few; how could we win?" He explained, however, "We had to have our own Party, our own army, our own people, and be our own leaders regardless of the difficulties." Two paths were present: "We could win quickly, in three to four or five years," or "the war could extend for ten to fifteen or twenty years." Opting for the first path, "We organized forces, attacked, and won in a period of five years. This was because of the Party. If the Party had not been absolute, with no correct line on strategy or tactics, we would not have won like that." [4] Throughout this speech, numerous themes are developed and repeated: that the CPK vanguard achieved victory through sheer determination, tenacity, and pursuit of a correct line; that the Khmer communist party fomented revolution without any assistance—including that of its Vietnamese counterparts; and that its revolution was unprecedented in both scale and scope. In many ways, the Khmer Rouge reading of history provides valuable insight into the specific policies and resultant programs that they would enact throughout their rule. Hence, in this chapter I provide a historical account of the rise of the Communist Party of Kampuchea. My purpose is not to provide an exhaustive chronology of the movement; that is a field already well plowed.[5] Instead, I want to interpret the Khmer communist revolution alongside a more conventional Marxist understanding of revolution—a task I hope will bear fruit for my subsequent presentation of CPK policy and practice.

Marx, History, and Revolution

Humans have developed different ways to work together to produce the things they need, notably, food, water, and shelter.[6] They have developed, in effect, different *modes of production*. Marx's clearest exposition of mode of production appears in his *Contribution to the Critique of Political Economy*, where he states: "In the social production of their existence, men inevitably enter into definite relations, which are independent of their will, namely *relations of production* appropriate to a given stage in the development of their material *forces of production*. The totality of these relations of production constitutes the *economic structure* of society, the real foundation, on which arises a legal and political *superstructure* and to which correspond definite forms of social consciousness. The mode of production of material life conditions the general process of social, political, and intellectual life."[7] Note, however, that the concept of a mode of production is an abstract and formal specification of relations that provides a tool for the analysis of historical and geographical experiences; it does not have any concrete existence in its "pure" form. Notably, there is no essential "capitalist" mode of production nor, for that matter, a "socialist" or "communist" mode of production. Bruce Berman explains that failure to recognize the conceptual limits of a mode of production leads to a desire to link immediately and perhaps superficial observable features of society directly to the defining features of various modes of production without setting them in their proper historical and geographical context.[8] As detailed later, it is mistaken to equate uncritically a few features of Democratic Kampuchea with abstract modes of production, such as Maoism or Stalinism.

With these caveats in mind, Marx presents a working model of society composed of two interrelated components: the base, or infrastructure, and the superstructure. The former, generally associated with economic, that is, productive, activities, is itself subdivided into two elements, these being the relations of production and the forces of production. The forces of production consist of humans (as laborers) but also the myriad means of production, such as raw materials, tools, and other instruments necessary for productive activity. The relations of production encompass specific class positions and their relations to one another, for example, peasants, serfs, slaves, waged workers, chieftains, employers, and so on. More precisely, the relations of production refer to the bonds that form between people in order to carry out production; these constitute, therefore, the social forms through which human labor and the means of production are united.[9] As Marx explains, "The particular form and mode in which this connection is effected is what distinguishes the various economic epochs of the social structure."[10]

Emanating from the infrastructure is the superstructure, comprising those institutions, relations, and practices that encompass politics, government, law, education, religion, and even the family. Here, it is important to stress that Marx does not say that the productive functions of society *determine* those relations and institutions assigned to the superstructure. Rather, as Ian Fraser and Lawrence Wilde explain, "The base-superstructure metaphor is used to offer a methodological guide to investigate how politics, law and culture develop in relation to the constantly changing economic structure."[11] Indeed, in the original German, Marx writes that the base "conditions" (*bestimmen*) the superstructure, thus positing a complex, dynamic relationship between the various components of society. In other words, Marx argues that people, working in and with a set of "social conditions of existence," create and shape the superstructure; the superstructure, therefore, is not determined in some mechanistic and autonomous way by the base but instead is produced by people within given enabling conditions defined by the totality of existing social relations.[12]

Every mode of production, Marx proposed, contains its own potential transformation. Following Hegelian logic, historical change—revolution— occurs when the relations of production impede the forces of production. As class antagonisms harden, a revolutionary transformation is initiated which ultimately results in the establishment of a new mode of production—a new society, a new way of life. It was at this point that Marx, based on his reading of European history, offered four broad epochs: primitive communism, slavery, feudalism, and capitalism. For Marx the designation of these epochs was not to develop a unified, linear metahistory but rather to call attention to the dialectics of societal change. Consider, for example, capitalism, an economic system in which the material conditions of existence are obtained primarily on the "free" market. Wage labor is a defining characteristic, as is private owner-ship of the means of production. Furthermore, capitalism is driven by certain systemic imperatives, namely those of competition and profit accumulation. Marx observed in England, France, and a handful of other European countries that capitalism had increased to the point that all basic material needs could be satisfied, yet throngs of men, women, and children lived in conditions of extreme poverty. Capitalists had enslaved the working class through their ap-propriation of the means of production and unfairly usurped the surplus value generated by the workers. Moreover, this form of exploitation was legal—but only from the standpoint that those who owned the means of production also had the means to determine law itself.

According to Marx, an exploitative system of production for exchange pre-cludes men and women—humanity as a whole—from developing an unalien-ated, un-estranged consciousness. As Ollman writes, "The human species is deprived of its reality, of what it requires to manifest itself as the human spe-cies." Indeed, the exploitative practices of a system built upon a system of pro-duction for exchange reduces humanity "to performing undifferentiated work on humanly indistinguishable objects among people deprived of their human variety and compassion."[13] Crucially, the fact that Marx locates the origins of alienation in the worker's relationship to work does not make this a narrow economic concept, in that for Marx labor is fundamental to every aspect of human existence.

Revolutions, according to Marx, are never simply about the seizure of power. This is a point that is all too often lost on would-be revolutionaries who see nothing beyond the immediacy of overturning the present form of govern-ment. For Marx the objective of socialist revolution, specifically, is the social and economic emancipation of the working class. However, the socialist revolu-tion also required (in today's parlance) a sustainable environment in which all humanity could live free and equal. To this end, we need to acknowledge that socialist revolutions, for Marx, constitute the restoration of an unalienated and non-exploitative metabolic interaction between humans and nature.

For Marx revolution in general refers to the processes of social change from one mode of production to another. More precisely, Marx postulates that revolutionary change is internal to society, based on the embedded dynamics of contradictions existing within each mode of production.[14] Class struggle, therefore, emerges as an inevitable feature of any society marked by divi-sions of labor. What, though, does Marx mean by *class*? Here, a social class refers simply to positions that people occupy in a system of production, in the broadest sense of both producing objects, that is, use-values, and providing services.[15] Societies of course divide along lines other than class position. Gender, ethnicity, and nationalism, for example, are significant markers upon which individuals and social groups identify and struggle; the key is to understand how these myriad subject positions intersect within any given society.

Each mode of production advances the material development of society, but only within the limits of existing social relations of production. When social relations hinder the development of material forces, class conflict and struggle results. For Marx revolutions are manifest in the material conditions—and contradictions—of society. To this end, in 1859 Marx outlined the broad historical preconditions for revolution: "At a certain stage of development, the material productive forces of society come into conflict with the existing relations of production or—this merely expresses the same thing in legal terms— with the property relations within the framework of which they have operated hitherto. From forms of development of the productive forces, these relations turn into their fetters. Then begins an era of social revolution."[16]

In reference to the emergence of capitalism, Marx explains, the modern bourgeois society that arose from the ruins of feudal society did not eliminate class antagonisms, such as the unequal relationship between lord and serf. Instead, capitalism established new classes, new conditions of oppression, and new forms of struggle. Marx and Engels elaborate: "Our epoch, the epoch of the bourgeoisie, possesses, however, this distinctive feature: it has simplified the class antagonisms. Society as a whole is more and more splitting up into two great hostile camps, into two great classes directly facing each other: bourgeoisie and proletariat."[17] In short, the fundamental cleavage of society, the basic and most defining struggle in capitalism, is the separation between those who own and therefore have access to the means of production and those who do not. This does not mean that workers and capitalists are the only classes in society. Marx never held a "two-class model." Indeed, he discussed at length other social groupings, including property owners, the petite bourgeoisie, the peasantry, and the lumpenproletariat. Marx did argue that there were two main classes—the bourgeois and proletariat—and the relationship between these two groups is primary "because there is a conflict of interest between workers and capitalists and because capitalists intensify exploitation in order to respond to competition."[18]

When Marx drafted the rules for the International Workingmen's Association (IWA) in 1864, he openly declared the primacy of the working class as revolutionary agent. "The emancipation of the working classes must be conquered by the working classes themselves," Marx wrote, noting further, "the struggle for the emancipation of the working classes means not a struggle for class privileges and monopolies, but for equal rights and duties, and the abolition of all class rule." Why, though, did Marx (and Engels) place such a great responsibility on the proletariat, the so-called working class? The answer rests in part on the alienated condition of the proletariat. In the aforementioned rules of the IWA, Marx explains that the economical subjugation of workers to those who control the means of labor lies at the bottom of servitude in all its forms, of all social misery, mental degradation, and political dependence.[19] This alone, however, is insufficient, for as Marx readily understood, many classes endure horrific conditions under capitalism. Crucial for Marx, however, was the fundamental contradiction that "by the nature of workers' role under capitalism—forced to sell their labor power in workplaces where they neither own nor control the means of production—workers came into conflict with the existing system and the bosses who own and control these workplaces."[20]

Capitalism enslaves and alienates the proletariat through the appropriation of the means of production. Class struggle in capitalism, therefore, emanates from the factory floor—that is, the point of contact between those who own the means of production and those denied. Because workers do not own or have insufficient access to the means of production, they cannot survive unless they sell their labor power to employers.[21] Capitalists, in turn, bring workers together in large workplaces, such as factories, where they must cooperate to produce goods or services. However, in the process, workers begin to view themselves in one another inside the factory; they *collectively* recognize their individuated, alienated lives. Subsequently, as alienation becomes more pronounced and capitalism produces ever more workers separated from the means of production, a working class materializes.

The proletarian revolution, in other words, pivots on a principle of self-emancipation. At some point, workers understand both that their options are limited and that their employers consider them costs of production to be ruthlessly controlled within strict parameters.[22] Workers begin to challenge capitalism because they seek security in their lives.[23] As Yates writes, "out of these realizations the germ of an idea takes hold." She elaborates, "As individuals, workers are powerless. But because they are so large in number and their employers so dependent on their labor, if they were to come together in solidarity, they could challenge the control to which they are subjugated."[24] Individual political consciousness thus forms out of solidarity while self-realization and emancipation proceeds through collective self-determination. The personal experience of alienation becomes the catalyst for political class-consciousness. Workers engage in strikes and other forms of work stoppages, and workers form unions and political parties, thereby expanding their concerns beyond the place of employment to affect regional and national affairs. In so doing, a revolutionary consciousness arises from the material conditions of alienated labor, paving the way for a communally based, postcapitalist society. Here we see the basis of Marx's famous dictum that revolutions are the locomotives of history. As workers recognize that the cause of their suffering, the source of their exploitation and misery, is not natural but instead social—a revolutionary transformation will arise.

The Russian Revolution opened a new chapter in Marxian political economy and effectively provided a blueprint for revolution where none had previously existed. As Michael Howard and John King explain, the immediacy of revolution and the overthrow of the czar placed the transition to socialism on the agenda as a practical issue. No longer was discussion of transitional periods an exercise in theory or speculation; revolutionaries in Russia confronted the stark reality of their actions. Indeed, the "revolutionary regime had inherited an economic catastrophe."[25] Consequently, events in Russia would dramatically affect subsequent revolutions throughout the twentieth century, including that of the Khmer Rouge.[26]

The Russian Marxists of the 1880s and 1890s unavoidably moved beyond the writings of Marx. Conditions in Russia were so at odds with the necessary preconditions spelled out by Marx that other measures would be required. Indeed, Russian theorists found little guidance in the writings of either Marx or Engels, certainly nothing that could address the dire conditions facing Russia.[27] Indeed, depending on one's perspective, in 1917 Russia was either the least industrialized of the great powers or the most industrially developed of the world's primary producing and exporting nations. In effect, Russia's economy was a motley amalgam of feudalist and capitalist forms. In industry and trade, for example, a limited number of giant cartels operated along with hundreds of thousands of artisan producers and market traders, and in agriculture, large latifundia existed side by side with millions of peasant farms.[28] Marxists such as Lenin, Nikolai Bukharin, Evgeny Preobrazhensky, and Leon Trotsky, among others, improvised policies and programs that often bore little resemblance to anything forwarded by Marx or Engels. In many respects, as Gramsci writes, the Russian Revolution was "a revolution against Karl Marx's *Capital*."[29] The practical result, John Merrington concludes, was "a catastrophic fatalism in the face of events, sustained by a blind belief in the "forces of history," in the inevitable collapse of capitalism due to its internal contradictions."[30]

Eschewing the spontaneous uprising of the proletariat, it fell upon Lenin and other revolutionaries to determine how to build socialism. To this end, Lenin favored the establishment of a subset of professional revolutionaries, a vanguard, whose task was "to train working class revolutionaries who will be on the same level in regard to Party activity as intellectual revolutionaries." Lenin elaborates that "attention must be devoted principally to the task of raising the workers to the level of revolutionaries, and not to degrading ourselves to the level of the 'laboring masses' . . . or necessarily to the level of the average worker." [31] Here, Lenin purportedly rejects Marx's postulate of proletarian self-emancipation. Lenin instead premises that workers cannot attain socialist consciousness on their own and that it is necessary for revolutionaries grounded in the theories of Marx to build socialism among the proletariat.

For subsequent Marxist-Leninists, the concept of a vanguard party was profound indeed. Revolutionaries (in both Russia and elsewhere) sought to create the conditions needed for a full and complete fulfillment of their ideals and to accomplish this in less time than Marx had premised.[32] In Russia the dictatorship of the proletariat became a dictatorship of the party.

The resulting idea of a dictatorship over the people in the name of the people was a radical, and tragic, redefinition of the meaning of socialism. Indeed, in 1904 Trotsky, in response to Lenin's forwarding of the vanguard, warned of the substitution of the party for the class, of the Central Committee substituting itself for the party, and finally of a dictator substituting himself for the Central Committee.[33] History would vindicate Trotsky's prophetic words, in the form of Stalin's Russia, Mao's China, and Pol Pot's Democratic Kampuchea. In name only were these totalitarian regimes Marxist.

The turn away from grassroots democracy toward the primacy of a vanguard marks a key transformation of Marxism. For Marx the socialist revolution was primarily about the negation of capitalism more than the construction of a postcapitalist society, whether we term this socialism or communism. Certainly, the ends and means are related, dialectically so, but the impetus is crucial. As Marx and Engels write in *The German Ideology*, "Communism is for us not a state of affairs which is to be established, an ideal to which reality [will] have to adjust itself. We call communism the real movement which abolishes the present state of things." [34] Thus, when Marx declares, "the philosophers have only interpreted the world in various ways; the point is to change it," Marx reveals his hand.[35] Marx's critique of capitalism was a condemnation of its inherent brutal contradictions, that labor under capitalism "produces for the rich wonderful things—but for the worker it produces privation. It produces palaces—but for the worker, hovels. It produces beauty—but for the worker, deformity." For this simple reason, Marx wanted to abolish the exploitative and alienating features of capitalism and to bring about a truly free, emancipated, and democratic society. The attempts by Russian Marxists—and the Khmer Marxists—to build socialism therefore constitutes an inversion of Marx's dialectics and a move away from his purpose. To build socialism is to engage in utopian politics, that is, an effort to will into existence, forcibly if necessary, a future society.

The vulgar rewriting of Marx after the Russian Revolution, however, provided a veneer of legitimacy to revolutionary upstarts and would-be dictators in that Marxism-Leninism came to define communism. The idea of socialism as the lower phase of and transition to communism based on state ownership of the means of production became the central and defining feature of socialist revolution throughout the twentieth century. Radical members of the intelligentsia accepted largely uncritically the inversion of Marx's writings by Lenin, Stalin, and myriad other so-called Marxists. This bastardized socialism, as Chattopadhyay concludes, had nothing in common with Marx's vision of postcapitalist society composed of an unalienated society of free and associated individuals with social ownership of the means of production and without state, commodity production, or wage labor.[36]

The Cambodian Revolution

The colonization of present-day Vietnam, Laos, and Cambodia by France began in August 1858 when a French naval force bombarded the Vietnamese port city of Da Nang, allegedly to obtain religious liberty for Catholics. The actual reason was to force the Vietnamese emperor to accept French trade and diplomatic representatives. By 1862 the Vietnamese ceded three southern provinces to the French, and over the next two decades, a French colonial presence encompassed the entirety of Vietnam. Administratively, the French partitioned Vietnam into the protectorates of Tonkin in the north and Annam in the center. The French ruled Cochinchina in the south directly as a colony. To these territories, the French added present-day Laos and Cambodia as protectorates. Together, Tonkin, Annam, Cochinchina, Laos, and Cambodia formed French Indochina.

The French emphasis on making Indochina self-sufficient and self-supporting contributed to wide-reaching and uneven transformations in local communities. Throughout the region as a whole, administrators imposed a new tax system, and officials established local budgets based on direct taxation to defray the costs of developing the entire colonial structure. High tariffs on goods imported into the colonies helped generate additional revenue, as did the organization of state-controlled monopolies that sold licenses for the production and distribution of opium, alcohol, and salt. In turn, these measures provided necessary funds for the construction of bridges, railroads, and harbors—necessary ingredients to exploit the raw materials offered by the colonies.[37] In addition, the French colonial government raised agricultural taxes and imposed a head tax payable in cash. This policy forced many peasant families to send their husbands, fathers, and sons to the cities, mines, and plantations in search of wage labor. In so doing, France created its own supply of surplus labor, for work in coal mines and rice and rubber plantations.[38]

Indochina as a whole would provide a source of raw materials for France, notably rubber and rice. The development of a manufacturing sector, consequently, was never prominent. However, French authorities approached the regional components of Indochina quite differently. In Cochinchina, for example, the French colonial administration adopted a narrow fiscal objective of balancing the colonial budget, paying the ever-expanding French administration personnel and, if possible, creating a profitable economy that would justify the costs of colonization. A major vehicle was the cultivation of rice for export.[39] Here, French officials introduced private ownership and the establishment of large landholdings. Collectively, these practices established the conditions conducive for social unrest. Rents, for example, usually represented 50 percent or more of the primary rice crop; moreover, loans extended for seeds, equipment, and draft animals could raise the property owners share to 70 or 80 percent.[40]

In Cambodia, French colonial authorities implemented a dual economic development policy based on the export of agricultural products, notably rice. Investors established large-scale rice plantations on land concessions, located chiefly in Battambang Province. To facilitate the distribution of rice, French authorities oversaw the construction of a rail line from Battambang City to Phnom Penh; from there, barges would carry rice to Saigon via the Mekong River. A second economic system consisted of almost the entire Khmer peasantry, who continued to grow rice using traditional methods on small farmholdings throughout the country. Here, the French acquired needed surpluses of rice through taxation; this became the largest source of governmental revenue.[41] Collectively, rice exports were to boost supply for the French agroprocessing facilities and international export trade system centered in Saigon.[42] In effect, Cambodia became a colony within a colony.

Throughout Southeast Asia, peasant rebellions were common occurrences. Even in the best of times, daily life was precarious, as farmers and fisherfolk dealt with the vagaries of weather and pestilence, environmental conditions that often meant the difference between feast and famine. Under the yoke of colonialism, however, conditions worsened with the imposition of high taxes, usury, land dispossession, and forced labor.[43] Anticolonial sentiment, however, emerged most vocally in the cities. Especially throughout Cochinchina, a grow-ing number of Vietnamese demanded greater political and economic opportu-nities. The men and women who formed the new intelligentsia from the 1920s onwards were products of a French educational system, with its emphasis on Western morals and values, and thus embodied the ideals of independence, liberty, and self-determination. Resentful of being second-class citizens in their own homeland, whether by reform or revolution, these men and women demanded equal economic and political rights. Most important, they began to agitate for a unified Vietnam, free of French colonial dominance.

In Cambodia political agitation was relatively subdued.[44] Chandler explains that French colonial rule "left most of Cambodia's institutions in place, and left most Cambodians alone, while insulating the people and their institutions from the political arena."[45] The vast majority of the Khmer remained rural, and, importantly, for the majority of rural Kampuchean families, land tenure was not a major problem. Most of the Khmer peasantry did not have a land-owning aristocracy pressing down on them, so French control of its posses-sions was largely secure.[46] This is not to present too rosy a picture of the French colonial presence in Cambodia. As Margaret Slocomb writes, "If Cambodian farmers were not actually starving, neither were they prosperous," and as a result, sporadic demonstrations and small-scale uprisings erupted in the early twentieth century.[47] Overt revolutionary activity, however, was restricted almost exclusively to the ethnic Vietnamese community, composed mostly of rubber plantation workers, government officials, and skilled workers.[48]

The Khmer communist movement was born in the struggle for indepen-dence from French colonial rule after World War II.[49] Composed initially of both communist and noncommunist factions, nationalist resistance groups—known as Issarak (Independent Khmer)—launched low-level, primarily rural campaigns against French oversight throughout the late 1940s. Increasingly, though, Vietnamese communists attempted to build a united front among the various resistance groups in Cambodia.[50] In essence, the Vietnamese communists believed that only the total defeat of the French from the en-tirety of the Southeast Asian mainland could assure their independence. The Vietnamese, to this end, provided aid to their Khmer comrades, mostly in support of their own liberation strategies. Vietnamese communists set up guerrilla bases throughout Cambodia, extending mostly over large areas in northwest, southwest, and southern Cambodia. Vietnamese cadre, working with Khmer, also established people's committees at district and village levels in many provinces in Cambodia and formed self-defense units to protect vil-lagers from the French army.

During the first Indochina War (1946–54), Vietnamese communists expected the Cambodian resistance fighters to model their movement on that of the Vietnamese. The Vietnamese cadre told their Khmer counterparts they could play a small but vital part in liberating Indochina, as part of a greater international movement capable of delivering equity and justice among the downtrodden nations.[51] In the process, Vietnamese communists gained more influence within the Khmer communist movement and subsequently utilized Cambodian territory in their own war against the French.[52] More formally, in 1951 the Vietnamese communists helped found the first communist organization in Cambodia, the Khmer People's Revolutionary Party (KPRP). The Vietnamese communities wrote the statutes for the KPRP and the draft platform, which they sent back to Cambodia for translation into the Khmer language and for approval.[53] Notably, the Vietnamese denounced Cambodian ideas of nationalism and local ways of organizing society as "feudal."[54] Indeed, the Vietnamese described the KPRP as "not the vanguard party of the working class but the vanguard party of the nation gathering together all the patriotic and progressive elements of the Khmer population."[55]

Official titles within communist movements are highly symbolic. Steve Heder explains that the Vietnamese choice of the formulation "Revolutionary People's Party" derived from Soviet communist terminology of the 1920s, according to which an external proletarian vanguard would lead a revolutionary people's party. Such nomenclature reflects a deep-seated chauvinism existing within the international communist bloc. The Comintern, for example, put forward the notion of a revolutionary people's party to apply to "backward," "primitive," or "tribal" areas; this reflected, in turn, "Stalin's conviction that the right of nations to self-determination should be understood in terms of proletarian self-determination, suggesting that those without proletariats had, at best, a qualified right to self-determination."[56] From the standpoint of the Vietnamese communists, material conditions in Cambodia precluded such self-determination. Relegated to second-class status, many Khmer revolutionaries bristled at this insult and thereafter harbored deep suspicions toward their communist neighbors.

As the fledgling Khmer communist movement actively resisted the French, Cambodia's monarch pursued an altogether different course of action. During the war, Cambodia's king, Sisowath Monivong, died and the French installed Prince Norodom Sihanouk to the throne. The move was surprising, in that Prince Monireth, Monivong's eldest son, was the logical heir apparent. French officials, however, determined that the young and inexperienced Sihanouk would best serve their interests.[57] Initially, the French were correct.

Throughout much of the war, Sihanouk spent his time in Phnom Penh and offered no visible resistance.[58] Far from the pliant pipsqueak the French believed him to be, though, Sihanouk quickly matured into a consummate politician. After World War II, Sihanouk adroitly bargained concessions from the French, including a written constitution that allowed for a democratically elected assembly in 1947 and, later, powers to set Cambodia's foreign policy in 1949. Domestically, Sihanouk marginalized political opposition and dissolved the national assembly in 1953 under the pretext of a national emergency.[59] Then, in February 1953, Sihanouk launched his "royal crusade" for independence. Traveling to France, Sihanouk avowed that he alone could establish a truly neutral and independent Cambodia. Moreover, and capitalizing on anticommunist sentiment throughout the Western world, Sihanouk hoped to demonstrate his resolve, promising a staunch anti-communist and pro-democratic agenda if only he had greater authority and freedom in his actions. French officials were nonplussed, but Sihanouk was determined and pleaded his case in Canada, the United States, and Japan, all the while affirming his anti-communist credentials and his ability to govern. The response of US Secretary of State John Foster Dulles is illustrative of most responses. Cambodian independence, Dulles explained, was meaningless without French economic and military support, for if left alone, communist forces would swallow Cambodia.[60]

Soon, though, the geopolitical winds would shift. As wartime costs mounted, in October 1953 French officials granted Sihanouk authority over judiciary and foreign affairs, as well as authority over Cambodia's armed forces. Sihanouk welcomed these overtures but saw an opportunity to push the envelope further. France retained an economic hold on the kingdom, especially the all-important rubber industry. Consequently, Sihanouk upped the ante and called for mass demonstrations throughout the country. Sihanouk's gambit paid off, and on November 9, 1953, Paris acquiesced.[61] Sihanouk's political maneuvering had apparently succeeded. The Kingdom of Cambodia was independent, and the expansion of the Indochina War into Khmer territory seemed to recede.

When Sihanouk secured independence, the future of the Khmer communist movement was very much in doubt. Sihanouk's crusade for independence had obviated, in the minds of many Khmer, the need for revolution. During the war against the French, most Khmer—including several members of the KRPR—were not fighting for communism; rather, the vast majority of Khmer resistance fights directed their revolutionary activities against French colonialism. To this end, as Chandler explains, most Khmer "were reluctant to become involved in rebellious politics after Cambodia's independence had been won."[62] Indeed, according to Chandler, the removal of the French probably meant little to most Cambodians, who continued to pay taxes to finance an unresponsive government in Phnom Penh. Consequently, because the people in the countryside had never been asked to play a part in any government, they saw few short-term rewards in resisting those in power, who were now at least Cambodians rather than French or Vietnamese.[63] Even had conditions been optimal, the Khmer communists were in no position to move forward. Numerically, the KPRP had perhaps a thousand members with another five thousand Khmers fighting alongside the Vietnamese.[64]

In 1954 defeat at Dien Bien Phu hastened the departure of France from Indochina entirely. The subsequent signing of the Geneva Accords, however, very much left the future of the region in question.[65] Most pressing was the decision to divide Vietnam into two political entities, the communist-dominated Democratic Republic of Vietnam (DRV) in the north and a US-supported Republic of Vietnam in the south. For many observers, the cessation of hostilities was but a respite as the region assumed greater importance in the rapidly expanding Cold War between the United States and the Soviet Union.

Military victory for the Vietnamese communists did not bring political victory. In the aftermath of the Geneva Conference, accordingly, the Vietnamese communists counseled postponement of the Khmer revolution until conditions *not in Cambodia* but in Vietnam warranted armed insurrection. Indeed, in their postwar planning, the leadership in Hanoi anticipated that communist parties in Laos and Cambodia would form the basis of parliamentary governments that would be independent but militarily and politically weak and thus reliant on the DRV for survival.[66] Simply put, the Vietnamese communists considered their revolution a people's democratic revolution, one that would sweep away feudalistic exploitation and build a foundation for socialism throughout Vietnam and beyond. The Cambodian revolution, conversely, was a national revolution, one that was not yet ready to build the foundation for socialism.[67] This meant, practically, that not only must the Khmer communists forestall overt revolutionary activities; they would also be required to support Sihanouk. Effectively, for the Vietnamese communists, it was imperative that Cambodia remain neutral—at least in the short term—to prevent the United States from establishing a base of operations on South Vietnam's western border.[68]

Meanwhile, Sihanouk capitalized on events to consolidate his own power in Cambodia. In 1955 the king sponsored a nationwide referendum, thereby cementing his popular mandate.[69] Next, in a surprise move, he abdicated the throne to contest the 1955 National Assembly elections as head of his newly formed party, the Sangkum Reastr Niyum (People's Socialist Community). Composed of various and disparate political elements, the Sangkum served as Sihanouk's personal vehicle to wield political power. Effectively, this ploy allowed Sihanouk both to enter the political arena directly and to preserve the monarchy.[70]

On the international stage, Sihanouk was committed to maintaining a neutral foreign policy, a stance marked by his 1955 participation at the Bandung Conference, whereupon he pledged his support of a non-aligned political-economic agenda. For Sihanouk Cambodia's very survival was continually under threat from its neighbors. Indeed, Sihanouk repeatedly described Cambodia as "a sheep surrounded by three wolves with long teeth."[71] Political events in Northern and Southern Vietnam, to be expected, posed an immediate threat, but in often complicated ways. For example, the existence of two separate Vietnams, north and south, posed one challenge for Sihanouk; he hoped to formalize the promises of both governments to respect Cambodia's territory and sovereignty. However, Sihanouk expressed concern over the prospect of a unified Vietnam. Here, Sihanouk's unease stemmed from the likelihood that a unified (and communist) Vietnam would emerge as a vassal of China. If this scenario materialized, only China could provide the necessary assurances for Cambodia.[72]

Far from a dogmatist, Sihanouk walked a fine line as storm clouds darkened the skies over Cambodia. On the one hand, Sihanouk welcomed economic and military aid from all comers, including France, West Germany, Australia, Japan, China, and the Soviet Union.[73] For example, between 1955 and 1963 Sihanouk accepted approximately US$400 million in military and economic aid from an increasingly skeptical and suspicious United States, an amount that constituted 30 percent of Cambodia's defense budget and 14 percent of its total budget.[74] On the other hand, while welcoming these funds, Sihanouk refused to enter into a more formal "security" pact with the United States. Such a move would have adversely affected subsequent relations with, notably, China, thus reducing significantly Sihanouk's room to maneuver.[75] Equally important, Sihanouk was suspicious of American intentions, believing that the United States supported and even encouraged Thai and Vietnamese incursions into his country.[76] Ultimately, though, Cambodia would only remain neutral and at peace for as long as its neutrality served the interests of other states.[77] Increasingly, this became more and more difficult as the conflict in Vietnam expanded in scale and scope.

From the signing of the Geneva Accords onward, insurgents in the US-supported Republic of Vietnam pressed the DRV for permission to wage armed rebellion and, repeatedly, senior leadership in the north refused these requests, worried that a hastily expanded insurgency might draw the United States into a protracted ground war. As such, the official position of the DRV was to limit revolutionary activities in the South to political agitation; indeed, only in 1956 were armed self-defense units formed.[78] Only in 1959 did the Vietnamese communists agree to the use of armed struggle with the founding of the National Liberation Front (NLF, colloquially known as the Viet Cong). Likewise, in Cambodia, Khmer communists agitated to wage armed revolution.

Conditions of Geneva Conference decreed that Khmer resistance forces would not be given control of any of their national territory in which to regroup; instead, they faced two unpalatable choices, namely to lay down their arms and participate in national elections organized by the Sihanouk government or retreat into exile in North Vietnam.[79] In the end, between one and two thousand Khmer communists traveled north to receive military and political training; these men and women would not return until the early 1970s. A second group of approximately one thousand Khmer revolutionaries remained in Cambodia. Of this latter group, some participated overtly in political opposition to Sihanouk while others worked covertly in an attempt to recruit party members. Significantly, this enabled the colonization of the KPRP by more radical members such as Pol Pot, Son Sen, Khieu Samphan, Ieng Sary, and Ieng Thirith. Unlike other veteran revolutionaries, these men and women had recently returned from university studies in Paris.

Pol Pot and other Khmer students had arrived in Paris when the political climate was vibrant and French intellectuals were shaping the themes that dominated postwar attitudes—a time when the French Communist Party was in turmoil following revelations of Stalin's atrocities. However, a burgeoning anti-Americanism replaced much disillusionment with Soviet politics. According to Becker, the Korean War, the American Marshall Plan for the reconstruction of Europe, and the continued American monopoly of the nuclear bomb combined to create an American menace in the eyes of many French Leftists.[80] This attitude permeated the youthful Khmer Marxists, a conviction that only deepened with overt American military intervention in Indochina. As such, they interpreted contemporary events in Cambodia and the world beyond through the writings of Stalin's "The National Question" and Lenin's "On Imperialism."

The knowledge and experiences gained in their studies abroad carried over to Cambodia. Pol Pot, for example, held semiclandestine seminars on civic virtue, justice, and corruption. Students, but also monks and military officials and bureaucrats disillusioned by the Sihanouk regime, attended many of these classes. Carefully, Pol Pot spoke of a new society but rarely mentioned communism. Pol Pot did not actively recruit members to the KPRP but rather encouraged participants to question and evaluate the political climate. Absent any direct support from their Vietnamese counterparts, however, the Khmer movement in Cambodia remained weak and vulnerable to intimidation and violence, as Sihanouk's secret police continued their suppression of known or suspected communists.[81] Betrayals and defections further hindered the movement. By the end of the decade, the Khmer communist movement lost nearly 90 percent of its rural cadre; some were murdered, many others quit from fear of retribution; and some simply disappeared.[82]

Since 1951 the Vietnamese communists had dictated the conditions of socialist revolution inside Cambodia. Military success in the south, Hanoi concluded, required the ability to provision the NLF and this required, in turn, continued access through Cambodia. In fact, even before the establishment of the NLF, military planners in Hanoi had initiated the construction of a series of supply lines through eastern Laos, the Central Highlands of Vietnam, and eastern Cambodia. Known as the Hồ Chí Minh Trail, this multicountry supply line consisted of thousands of miles of roads and footpaths carved out of dense forest vegetation whereby tens of thousands of men and women transported food, weapons, medicines, and other supplies. Eventually, fully armed North Vietnamese Army troops would utilize the trail to conduct military operations in both South Vietnam and Cambodia.

North Vietnamese access through Cambodia was conditional upon Sihanouk's assurance, or at minimum, his acceptance, of neutrality. This explains in part Hanoi's refusal to abide the demands of the Khmer Rouge. Vietnamese communists were unwilling to jeopardize their prime directive, a unified Vietnam. As such, when Khmer Rouge leaders requested support to move against Sihanouk, senior leaders of the Vietnamese communist party refused. To this end, the objectives of the communist Vietnamese and the neutralist Sihanouk aligned, to the frustration of the Khmer revolutionaries. This meant, practically, that not only were the Khmer communists to forestall armed insurrection, they would also be expected to support the ostensibly neutralist Sihanouk. For the Vietnamese, the brewing struggle against the United States was all-important, and it was imperative that Cambodia remain neutral—at least in the short term—so as to prevent the United States from establishing a base of operations on Vietnam's western border. However, Sihanouk's incessant purge of suspected communists coupled with his apparent deference to his communist neighbors hindered Pol Pot's efforts to expand their movement and, in certain respects, threatened to extinguish the revolution altogether.

In 1960 delegates of the moribund KPRP met secretively in a Phnom Penh railway yard to elect new leaders and to draft a political agenda. The meeting marked the first convention of the KPRP in nine years and, significantly, marked the first concerted effort to step outside the Vietnamese communists' shadow. Renaming themselves the Workers' Party of Kampuchea (WPK), the Khmer communists symbolically set themselves on equal footing with the Vietnamese Workers' Party. In addition, attendees agreed upon a platform that clearly departed from the Vietnamese by declaring Sihanouk and the "ruling feudal class" to be "the most important enemy of the Kampuchean revolution." [83] Party members appointed veteran revolutionary Tou Samouth as party secretary, with Nuon Chea and Pol Pot elected as the second and third highest-ranking members, respectively. However, internal dissent and growing factions hindered the effectiveness of the WPK over the next two years, until the sudden disappearance of Tou Samouth opened the door for Pol Pot and his allies to assume greater power. At a meeting convened in 1963, delegates formally installed Pol Pot as secretary general, and he, in turn, initiated a new course of incremental but unswerving steps toward armed revolution. [84] The vanguard, known as Angkar, had formed. Years later Pol Pot would explain that they had achieved victory through "the implementation of the Party's dictatorship of the proletariat in all areas of . . . revolutionary activity." [85]

In June 1965 Pol Pot traveled to Hanoi. He used the opportunity to conduct several lectures and study sessions about the political situation in Cambodia, to discuss the state of the Khmer resistance movement, and to coordinate tactics for the coming years. Additionally, Pol Pot presented to his Vietnamese counterparts drafts of his political platform, including a resolution that emphasized self-reliance and endorsing all forms of struggle, including armed violence. [86] Pol Pot likely expected support from his Vietnamese counterparts to make contingency plans for armed struggle in Cambodia against Sihanouk. At the very least, Pol Pot probably hoped to acquire weapons needed for revolution. [87] In the end, Pol Pot's expectations were unfulfilled, as his Vietnamese counterparts continued to view a neutral Cambodia as necessary to their immediate and most pressing objective of reunification. The Vietnamese leadership berated the Khmer communists for pursuing a nationalist agenda and for allegedly wanting to put the Cambodian revolution ahead of the collective goal of a socialist Indochina. Lê Duẩn, secretary general of the Vietnamese communists, for example, stressed that the Khmer's strategy of "self-reliant struggle" was inappropriate and defeating; moreover, as a revolutionary party the Khmer Rouge were subordinate to the Vietnamese and thus in no position to make such demands. [88] To this end, Lê Duẩn "recommended that the

Cambodians combine building revolutionary bases in the countryside through unarmed mass mobilization with continued infiltration of parliament and government, in order to position the Party to make a bid for power, perhaps through violence, once the Vietnamese had won the war."[89] Ultimately, Hanoi stressed the need for continued access to sanctuaries within Cambodia and for the ability to transport troops and supplies into southern Vietnam along the Hồ Chí Minh Trail. In fact, the Vietnamese communists had recently reached an agreement with Sihanouk that allowed the NLF access to Cambodian territory; in exchange, the Vietnamese pledged to honor all territorial borders at war's end. Given the enfeebled state of the Khmer resistance, the Vietnamese presciently believed that if anything should happen to Sihanouk, he would be replaced not with a socialist government but a right-wing regime that would ally itself with the United States.[90]

Having failed in his attempt to secure the go-ahead for armed rebellion, Pol Pot and his entourage traveled to China to meet with several high-ranking officials of the Communist Party of China, including Deng Xiaoping and Liu Shaoqi.[91] The Chinese communists viewed Cambodia as an important piece in the grand scheme of geopolitics but, similar to the Vietnamese, concluded it was not the decisive piece. Beijing did anticipate, however, a very different future role for the Khmer Rouge than did Hanoi. Although China and the DRV shared the goal of defeating the United States, they had divergent strategic interests in postwar arrangements. While the Vietnamese saw a united Indochinese communist front as the best way to guarantee Hanoi's regional influence, a diffused power structure among Vietnam, Laos, and Cambodia best served China's strategic interests.[92] As such, the Chinese counseled, the Khmer Rouge should suppress its nationalist aspirations for the greater good, that is, the defeat of the Americans. In practice, this meant not only that support for armed revolution was not forthcoming but that the Khmer Rouge could not strike against Sihanouk.

Although denied immediate support and assistance for armed insurrection, Pol Pot returned to Cambodia with high hopes. Proclaiming his alliance with China as the path to victory, Pol Pot informed his inner circle, "We need have no more doubts about the correctness of what we are doing."[93] To this end, in September 1966 Pol Pot convened a plenum to draft a new party program. The party officially changed its name to the Communist Party of Kampuchea, thereby elevating itself to the level of the Chinese Communist Party (CCP) and surpassing that of its Vietnamese counterparts.[94] More concretely, Pol Pot relocated his headquarters to the highlands of northeast Cambodia, a consequential move for two reasons. On the one hand, the relocation was practical, as the Khmer Rouge could avoid both increased US bombing and the coaching of Vietnamese counterparts. On the other hand, senior leadership of the CPK benefited from their everyday interactions with the tribal minorities among whom they lived. Over the years, the non-Khmer peoples of Ratanakiri, Mondulkiri, and Kratié had grown increasingly hostile to the Phnom Penh government, as roads, rubber plantations, settlers, and foresters moved onto their traditional lands. Importantly for the Khmer communists, however, the minority peoples seemed to offer an example of a pristine communal society, one that was uncorrupted by social differentiation or currency. Indeed, without access to money, markets, or the state, for Pol Pot and his associates, the inhabitants of the highland forests enjoyed what appeared to be deeply rooted traditions of autonomy, solidarity, and mutual aid.[95] These practical observations, read through the lens of Marx, most likely informed subsequent CPK policy and practice.

In 1967 localized protests broke out in rural Samlaut in western Cambodia against government-backed rice purchasing schemes, fed by long-standing resentment of government clientelism, corruption, and inequality.[96] In that year, and in response to a worsening economy, Sihanouk announced the devaluation of the riel and imposed a program of austerity. These policies had two immediate effects. First, merchants in Cambodia, regardless of ideology or loyalties, were anxious to sell rice and other goods directly to the Vietnamese communists on the black market because the latter paid for goods in American dollars at international rates. Effectively, the Vietnamese communists, having obtained dollars from Hong Kong through the Chinese embassy in Phnom Penh, outbid the Cambodian government in its own market. Second, the imposition of fixed prices discouraged peasants who did not trade on the black market from growing rice for more than minimal needs. In other words, the fixed prices established by the government made the legal sale of rice unprofitable.[97]

Consequently, desperate for revenues generated through the production and exchange of rice, the Sihanouk government introduced in 1967 a new rice collection system. Known as *ramassage du paddy*, government officials forced peasants to sell rice to the government at artificially low prices. Villagers seized arms, destroyed government property, and killed several government officials, sparking unrest in other provinces among the disaffected rural poor.[98] Sihanouk responded in force, ordering the Cambodian military to wage a bloody counterattack on the Khmers Rouges, a derogatory term he coined in reference to the protestors. Retribution became spectacle with the public execution of suspected leaders and the screening of graphic films of the killings throughout the country. Years later Sihanouk conceded, unapologetically, that the government was responsible for killing upwards of ten thousand peasants.[99]

For many among the rural poor, Manning suggests, the connection between localized experiences of state and elite repression and the attraction of a growing communist insurgency, which had called for a nationwide uprising earlier that year, was sealed from this moment onward.[100] Indeed, the violent uprisings were significant, but they also direct attention to the haziness of the Khmer communist revolution. Indeed, the protests caught Pol Pot and other members of the inexperienced CPK unaware. As Chandler writes, Samlaut was the product of "local grievances against injustice and social change, corruption, and ham-fisted government behavior." This is not to deny that leaders on the Left moved quickly to capitalize on the unrest. Indeed, in January 1968 leaders of the CPK officially formed the Revolutionary Army of Kampuchea and launched their first military operations. These were mostly small-scale operations, directed primarily toward the seizure of weapons from Cambodian armories, but marked a crucial turning point in the revolution. Ominously, the armed insurrections initiated by the Khmer Rouge after the Samlaut rebellion represented the end of an era during which Khmer communists dutifully adhered to a policy of peaceful resistance and political participation handed down by their "elder" brothers in the DRV.[101]

The establishment of the Khmer Rouge as a military force coincided with the escalation of the Vietnam War. Beginning in 1965, the United States engaged in sustained aerial bombing campaigns against the DRV, and the first contingent of US ground combat troops arrived that same year. Parallel to these actions, US military offenses conducted on Cambodian territory intensified greatly. In 1967 American military advisors initiated Operation Salem House, whereby teams of six to eight Americans and South Vietnamese would enter Cambodia seeking tactical intelligence. At first, these teams were limited in their geographic coverage, restricted to the northeastern tip of Cambodia. Over time, however, these operations (originally named Daniel Boone) expanded to encompass the entire Cambodian-Vietnamese border region. By October 1968 the number of covert missions had increased in both scale and scope. By 1969 US forces had conducted 454 covert missions in Cambodia.[102] More devastating, in 1969 Nixon approved Operation Menu, a highly classified military operation that would last for more than fifteen months, during which time American pilots flew more than 3,800 sorties and dropped more than 100,000 tons of bombs on the Cambodian countryside.[103] The objective was allegedly to eliminate NLF and North Vietnamese Army sanctuaries inside Cambodia and to destroy the Hồ Chí Minh Trail.[104]

The widening war heralded the downfall of Sihanouk. In 1970, while Sihanouk was traveling in France, republican forces under leadership of Lon Nol and the deputy prime minister, Prince Sisowath Sirik Matak, staged a bloodless coup. Matak, the most prominent of the conspirators, was impatient with Sihanouk's mismanagement of the economy and dismayed by the presence of Vietnamese bases on Cambodian soil.[105] The removal of Sihanouk from power dramatically transformed events in Cambodia. On April 30, 1970, Nixon authorized—with Lon Nol's acquiescence—the use of US and allied South Vietnamese ground forces on Cambodian territory. In less than a year, "events surrounding Cambodia had moved essentially full-circle. From a nation that physically had been relatively untouched by the adjacent war, Cambodia was transformed into the center of the maelstrom."[106] Indeed, as Laura Summers concludes, the coup alone might not have precipitated a civil war, but violent invasion made it difficult to avoid.[107]

Soviet reaction to the coup was tepid but calculative. Wanting to avoid either a US- or Chinese-controlled Cambodia, the Soviets joined other third-party nations calling for an international conference to restore order in Cambodia and to guarantee its neutrality in the Vietnamese-American war.[108] The CCP, also, recalibrated their approach. Committed to a postponement of the Khmer communist revolution to help the Vietnamese defeat the United States, the Chinese Politburo attempted to establish relations with the Lon Nol government, thereby guaranteeing continued NLF and North Vietnamese Army access to bases in Cambodia. Lon Nol, however, declined the overture, and Chinese officials subsequently called upon the deposed monarch, Sihanouk, to form a military alliance with the Cambodian communists and to lead a government-in-exile. Subsequently, Sihanouk declared publicly his alliance with the Khmer Rouge and called upon the people of Cambodia to join the revolution. Pro-Sihanouk demonstrations erupted throughout the countryside, and thousands of young men and women rallied to the monarch's appeal to join ranks and overthrow the Lon Nol regime. Within two years, Khmer Rouge forces counted more than twenty thousand soldiers. Significantly, the motivation for revolution among the rank-and-file new recruits hinged less on the perceived attractiveness of a communist society and more on the desire to restore the prince and end armed conflict. Terrorized and traumatized by war, in ever-growing numbers Khmer peasants traded plowshares for rifles.

Several veteran Khmer revolutionaries also returned to Cambodia at this time to take up the fight. Having lived and trained in Hanoi since 1954, more than a thousand Issarak veterans, 822 of whom were now apparently CPK members, made the long and dangerous trek along the Hồ Chí Minh Trail to join their communist brethren.[109] Most were unaware, however, of the significant changes that had developed within the Khmer communist movement, namely the ascension of Pol Pot and his closest supporters. Nor could they anticipate the ruthless reception awaiting their return, for the xenophobic Pol Pot viewed the veterans as Vietnamese disguised in Khmer bodies. However, while in North Vietnam, these veteran revolutionaries engaged in political studies of Marxism-Leninism; many also had received military training. By comparison, the badly equipped and raw Khmer Rouge recruits lacked proper training and military discipline. Pol Pot correctly surmised the value provided by the returning veterans.[110] Consequently, as these Khmer communists returned, they were disarmed and assigned low-ranking positions, responsibly mostly for the training of new recruits. Soon thereafter, though, Pol Pot authorized the purge of the returnees. By 1977 all but a dozen of the Hanoi-trained Khmer were dead.[111]

Civil war raged across Cambodia between 1970 and 1975. During this time, the Khmer Rouge matured into an effective military force. Ongoing bombing campaigns waged by the United States generated popular support for the Khmer Rouge. What is more, the mounting death toll and suffering fueled resentment and a desire for revenge among the recruits.[112] For Ben Kiernan, the bombing served to harden, radicalize, and legitimize the extreme policy ambitions in the minds of the CPK leadership.[113] For example, as Khmer Rouge forces "liberated" territory, soldiers evacuated towns and villages, with the inhabitants forced onto small-scale cooperatives. Steadily, ever-more-draconian policies materialized, including the prohibition of religious practice, the introduction of "moral" codes, and the conscription of labor for building dams and canals for irrigation. To ensure discipline, Khmer Rouge cadre established security centers and publicly executed persons deemed to be enemies of the revolution.

On April 17, 1975, Khmer Rouge forces entered Phnom Penh. Their victory was anything but certain, and the nature of their victory would decidedly influence postrevolutionary society. During the civil war, the Khmer Rouge kept hidden their more radical programs and effectively concealed their identity as communists. Subsequently, when they took control of the country, they still kept their leaders hidden and their party's identity a secret, instead saying only that the "organization" (angkar) was in power.[114] Within a climate of uncertainty and fear, CPK officials set in motion a series of programs initiated during the war: the evacuation of towns and villages, the confiscation of private property, and forced collectivization. In time these initiatives would destroy their popular base, setting in motion a violent downward spiral that culminated in lingering famine and murderous purges. It is sadly ironic that the postrevolution utopia imagined by Khmer Rouge cadre materialized as a horrific dystopia and the death of approximately a quarter of its population.

Conclusions

Neither Marx nor Engels favored the idea of a vanguard or of any nondemocratic form of rule. Both men expressed distain toward the idea of a "program which divided the movement into those who monopolized the revolutionary idea and those who served as cannon fodder." Moreover, both Marx and Engels "struck at the essence of the vanguard idea, which implicitly or explicitly denies the capacity of the masses to emancipate themselves and therefore assigns the responsibility for thinking and leading to a self-appointed general staff drawn—inevitably—from the educated classes."[115] To think otherwise would mean a "utopian" and not a "scientific" approach to socialist revolution; such a conception of history would, for Marx and Engels, introduce an idealist element into their understanding of class struggle and thus negate the materialist foundation of revolution.[116]

The idea of a proletarian revolution, however, led by an intellectual vanguard and "occurring in a technologically backward society, where the proletariat constitutes only a small part of society, gained its *droit de cité* through a theory propagated around the time of the First World War."[117] Indeed, after the Russian Revolution, several communists believed a socialist revolution had indeed taken place in 1917. The Russian Revolution supposedly disproved Marx's prognostication of a *proletarian* revolution and thus afforded legitimacy to their actions.[118] Such was the prestige of the Russian Revolution that communists in China and throughout the Third World, including those in Cambodia, modeled but did not copy their revolutions on the Soviet model.

The socialist revolution waged by the Khmer Rouge was a peasant-dominant but not peasant-dominated revolution. Peasants comprised the majority of participants in the revolution, but they were neither the initiators nor the inheritors. Rather, the Khmer Rouge revolution materialized not from ideological unity with the Khmer populace but instead because of the actions of a repressive cadre of men (and some women) who brutally outmaneuvered both their political opponents and erstwhile allies. The communist revolution engineered by Pol Pot's vanguard was neither a populist uprising nor a spontaneous grassroots movement—though certainly some conditions were present, as evidenced by the rebellion in Samlaut. However, the decades-long communist movement in Cambodia never attracted much popular support. It was not until the devastation wrought by the American bombing campaign and the coup of Sihanouk that the peasantry rallied in any significant number to the Khmer Rouge. The rise of Pol Pot and his supporters signifies an elitist movement that coopted the grievances of the masses while dismissing the aspirations of the masses.[119] This is a point that bears emphasis because the Khmer Rouge—having taken power—never believed it enjoyed the popular support of the men and women it governed. And in fact, it never did. As Chandler concludes, few people were willing to overturn their lives as completely as the CPK demanded.[120]

In April 1976 Khieu Samphan assumed the post of president of the State Presidium of Democratic Kampuchea. Speaking before the newly created and completely symbolic Peoples' Representative Assembly, the longtime revolutionary declared a day of great victory. "Never before in the thousands of years of the history of our Kampuchean nation," Khieu Samphan announced, "have the worker-peasant class and other laborers risen to hold power like this." The president explained that the revolutionary movement "was a necessity, the result of the long, pitiful, difficult and untiring thousands of years of struggle of our Kampuchean nation and people to oppose imperialism, colonialism and the other oppressor classes." Khieu Samphan celebrated the recent national liberation of Cambodia and remarked on the "sacrifices" of the Khmer people, "male and female, young and old," of whom more than one million "gave up their lives, were wounded, or were crippled in the war of destruction by Imperialist America and its servants."[121]

Khieu Samphan's speech is important mostly for what he did not say. Absent from his remarks are any references to Marxism-Leninism. Nor is there mention of Vietnam, China, or the Soviet Union. Indeed, the president's speech is part of a narrative of both the Khmer communist revolution and the CPK. Until 1977 CPK leaders made no public pronouncement of their adherence to Marxism-Leninism, preferring instead to educate their citizens on the value of communism devoid of political context. So too did the leaders promote a mythology that they had achieved victory unaided by any foreign government and that their revolutionary movement was unparalleled in history. In their comments, both public and private, CPK officials frequently and vehemently denied any assistance in fomenting revolution in Cambodia. Pol Pot, for example, affirmed in September 1977 that the party had achieved victory singlehandedly, that it was the perseverance and tenacity of the revolutionary masses that defeated the combined forces of the former government and its imperial handmaidens, the French and the Americans.[122] Notably, the material reality of revolution circumscribed postrevolutionary policy and practice.

A captured Khmer Rouge document dated 1975 reads, "The immediate goal of the party is to lead the people to succeed in the national democratic revolution, to exterminate the imperialists, feudalists, and capitalists, and to form a national revolutionary state in Cambodia." The document continues, "The long range goal of the party is to lead the people in creating a socialist revolution and a communist society in Cambodia." [123] Effectively, leading members of the CPK viewed themselves as forming a dictatorship of the proletariat. They also acknowledged that conditions for revolution had not been optimal—that the people had not yet adopted a proper political consciousness. The immediate postrevolutionary task, therefore, was to "build socialism" among the masses.

CHAPTER 2

"Be Masters of Your Own Destiny!"

The various plans and propositions put forward in the name of the Communist Party of Kampuchea did not materialize in a vacuum but instead were part and parcel of a deliberate attempt to transform Cambodia's political economy and its subjects. The Khmer Rouge came to power during the height of the Cold War, an era marked by anticolonial and decolonization movements throughout the Global South. Senior CPK leaders learned concrete lessons from so-called Marxist revolutions in Russia, China, and Vietnam and fashioned their own revolution in response to specific conditions manifest in Cambodia. Consequently, international treaties and the establishment of foreign relations were not anathema to the CPK, and Democratic Kampuchea was anything but the isolated state routinely and erroneously portrayed in the literature. To this end, members of the CPK negotiated a fine line between necessary engagements on the international stage while maintaining their independence and self-rule domestically. This balancing act of external alliances and internal autonomy profoundly shaped Khmer Rouge agricultural policies and programs. Of paramount importance is the quixotic relationship evidenced by senior leaders of the CPK toward the Non-Aligned Movement.

Much genocide research operates on assumptions that narrow the framework of interpretation and mitigate against an appropriately broad international understanding.[1] The study of the Cambodian genocide is no exception. Repeated and inappropriate references to "autogenocide," for example, attenuate our understanding of the international coordinates of CPK policy and practice. As such, scholars of Democratic Kampuchea have heretofore neglected to situate adequately the policies and practices of the CPK within the broader historiography of the Non-Aligned Movement and "Third Worldism." In opposition, I argue that we must understand the political economy of Democratic Kampuchea, and especially the agrarian transformations affected by the Khmer Rouge, from the vantage point of Third World developmentalism. Programmatically, CPK party officials pursued a variant of state capitalism, an approach based on a nationalist-informed socialism. Such a perspective provides crucial insight into the policies and practices, both domestic and foreign, proposed and implemented by the CPK. Accordingly, in this chapter I present a historical overview both of "socialism in one country" and the Non-Aligned Movement. Drawing on Michel Foucault's concept of governmentality, I argue that the particular mode of governance installed by CPK party leaders constitutes a regime of practice oriented toward the collectivization of agriculture and state-guided industrialization informed by Third-World socialism.[2]

Nationalism and Third-World Socialism

Revolution for Marx was necessarily a bottom-up project, that is, an inherently democratic, grassroots movement. The central premise for Marx is that collective determination emanates from self-realization: the proletariat gains awareness of its personal exploitation through solidarity with other alienated workers. Worker solidarity would proceed globally and communism would ultimately negate nationalism. Revolution in Russia (and later in China, Vietnam, and Cambodia) did not follow this path; instead, a self-proclaimed vanguard carried out a top-down, nondemocratic coup. Thus, given that the Russian Revolution did not conform to that postulated by Marx, Bolshevik leaders faced a very practical question: could an isolated communist government survive without contemporaneous socialist revolutions elsewhere in Europe? Crucially, postrevolution governance in Russia was a practical matter, and the scattered writings of Marx provided little in the way of guidance. To this end, the question of socialism in one country divided Russian Marxists.[3] For the more orthodox Russian Marxists, such as Trotsky, the establishment of socialism in country was impossible. Marx and Engels, for example, had argued against the feasibility of a socialist project in one country, averring that if an isolated country, such as France, should ever establish communism, it would soon collapse. In agreement, Trotsky reasoned that in the case of a prolonged isolated existence, Soviet Russia would collapse under economic or military pressure from outside Western powers. Other Bolsheviks, such as Lenin, held that socialism in one country was possible but that an autarkic socialism would remain unfinished without associated socialist revolutions elsewhere. Lenin, in fact, concluded near the end of his life that Russia's transition to socialism would remain incomplete until a world revolution enabled workers to provide each other active support in completing their socialist societies. Lastly, some leaders, notably Bukharin and Stalin, premised not only that socialism was possible in one country but that in certain respects it was desirable. Stalin in particular argued that Russian socialism would not collapse of its own weakness in the absence of revolution elsewhere, and, in fact, through a prolonged period of isolation Russia had a good chance of building a strong socialist society. In the end, Stalin's thesis won out. The idea that a complete socialist society in one country was a viable project signified a momentous change in Bolshevik doctrine, a shift that greatly affected subsequent communist revolutions throughout the twentieth century.[4]

Throughout the Soviet Union, socialism became a technical project that presupposed the accumulation of capital and creation of appropriate strategies to increase productive capacity. In turn, the experiences of Stalinism and a bourgeoning Russian state capitalism informed and shaped subsequent efforts to promote socialism in the third world, thus marking an important moment in the articulation of nationalism with socialism. Indeed, after 1945 a nationalist interpretation of socialism became one of the dominant political idioms of social change and development as the centers of gravity of both socialism and nationalism moved from the West toward Asia, Africa, and Latin America.[5]

After World War II Western powers challenged and opposed demands for political and economic independence raised by their former colonies. Often, deadly conflict erupted as nationalist leaders, including those in Indochina, resisted the reimposition of colonialism. However, Western powers responded also with newer forms of imperialism, often shrouded under the guise of modernization and development.[6] For example, the establishment of international organizations, such as the World Bank and the International Monetary Fund, imposed countless structural programs designed to incorporate Western technology and methods of production into the so-called developing world. To be sure, numerous leaders throughout the Global South welcomed the inflow of foreign aid. For many other nationalists, however, Western-imposed economic programs constituted nothing more than a renewed form of imperial domination. For these nationalists, the realities of aid interventionism belied the humanitarian rhetoric that accompanied such programs, and they decried both the hypocrisy and material inequalities that followed modernization.

Anticolonialism was not necessarily synonymous with anti-capitalism, but the affinity of the two positions was palpable. Notable in this regard are those theorists and revolutionaries who adhered to and promoted the so-called dependency school of development.[7] Far from a unified paradigm, the various forms of dependency theory shared an explanation for the continuing inequalities between North and South and for the widening gap between rich and poor.[8] Exemplified in the writings of Osvaldo Sunkel, André Gunder Frank, Theotônio dos Santos, Fernando Cardoso, and Johan Galtung, among others, dependency theory placed the logic of underdevelopment within a globally articulated historical-geographical context.[9] That is, an understanding of underdevelopment requires us to see it both as process and as relation, as part of a system of global economic relations marked by the monopolistic control of capital and technology at national and international levels.[10] Dependency theory represented but one among many strands of Marxist and Marxist-influenced engagements with questions of imperialism, a world capitalist system, and the persistence and production of underdevelopment.[11] Most importantly, these critiques helped legitimize a common agenda for changing the structure of international relations as the collective identity of most Asian, African, and Latin American countries in international relations became expressed through demands for reform in the institutional structure of the international economy.[12] Accordingly, during the Cold War nationalist leaders of many former and existing colonies sought to promote a sense of solidarity centered on a foundational principle, this being the forceful condemnation of colonialism in its many forms and the fundamental right to self-determination, state sovereignty, and national independence as the sine qua non of international development.[13]

Nationalist demands for economic and political independence fueled the rise of the revolutionary concept of Third Worldism.[14] The term *third world*, coined in 1952 by Alfred Sauvy, originally held two distinct but related meanings. The first usage encapsulated the many liberation movements of former and current colonies that challenged the capitalist first world and the communist second world. Importantly, for Sauvy, himself a social democrat, the *troisième monde* was a space of underdevelopment.[15] However, analogous to the *tiers état* and the French Revolution, Sauvy reconceptualized these spaces and coined the term *tiers monde*. So conceived, the idea of the *tiers monde* came to signify a potentially powerful revolutionary force, a meaning subsequently adopted by colonized nationalists. Indeed, the *tiers monde* provided a rallying cry for anticolonial movements active especially throughout Africa and Asia, including those in Indochina.[16] Frantz Fanon captures these sentiments in his 1961 classic, *The Wretched of the Earth*, writing, the Third World must start over a new history of humanity. Such an endeavor must take account of not only Europe's accomplishments but also its crimes committed on "the immense scale of humanity," including "racial hatred, slavery, exploitation and, above all, the bloodless genocide whereby one and a half billion men have been written off." For Fanon, the third world represented a global revolutionary force, a global movement that, in solidarity, composed an alternative to the rapacious path of underdevelopment associated with so-called Western civilization. Fanon concludes: "If we want to transform Africa into a new Europe . . .

then let us entrust the destinies of our countries to the Europeans. . . . But if we want humanity to take one step forward, if we want to take it to another level than one where Europe has placed it, then we must innovate, we must be pioneers."[17]

Increasingly, throughout the late 1950s and early 1960s, liberation movements and governments in Africa, Asia, and Latin America used the concept of the third world in their struggles for independence and autochthonous development and in so doing reinterpreted socialism itself.[18] Understood through the lens of third-world orthodoxy, socialism appeared as a promising program to overcome the wretchedness of underdevelopment and to achieve independent and national socioeconomic development. In so doing, the integration of revolutionary nationalism into socialism throughout the third world opened the door to new revisions—far removed from those expounded by Marx—within socialist ideology.[19]

A key moment in the emergence of Third Worldism was the 1955 Asian-African Conference held in Bandung, Indonesia. Taking place in the aftermath of France's defeat in the Franco–Việt Minh War, the Bandung Conference marked the first time that former colonies of Asia and Africa "assembled to discuss common problems and attempted to formulate a united approach to international relations."[20] In attendance were many of the most outspoken and respected representatives of both colonies and former colonies. These included Sukarno, Jawaharlal Nehru, Gamal Abdel Nasser, Hồ Chí Minh, Kwame Nkrumah, and Zhou Enlai. In total, delegations from twenty-nine primarily new nation-states or nationalist movements from Asia and Africa participated.[21] The solidarity evinced by these leaders stemmed from a mutual frustration with the wider international community. In particular, participants called out their lack of representation within the United Nations—an international body increasingly seen as catering to the more economically and militarily powerful states. In the context of the nuclear arms race of the 1950s and the danger of a worldwide nuclear conflagration, Lorenz Lüthi explains, these leaders believed they had to "contribute to the solution of the problem even if they were neither the reason for nor a part of it. Being a potential victim in a future global war was sufficient to claim a voice in the debate at that time."[22] Participants also denounced colonialism in all its myriad forms. Indeed, the final communiqué of the conference condemned all manifestations of colonialism and was widely viewed as an attack not only on the formal colonialism of the Western European powers but also on the Soviet occupation of Eastern Europe and the information colonialism, or neocolonialism, of the United States.[23]

A presumed unity and shared historical colonial legacy provided a touch-stone for Third Worldism. In practice, however, coherence was illusory, and so in many ways the Bandung Conference was more symbolic than substantive. Schisms among its members were visible from the beginning. Most govern-ments in attendance at Bandung aligned politically with one of the two super-powers (either the United States or the Soviet Union) and were nonplussed in their commitment to an alternative economic route between capitalism and socialism.[24] Geopolitical divisions between those nations whose leaders advocated nonalignment (e.g., India and Ceylon) and those who sided with the United States (e.g., Pakistan, the Philippines, and Thailand) or the Soviet Union (e.g., Democratic Republic of Vietnam) were readily apparent. Moreover, the growing rift between China and the Soviet Union in addition to a series of recurrent military conflicts between India and China (1962) and India and Pakistan (1956, 1965, 1971) augmented the factions.[25] In the end, there was no direct follow up to the Bandung Conference. In fact, the Bandung Conference failed to lead directly to any long-term organizational initiatives.[26]

The spirit of Third Worldism persisted, however. In the shadows of the Bandung Conference many nationalist proponents of Third Worldism, such as Nehru, Sukarno, and Nasser, advocated a synthesis of nationalism and socialism in one country. This approach made it possible to develop a strong discourse on political and economic independence, thereby linking national-ism, economic development, and industrialization to the struggle against neo-colonialism.[27] Accordingly, when the Yugoslav leader Josip Broz Tito called for the creation of a new international movement at the UN General Assembly in the fall of 1960, he sought cooperation among "non-bloc" or "neutralist" countries.[28] Consequently, when the First Conference of Heads of State or Government of Non-Aligned Countries convened in Belgrade, officials from twenty-five governments and representatives from nineteen national lib-eration movements attended. For many historians, the Belgrade Conference marked the proper origins of the Non-Aligned Movement and eventually paved the way for revolutionary socialism.[29]

The Non-Aligned Movement was a product of the Cold War.[30] Nevertheless, members struggled to define their movement as something more than a caucus of states neutral in the Cold War.[31] Proponents deployed the idea of Third Worldism to generate unity and support as they sought to displace the "East-West" conflicts and to foreground the "North-South" conflict, that is, between so-called oppressor and oppressed regimes.[32] Programmatically, members for-warded initiatives to promote and implement economic growth and develop-ment, often but not always within existing institutional structures. For several leaders, however, the historical model for national development was Stalin's state-guided industrialization. In time, the imperatives of socialism in one country replaced the call for world revolution and the meaning of socialism changed from self-emancipation of the working class to national economic development. In this way, revolutionary nationalists rendered socialism a strategy that would guide nations in the struggle to overcome underdevelopment. Robbed of Marx's humanism, socialism in practice often became a technical project that presupposed the creation of appropriate tools to increase productive capital.[33] Against this backdrop, senior officials of the Khmer Rouge drew inspiration and guidance.

Nonalignment and the Khmer Rouge

Between August 16 and 19, 1976, delegates from eighty-six member states of the Non-Aligned Movement convened in Colombo, Sri Lanka. The setting was symbolic, as it marked the first summit of non-aligned countries held on the Asian continent. The resultant Colombo Declaration reflects this: "The history of Asia had been marked by successive periods of foreign conquest and colonial domination, which had created in the peoples of Asia a determination to preserve and defend their freedom by eschewing involvement in military blocs and alliances." The declaration continues, "The struggles of the Asian peoples for freedom, justice and equality have been victorious. A resurgent Asia enters the last quarter of the twentieth century with its peoples united in their determination . . . to overcome the problems of under-development and the adverse consequences, economic, technological and cultural, resulting from long subjugation to colonial rule."[34]

Sixteen months earlier a resurgent Asia witnessed the victory of the Khmer Rouge. Remarkably, this event seemingly heralded a broader victory of Third Worldism over colonialism and neocolonialism. Member states of the Non-Aligned Movement understood the CPK's *national* struggle as part of an *international* struggle that included other revolutionary movements in Asia and Africa. As stated in the declaration, member states "welcomed the triumph of the struggle of the peoples of Democratic Kampuchea, Lao People's Democratic Republic and the Socialist Republic of Vietnam against United States' imperialist aggression." The conference "congratulated Democratic Kampuchea on having remained faithful to the principles of Non-Alignment and paid tribute to its constant determination to defend them."[35] The struggles of Democratic Kampuchea, notably, stood alongside "the success of the liberation struggle of Guinea-Bissau, Cape Verde, Mozambique, Angola, and Sao Tome and Principe."

The context and intonation of the conference is important for understanding postrevolution CPK economic policy. Throughout the early to mid-1970s, many liberal economic strategies and financial institutions advocated the modernist view that developing countries could and should pay for essential imports by borrowing extensively from private banks, and subsequently many countries of the Global South did borrow sizable amounts to import industrial goods. The policies, in turn, contributed to high levels of indiscriminate borrowing and a growing global debt crisis. As such, participants at the Colombo Conference, including representatives of the CPK, voiced their support for the formation of a New International Economic Order to counter the exploitative structures forwarded by the Global North.

A summary text of the conference later published by the embassy of Democratic Kampuchea in Berlin, East Germany, illustrates CPK rhetoric well. The conference "achieved brilliant victories," the text explains, including a suite of resolutions that "reinforce the principles of non-alignment, enhance the role of this Movement and confirm the resolute solidarity of the non-aligned countries in the common struggle against imperialism, colonialism, neo-colonialism and against the interferences, interventions, aggressions and against the expansionism of the rich great powers, for independence, sovereignty, territorial integrity and the right of each people to determine the destiny of its nation by itself in full independence and sovereignty." The text continues: "The struggle to establish a new international economic order is a political struggle of far-reaching consequences and that the great powers are entirely responsible for the grave situation existing in the development countries." Thus, "to bring about the establishment of a new international economic order, the non-aligned countries must therefore actively unite to wage a struggle against the aggressions and interferences, committed under whatever pretext, by the rich great powers. At the same time[,] they must undertake every effort to overcome all obstacles, build up their own national economy and strengthen their cooperation based on the principle of mutual respect."[36]

Having acknowledged the global importance of the Non-Aligned Movement, the CPK text concludes with reference to Democratic Kampuchea's unconditional support: "The people of Kampuchea warmly hails the victories of the 5th Summit Conference of Non-Aligned Countries which consolidate the non-aligned principles, enhance the non-aligned movement and strengthen the solidarity within its ranks." To this end, "In contributing to the revolutionary struggle of the peoples of the world, to the liberation struggle of the brotherly countries of the Third World and to the strengthening of the cause of the great non-aligned family, the people of Kampuchea is determined to carry out the revolution successfully in its own country, to build up its economy and edify its country according to the principles of independence, sovereignty and self-reliance."[37]

In hindsight, one may question the sincerity of the CPK delegates at Colombo. As representatives of the CPK waxed elegantly about justice and democracy at the conference, Khmer Rouge soldiers were purging thousands of Cambodians. Indeed, in the month of August 1976 alone, Khmer Rouge cadres arrested, detained, and executed upwards of 155 men and women at the infamous S-21 Security Center.[38] None of these detainees appeared in a court of law. In fact, in Democratic Kampuchea, there were no judges, juries, or lawyers. Still, the rhetoric of the CPK is important, hyperbole notwithstanding, for the alleged alliance of the CPK to the principles of nonalignment does inform their conception of postrevolutionary society.

Ieng Sary, deputy prime minister of foreign affairs, echoed these sentiments two months later. Speaking before the 31st Session of the United Nations General Assembly in New York, Ieng Sary evoked the spirit of the Colombo Conference. The present assembly, Ieng Sary explained, "takes place at a time when all the peoples of the world of the non-aligned countries and of the Third World are waging a victorious struggle everywhere against imperialism, colonialism, neo-colonialism, Zionism and all forms of foreign interference, aggression, expansionism and exploitation, for independence, sovereignty, territorial integrity, for the right to determine their own destiny and for the establishment of a new international economic order on the basis of justice and equality." Again, we see a senior CPK official explicitly position Cambodia's revolution alongside other liberation movements throughout Asia, Africa, and Latin America. "Dozens of new independent states are arising from the ruins of colonialism," the deputy prime minister affirmed, "determined to engage in the struggle to defend and consolidate their political and economic independence, their sovereignty and territorial integrity against all acts of domination, exploitation, interference and aggression on the part of the rich great powers. . . . Scarred by the same fate in the past under colonialist regimes, linked together by common goals and interests, these independent states of the Third World reject by common consent the outlived international relations which are based upon inequality and dependence." Repeatedly, Ieng Sary professed on behalf of the CPK a commitment to solidarity against the imperialist powers. The precepts of Third Worldism reverberated with each passage. He continued: "Born from the categorical rejection of bloc politics and from the compelling necessity for the newly independent states to preserve and consolidate their hard-earned liberty and sovereignty against the ambitions, the greed and the expansionist designs of the rich great powers, the Non-Aligned Movement demonstrated its vitality and energy once again at the recent 5th Summit Conference of Colombo."[39]

Democratic Kampuchea, Ieng Sary blunted stated, was born of these struggles. He explained,

> The people of Kampuchea has not kept aside from the world's upheavals. Together with all the other peoples, it has actively taken part in the common struggle against imperialism, colonialism, and neo-colonialism in order to liberate itself from all forms of domination, oppression and exploitation. Our people never accepted the yoke of the colonialist and neo-colonialist system which was imposed on us for over a century and against which our people fought from the beginning, gaining successive victories in a long, difficult and unyielding struggle on the political, military and diplomatic levels, leading to the total victory over the American imperialists' war of aggression on April 17, 1975.

For Ieng Sary, the victory over colonialism in Cambodia was a victory for all Third World nations: "April 17, 1975 is also a victory of the unwavering solidarity with the struggle of the people of Kampuchea shown by the non-aligned and Third World peoples and countries and by all peace- and justice-loving peoples and countries in the world. . . . [It] is a victory of the policy of independence, peace and non-alignment over the politics of domination, oppression, exploitation, interference and aggression."[40] Victory in Cambodia came with a steep price. According to Ieng Sary, "More than one million inhabitants were killed or wounded, that is about 13% of the total population. The economy was devastated. The means and instruments of production were largely destroyed: hundreds of thousands of cattle and water buffaloes, necessary for agricultural work, were killed; 7–80% of the factories, plantations lands, rice-fields, forests were destroyed; 60–80% of the means of communication (bridges, roads, railroads, harbors. . . .); hundreds of villages and urban settlements were razed to the ground and wiped off the map."[41] Ieng Sary was not in error. Outside observers detailed that the war destroyed approximately one-third of the country's bridges and left two-fifths of the road network unusable. The railroad was mostly inoperable and much of the country's productive infrastructure had ceased working. Indeed, only 300 of 1,400 rice mills and 60 of 240 sawmills were functioning, and both timber and rubber production had declined to one-fifth of prewar production levels.[42]

Ieng Sary vowed that reconstruction would take place conforming to the principles of the Non-Aligned Movement. He explained,

> Democratic Kampuchea will always continue to follow a policy of independence, peace, neutrality and non-alignment. . . . Democratic Kampuchea participates neither in any alliance nor in any regional association. She resists the establishment of any foreign military bases on her territory and all forms of intervention and interference with her internal affairs. Our people resolutely defends its independence, national sovereignty, territorial integrity and its inalienable right to determine its own destiny. . . . At the same time, Democratic Kampuchea continues her efforts to establish and maintain close relations with her neighbors and with all the other countries of the world, based on the strict mutual respect for independence, sovereignty, territorial integrity, of the principle of equality and mutual advantages.[43]

Throughout 1976, for example, several foreign diplomats, envoys, and trade delegates traveled to Democratic Kampuchea. In February 1976 six envoys stationed in Beijing toured the newly liberated country; these included the ambassadors of Zambia, Sweden, Egypt, Tunisia, and Afghanistan and the special representative of the Palestine Liberation Organization. The following month, the special envoy of Mauritania and a delegation from Beijing made a visit. Meetings with the ambassadors of Cuba, Egypt, Laos, Mali, Pakistan, and Tanzania, envoys from Guinea and Senegal, an emissary from Iraq, and a representative of Romania soon followed. Likewise, several officials of the CPK made visits to allied countries and participated in select international conventions. In an effort to establish diplomatic relations with selected noncommunist states, the CPK sent delegations to Burma, Côte d'Ivoire, Malaysia, Mexico, Nigeria, Peru, the Philippines, and Singapore. CPK officials established also formal relations with Austria, Finland, Greece, Japan, and the United Kingdom. Nine countries had permanent representatives or ambassadors stationed in Phnom Penh: Albania, China, Cuba, Egypt, Laos, North Korea, Romania, Vietnam, and Yugoslavia.[44] Surely, many of these diplomatic exchanges were perfunctory, serving more a symbolic than material purpose. Nevertheless, these overtures reflect an attempt on behalf of the CPK to engage selectively, purposefully, and on their own terms with members of the wider international community. Conforming to the principles of the Non-Aligned Movement, the Khmer Rouge, as nationalists, pursued selective internationalism, not isolation.

That senior leaders of the CPK aligned their state-building project with the Non-Aligned Movement is beyond doubt. Indeed, they codified their adherence to the movement in the Constitution of Democratic Kampuchea. Of significance, these officials positioned their victory and subsequent government not as an aberration but as a defining moment in the broader anticolonial movement. Certainly, words may ring hollow, and documentary evidence demonstrates that the rhetoric of the CPK often failed to match reality. Nevertheless, the argument holds that policies forwarded by the top echelons of the CPK adhered to the broad coordinates of the Non-Aligned Movement. It is necessary, therefore, to evaluate postrevolutionary CPK governance within the parameters of Third Worldism.

Khmer Rouge Governance

A captured Khmer Rouge document from early 1975 reads, "The immediate goal of the party is to lead the people to succeed in the national democratic revolution, to exterminate the imperialists, feudalists, and capitalists, and to form a national revolutionary state in Cambodia." The document continues, "The long range goal of the party is to lead the people in creating a socialist and a communist society in Cambodia."[45] Upon seizing power, however, senior officials of the CPK conceded that conditions for revolution had not been optimal. They recognized that the people of Cambodia had not yet adopted a proper political consciousness. For the CPK, formed as a vanguard of revolution, it was essential to "build socialism" among the masses. This effort required, in turn, a form of governance sensitive to both material and ideological needs.

Scholars have long debated the political nature of Democratic Kampuchea. Heretofore, scholars have labeled the CPK Marxist-Leninist, Maoist, Stalinist, peasant-populist, national chauvinist, and even fascist.[46] Such attempts are somewhat misguided, however, and too often fail to separate rhetoric from reality. My concern, rather, focuses more on what they did as opposed to what they were. A promising course, and one that I follow in the remaining sections of this chapter, is to document and detail Khmer Rouge governmentality, that is, the *regimes of practice* introduced and put into operation by the Khmer Rouge. Conceptually, governmentality is associated with the French philosopher Michel Foucault and his understanding of government as the "conduct of conduct," that is, "the way in which the conduct of individuals or of groups might be directed." As Mitchell Dean explains, "to conduct" means to lead, to direct or to guide, and perhaps implies some sort of calculation. To govern, therefore, "is to structure the possible field of action of others." In short, governmentality appears as a form of vanguardism, as a select group of individuals any attempt to shape with some degree of deliberation aspects of human behavior according to particular sets of norms and for a variety of ends.[47] For senior leaders of the CPK, this meant the very deliberate attempt to build socialism through governance.

At the core of the Non-Aligned Movement was a demand for democratic participation, that is, for the peoples of the Third World to have a say in determining their own future. In practice, this demand translated into various experimentations with participatory forms of government. For those states guided by Marxist-Leninist ideology, *democratic centralism* assumed prominence.[48] Not found in the writings of Marx or Engels, democratic centralism is a twentieth-century concept. In the years before the Russian Revolution of 1917, both the Bolshevik and Menshevik factions of the Russian Social Democratic Labor Party advanced democratic centralism as their organizing principle, whereby the proletariat would democratically govern postrevolutionary society.[49] According to Lenin, this form of representative democratic politics would extend into other spheres of society, including that of the economy, whereby workers would assume the decision-making role with respect to production and distribution. Consequently, the centralization of governance within the proletariat would lead to the gradual withering away of the former bourgeois bureaucracy. Thus, when Lenin writes that "the proletariat needs state power, the centralized organization of force, the organization of violence, for the purpose of crushing the resistance of the exploiters and for the purpose of leading the great mass of the population," he is not referring not to the "state" as commonly understood. Rather, for Lenin, governance assumes a "special form of organization."[50] Under Stalin, however, a totalitarian state-party forcibly replaced Lenin's proletarian-led democratic centralism.[51] This shift accompanied a broader transformation in Soviet policy whereupon official priorities expanded from a focus on the mechanical aspects of industrialization to the training of a loyal, capable workforce."[52] In so doing, Stalin codified a more potent form of building socialism. The governance of Democratic Kampuchea, on paper, reflected the principles of an idealized democratic centralism. On the ground, Khmer Rouge governance resembled more a Soviet, and specifically Stalinist, bureaucratic dictatorship.[53]

On December 14, 1975, eight months into their reign, senior CPK leaders drafted the Constitution of Democratic Kampuchea and promulgated the document on January 5, 1976. According to Khieu Samphan, then deputy prime minister, the people—the workers, peasants, and soldiers—of Democratic

Kampuchea wrote the constitution.[54] In reality, members of the CPK authored the document and positioned Democratic Kampuchea as "an independent, united, peaceful, neutral, non-aligned, sovereign and democratic state with territorial integrity." Tellingly, the framers of the constitution declared, "The State of Kampuchea is the State of the workers, peasants and other laborers of Kampuchea." In addition, the constitution affirms, "All important means of production are the collective property of the people's State and the collective property of the communally organized people."[55] Such rhetoric glosses over material practice and, following David Chandler's cautionary remarks, "it is important to notice what is omitted."[56]

For Chandler, the document is a manifesto, and as such, the framers directed the text especially at those who believed it in already, that is, members of the CPK, and at those whom the members were educating, in other words, those men and women lacking a proper political consciousness.[57] Crucially, the document leaves out what most other constitutions put in, notably, the specific rights of citizens and the obligations and institutions of the government.[58] Article 9, as case in point, affirms, "Every citizen of Kampuchea has the full right to enjoy material, moral and cultural life."[59] Superficially, the constitution presents a legal order devoid of citizenship and, hence, class distinctions. Elsewhere, however, a decidedly unequal sociolegal hierarchy is apparent, as illustrated for example in the 1976 statutes of the CPK, which codify the "ideology, membership, structure and organization of the Party."[60] Party membership is exclusionary, and by implication, so too is participation in society.

In principle, anyone aged eighteen or older could join the CPK. According to CPK statutes, however, membership was conditional upon the fulfillment of two criteria.[61] First, prospective members were required to satisfy a suite of conditions, notably but not solely prior revolutionary work in unions, cooperatives, and the military; a good class pedigree; and proper morals. Second, prospective members were required to undergo a particularly intrusive screening process to demonstrate conformity with the aforementioned criteria. Moreover, to ascend to a leadership role in the party, prospective members needed to satisfy ten conditions, such as strong revolutionary stances on the party's political line, party solidarity and unity, and proletarian ideology. Loyalty, vigilance, self-reliance, and self-mastery also were stalwarts necessary for consideration of party leadership positions. Subsequent articles expounded upon these criteria. For example, cadre were to have "a correct and strong proletarian class stance," exhibit a "high and absolute stance of sacrifice of private ownership," and demonstrate vigilance toward the "building of socialism."[62]

Nowhere in the constitution nor the party statues was the most basic social division within society codified, this being the distinction between "new" people and "base" people. Here, the latter referred to those people who came under Khmer Rouge control during the civil war, that is, before April 17, 1975. In general, Khmer Rouge cadre perceived base people as more loyal and hence more trustworthy. Those designated as new people, conversely, were those who either did not live in liberated areas prior to the date of victory or did not actively support the Khmer Rouge. Also known as "17 April" people, new people inhabited a political space far below that of base people and party members. As such, while the constitution extolled that "every citizen of Kampuchea has all his means of existence fully secured," reality was vastly different.[63]

Party leaders did address in limited ways the matter of rights, and by extension participation, in their drafting of the 1976 statutes. According to this document, individual members could not make decisions by themselves, but only in concert with other members. Of particular significance is the designation of rights afforded to party members. Full-rights status meant that members were permitted to "consider and discuss and join in decision making" on all party affairs, unlike candidate members, who were allowed only to participate in meetings, without the right of decision-making.[64] In so doing, CPK officials introduced a mode of governance whereby the majority of its citizens retained very few rights but were burdened with countless (and unwritten) obligations. Workers provided the necessary labor and loyalty to the party and the state, and in turn the party provided food, water, shelter, and clothing. Other expectations followed. Workers attended party-led meetings and training sessions, and workers were to conduct themselves appropriately, disciplined and punished as necessary by Khmer Rouge cadre.

Although varying from government to government, two guiding principles of democratic centralism include the hierarchical structure of governance, that is, the unconditionally binding nature of the decisions of higher bodies upon lower ones and the subordination of the minority to the majority.[65] In Democratic Kampuchea members of the CPK retained the former and inverted the latter. Organizationally, the CPK governed via a territorially defined vertical structure composed of zones (*phumipeak*), regions (*damban*), districts (*srok*), communes (*khum*), and villages (*phum*). By way of illustration, the Northwest Zone was composed of seven regions, numbered one through seven; in turn, Region 5, located north of Battambang City, was composed of four districts (Serey Sophoan, Preah Neth Preah, Phnom Srok, and Thma Puok), and these districts were composed of several communes. Phnom Srok, for example, contained five communes, while Thma Puok was composed of nine communes. Each commune, in turn, was composed of a number of villages, such as the commune of Sreh Chik, in the district of Phnom Srok, which consisted of fifteen villages. Materially, communes, districts, regions, and zones were virtual; that is, they existed purely in administrative form. Villages only had a concrete existence, though villagers participated in myriad commune-, district-, region-, and zone-level activities.

Initially, Democratic Kampuchea consisted of five zones: the Northeast, North, Northwest, Southwest, and East, including a special zone surrounding Phnom Penh. In the ensuing months and years, administrative divisions, notably zones, changed often, usually resultant from internal purges or power plays among CPK leaders. Toward the end of 1975, for example, the Southwest Zone was split in two, forming a new West Zone and a smaller Southwest Zone. CPK leaders also dissolved the Phnom Penh special zone, which they subsequently ruled as a distinct territory not within the formal administrative structures. The port facility at Kampong Som also existed as a separate administrative entity ruled directly by CPK leadership. Later, two autonomous regions came into existence: Region 106, consisting mostly of the former Siem Reap and Oddar Meanchey provinces, and Region 103, composed of the former Preah Vihear province. Toward late 1976 and early 1977, a seventh zone was created as Regions 103 and 106 were merged to form a new North Zone, and in the process the old North Zone was renamed the Central Zone.[66]

Governance throughout Democratic Kampuchea was almost entirely hierarchical, as policies, programs, and pronouncements flowed top to bottom. A three-person committee, consisting of a secretary, deputy secretary, and member, administered each political division; these individuals were responsible for politics, security, and economics, respectively. In this way, party members effectively controlled all aspects of society. The zone committee, for example, was responsible for overseeing the implementation of CPK plans and policies throughout its respective zone and for delegating plans and policies to all other levels (e.g., regions, districts) in its zone. The committees at the region, district, and commune levels fulfilled similar functions of implementing tasks designated by the higher levels. In addition, all political divisions from the commune level up included various three-person subcommittees, each responsible for specific tasks. Economic committees, for example, administered the collection and warehousing of rice, while finance committees managed all other agriculture products. Apart from these relatively fixed governing bodies, the CPK introduced also innumerable mobile committees, responsible for the deployment of work brigades to undertake specific projects, such as the construction of a canal, the clearance of forest, or the harvesting of fields.

A key function of governance is the establishment of concrete devices, that is, institutions, that allow for the exercise of power.[67] In Democratic Kampuchea senior CPK leaders formed several ministries—separate political bodies—designed to address specific areas of governance.[68] These included the Ministries of Foreign Affairs (headed by Ieng Sary), Economy (Vorn Vet), Defense (Son Sen), Information and Propaganda (Hu Nim), Health (Thiounn Thioeun), Social Affairs (Ieng Thirith), Public Works (Touch Phoeun), Culture, Education, and National Studies (Yun Yat), and Interior, Cooperatives, and Communes (Hou Yuon).[69] These ministries, in turn, may consist of several internal divisions, as, for example, the Ministry of the Economy, which consisted of six subcommittees: agriculture, industry, commerce, rubber plantations, transportation, and energy.[70]

Whereas democratic centralism in theory permits greater representation of the people, as practiced in Democratic Kampuchea power was concentrated among a decidedly small minority of party members. By statute, the Central Committee was the highest decision-making body in Democratic Kampuchea.[71] Moreover, as a broadly representative body, the Central Committee was (on paper) responsible for the implementation of the party's political line and the oversight of cadres and party members.[72] In reality, the Central Committee was subservient to an ever-smaller governing body, the Standing Committee. Dominated by Pol Pot, Nuon Chea, Son Sen, and Ieng Sary, the Standing Committee was the true locus of sovereign power. Initially, the Standing Committee included Pol Pot (secretary general), Nuon Chea (deputy secretary general and vice-chair of the Military Commission), Ieng Sary (deputy prime minister of foreign affairs), So Phim (secretary, Eastern Zone), Vorn Vet (deputy prime minister for the economy), Ros Nhim (secretary, Northwest Zone), Ta Mok (secretary, Southwest Zone), and Son Sen (deputy prime minister for defense).[73]

The hierarchical social structure of CPK governance permitted the Standing Committee to exercise near total control throughout society. In practice, the administrative divisions of zones, regions, districts, and communes functioned as an *integrated hierarchy*, in that the flow of information, supplies, and so on moved hierarchically through the three-person committees, with ultimate control overseen by the Standing Committee. Lower-level cadre, for example those governing at the district level, were required to channel all requests via messenger or telegram to their immediate supervisors at the regional level; these cadre would, in turn, forward the request to the zone level, where it would then be routed (often via telegram) to the relevant ministries of the CPK. There were to be no "horizontal" relations; hence, a district secretary in the Northwest Zone could not request supplies from a neighboring district secretary in the same zone. He or she would in theory have to route the request through the zone committee (and hence to the Standing Committee) before it would be rerouted to the other district cadre.

Statutes and internal memorandums provided, ostensibly, a degree of autonomy. On October 9, 1975, for example, members of the Standing Committee concluded, "each [administrative unit] must have total mastery in the sense of implementing the Party line and the decisions of the Party, with initiative, being on the offensive to arrange carefully and in detail, quickly, and in succession." In other words, the Standing Committee granted a limited amount of latitude among sone, region, and district secretaries. Indeed, members acknowledged, "there would be no concentrated democracy" if decision-making powers were held solely by the Standing Committee. However, consultation with the Standing Committee was imperative, as made clear in the following directive: "When a telegram comes in, immediately when it is received the office must hand it to the responsible section immediately, so they can examine and consider it and make proposals to the Standing Committee."[74]

Governmentality consists of myriad apparatuses that allow for the exercise of power. In Democratic Kampuchea, key leaders of the Standing Committee established a specific mode of governance that promised a representative form of government but delivered a highly centralized and increasingly dogmatic rule of the majority by minority. Far from the idealized mode of governance envisioned, for example, by Lenin, the political institutions fashioned by the CPK were more reflective of the bureaucratic regime imposed by Stalin in the Soviet Union.[75] To this end, the administrative structure imposed by the CPK, itself informed by not determined by the imperatives of socialism in one country and the Non-Aligned Movement, greatly affected specific economic programs introduced and implemented throughout Democratic Kampuchea. I turn now to these programs before addressing, in chapter 3, the particularities of agriculture.

Economic Development in Democratic Kampuchea

An analytics of governmentalities demands that we pay attention to how governments define and address key problems.[76] For an understanding of Democratic Kampuchea, this requires an analysis of the CPK's Four-Year

Plan, drafted by members of the Standing Committee between July 21 and August 2, 1976. Here, senior leaders identified two prime objectives underlying their effort to build socialism: to serve the people's livelihood and to raise the people's standard of living and to seek, gather, save, and increase capital from agriculture in order to expand industry and defense.[77] On the surface, these goals are straightforward and uncontroversial. A closer inspection, however, reveals fundamental tensions, indeed, a series of contradictions that continually plagued CPK governance and conditioned ominously the health and well-being of all men, women, and children who lived under their reign. I address these in considerable detail throughout chapters 3 and 4; now, suffice it to say that the Four-Year Plan established the parameters by which the political economy of Democratic Kampuchea functioned.

A key feature of government, Dean identifies, is that officials "must ask questions of themselves, must employ plans, forms of knowledge and know-how, and must adopt visions and objectives of what they seek to achieve." Even the most brutal of regimes, Dean reminds us, has an intrinsically programmatic character as it attempts to regulate, reform, organize and improve what happens in the context of a specific set of objectives.[78] Accordingly, the CPK's Four-Year Plan provides insight into the idealized communist society envisioned by its framers. As Chandler finds, the tone of the document is relatively optimistic; the men and women who compiled it probably believed that the party's assumption of power a few months before, and their own retention of key positions within the CPK, would facilitate a rapid and effective socialist transformation of society.[79]

The plan itself, while meticulously detailed, is also frustratingly vague. Indeed, many sections read as a wish list of projects to be undertaken. Thus, we learn, "Sea wharves must be strengthened and expanded step-by-step each year to master the increasing import and export requirements." Also: "Must extend the old railway lines and add more carriages" and "prepare engines, administration, strengthen and expand civil aviation (with foreign planes)."[80] Such limitations were understood by CPK leadership, however, as indicated by the repeated calls for detailed information of the country. During a zone assembly held from June 3 to June 7, 1976, a party official—possibly Pol Pot—directed the audience "to make maps and give the figures for the area of land in each Region and the figures for each sector of the economy: statistics sector by sector, period by period." The speaker continued: "If we do this, the Zone Committee can grasp things and so can other people. At a glance we see things clearly, and so we know how far the Zone has gone, what progress it has made, how all the Regions compare." The demand for and use of information, in other words, followed the CPK's overall approach to governance—at least, in the early months. Here, party leaders entreated cadre to compile, assemble, and act on vast quantities of data to ensure effective political and economic programs. "These figures are not just to have figures on paper," the aforementioned speaker explains; "they are to further our leadership."[81] Thus, the leadership required all levels of government to provide, on a regular basis, statistical information used for planning purposes.

A recurrent theme in myriad CPK documents is the pursuit of independence, self-reliance, and self-mastery. Repeatedly, members of the CPK claimed the uniqueness of their revolution. Party leaders affirmed often the exceptionality of their economic programs envisioned for postrevolutionary society. For example, minutes of a meeting convened by members of the Standing Committee on January 9, 1976, for example, indicate that the party "must really strive on our own to build the country and solve the livelihood [problem] of the people."[82] Such pronouncements are readily apparent in the Four-Year Plan: "Our revolutionary movement is a new experience, and an important one in the whole world, because we don't perform like others. . . . Ours is a new experience, and people are observing it. We don't follow any book. We act according to the actual situation in our country."[83]

In key respects, the governance, and by extension, the economic programs introduced by members of CPK are unique. This statement, though, requires some qualifications. In concrete ways, the initiatives forwarded and implemented by the Khmer Rouge do stand alone, yet in the abstract, the various projects are entirely consistent with those initiated by their communist forbears. For example, the collectivization of agricultural workers, detailed in chapter 3, was a stalwart feature of the Soviet Union, China, Vietnam, and many other governments that claimed adherence to Marxism-Leninism. However, the particular form of collectivism in Democratic Kampuchea did differ markedly from these others. Ultimately, we should evaluate CPK practices on their own terms, but understood within a broader historiography of both communism and Third Worldism.

The forwarding of self-reliance is especially pertinent in this regard. Frequently, scholars afford considerable weight to the bombastic claims of CPK spokespersons. Karl Jackson, for example, explains, "The Khmer revolutionaries were trying to establish total sovereignty and self-reliance in the cultural, economic, and political realms" and that their "application of the doctrine of self-reliance led the revolutionaries to seal Cambodia off from all but a very few close allies."[84] Charles Twining likewise concludes that CPK leaders "wanted genuinely to create a country totally independent from every point of view.

To achieve this state, Cambodia must be self-contained and self-reliant to the point of autarky."[85] Accordingly, scholars routinely describe the Khmer Rouge as extreme, radical, and exceptional. Viewed within the nationalist context of third-world socialism, however, these conclusions come under question; evaluated within the context of documentary evidence, they dissolve entirely. As we have seen, third-world leaders, particularly from the 1960s onward, advocated national development programs informed by state-guided industrialization. Accordingly, reference to self-reliance does not preclude international exchanges or the acceptance of external assistance. It does mean, in practice, a commitment to a policy of non-aligned development that does not engage in the type of transactions that undermines sovereignty.[86] In short, self-reliance entails the "autonomy of decision-making and full mobilization of a society's own resources under its own initiative and direction."[87] That said, and echoing the long-standing tensions inherent between internationalism and socialism in one country, *national* self-reliance does rest uneasily with *international* solidarity. Indeed, as Friedrich Wu explains, "The most contentious issue regarding self-reliance is how and at what level a country should set its threshold of participation in international exchanges and allow external involvement in its domestic economy."[88] Consequently, adherents to the Non-Aligned Movement championed the idea of *self-determination*. In other words, leaders throughout the Third World demanded the right to determine participation in the global economy on their own terms. This meant, in practice, that while many member states of the Non-Aligned Movement sought to increase cooperative relations in and among third-world states and to reduce their individual and collective dependence on either the Western powers or the Soviet Union, other members could choose to align with either superpower.

In Democratic Kampuchea, senior CPK leaders advocated both self-reliance and self-determination, not in an effort to isolate their country from the wider global economy but instead to participate on terms of their own choosing. Party members, for example, affirmed that foreign aid may be accepted; however, such offers would be refused if accepting them would affect their commitment to political-economic independence and mastery.[89] Accordingly, domestic objectives, such as the raising of people's standard of living, elided with structural objectives, such as the accumulation of capital. In theory, self-reliance affords primacy to the national objective of meeting basic human needs, such as the provision of food, shelter, housing, education, health care, and jobs.[90] Self-determination, relatedly, emphasizes international cooperation among like-minded governments. In concrete form, this dialectic of self-reliance and self-determine manifests as import-substitution industrialization.

Import-substitution industrialization prevailed in many third-world countries during the 1950s and 1970s.[91] As colonial empires collapsed and the substantial economic inequalities between the first and third worlds grew visible, the most pressing issue confronting the former colonies—including Democratic Kampuchea—was to raise productivity and accumulate capital. For decades if not centuries the economies of colonies were held in check by unfair trade arrangements and production processes that consigned the colonies to positions of subservience and dependence within the global economy. Colonies and former colonies historically imported most of their manufactured goods in return for the export of primary products, such as sugar, bananas, coffee, tea, and cotton. Following independence, however, innumerable difficulties, notably the asymmetry of existing infrastructure, threatened participation in the global economy and, by extension, domestic economic development. Consequently, in an effort to minimize future dependency, many nationalists throughout the third world attempted to protect their fragile economies through tariffs, quotas, and other protectionist policies while simultaneously investing in the manufacture of products currently imported.[92] In short, import-substitution industrialization constituted an economic strategy predicated on self-reliance.

In practice if not word, the leadership of the CPK pursued an economic program of import-substitution industrialization. Such an approach is readily apparent in many CPK documents. For example, minutes from a meeting held on May 8, 1976 state, "We will decrease importing items next year, including cotton and jute, because we are working hard to produce ours. We will import only some important items such as chemical fertilizer, plastic, acid, iron factory, and other raw materials." Apparently, CPK officials deemed this strategy most appropriate, in that solutions were not to be found "by taking loans from the West or Eastern Europe," for in so doing the CPK would lose its "self-reliant stance."[93] However, adoption of import-substitution industrialization required key calculations, notably, what the country could produce locally and what required to be imported. To this end, CPK officials premised Democratic Kampuchea as brimming with "such things as land, livestock, natural resource, water sources such as lakes, river and ponds" and that these afforded their country "great advantages compared with China, Vietnam, or Africa."[94] In other words, the CPK leadership perceived Democratic Kampuchea in *market competition* with other states and as such required a comparative advantage in order to succeed.

In a documented entitled "Report of Activities of the Party Center according to the General Political Tasks of 1976," it is noted, "We can export and sell many products such as kapok, shrimp, squid, elephant fish, and turtles. All of these products can earn foreign exchange. There are great possibilities for exporting peanuts, wheat, corn, sesame, and beans. The objective would be to save up these products for export. Almost anything can be exported, so long as we don't consume it ourselves, but set it aside."[95] The report further details, "We have the potential to achieve full quotas in rubber, cement, railroads and salt. We have progressed nicely, almost with empty hands. We have achieved good results. But the possibilities are even greater. We must expand the Plan. Our line is to stress industry and the working class as the basis."[96] Under colonial rule, French officials looked to the export of agricultural products, especially rice but also rubber, to fill their coffers; Sihanouk likewise tried to gain necessary capital through the export of rice and rubber. It is thus hardly to surprising that senior members of the CPK turned also to agriculture, notably rice and rubber, as their country's comparative advantage. For example, during the aforementioned zone assembly held in June 1976, a senior party member identified rapid agricultural development as crucial to the postrevolutionary success of Democratic Kampuchea. The speaker explained, "National construction proceeds along the lines laid down by the Party. The important point of this is building up our agriculture, which is backward, into modern agriculture within ten to fifteen years."[97] This is a key refrain of CPK documentation: the modernization of agriculture. A speech delivered in August 1976, for example, reaffirmed the need to "transform agriculture from a backward type to a modern type in ten to fifteen years."[98]

From a material standpoint, the objectives of the CPK are clear: to establish a modern agricultural system premised upon efficiency and the market-logics of capital accumulation. This was no desire to construct of agrarian utopia, nor was this an attempt to model Cambodia after the ancient empire of Angkor. Rather, senior officials proposed and implemented plans to transform rapidly—from their vantage point—a backward and inefficient farming system into a modern, highly efficient agricultural system that would furnish the necessary capital for rapid industrialization. Consequently, party officials planned to purchase key inputs necessary for the expansion of rice, including fertilizers, pesticides, and farming implements from foreign markets in exchange for rice. Increases in agricultural productivity in turn would result in the increase in the quantity of rice available for exchange and provide the necessary injections of capital to spur industrial growth. Domestically, plans called for the promotion of items necessary to facilitate the people's livelihood: plates, pots, spoons, mosquito nets, shovels, hoes, and so on. In practice, most of these industries never materialized, although textile factories and some machine shops were in operation. Party leaders also did not neglect other agricultural commodities, as they identified many other non-rice products for potential export: rubber, corns, beans, fish, and other forest products. However, for the CPK, "these products are only complimentary." Their argument was profit-based: "For 100,000 tons of milled rice, we would get [US] $20 million; if we had 500,000 tons we'd get $100 million. . . . We must increase rice production in order to obtain capital. Other products, which are only complimentary[,] will be increased in the future."[99] In practice, the CPK failed to deliver according to plan. Nonetheless, these plans provide insight into the decision-making processes, at least throughout 1976, as to the anticipated economic organization of Democratic Kampuchea—a topic I explore in detail in the next two chapters.

Conclusions

The 1970s was the great age of third-world rhetoric of common cause and common action.[100] The decade witnessed a growing number of leaders throughout Asia, Africa, and Latin America—including many senior officials of the CPK—adopt a distinctly revolutionary tone and outlook that stressed self-reliance and self-determination.[101] As Khieu Samphan affirmed, "Democratic Kampuchea resolutely remains in the great family of non-aligned countries."[102]

Previous scholarship has downplayed the salience of the CPK's position as a member of the Non-Aligned Movement. This inattention has led to considerable misunderstandings of subsequent policies forwarded by the CPK, and consequently scholars too often fail to contextualize properly the international dimensions of CPK domestic policies. Indeed, hyperbolic statements of autarky belie the global context of Democratic Kampuchea's political economy and CPK governance. Far from being an inward-looking regime marked by isolationist tendencies, senior leaders of the CPK heralded Democratic Kampuchea as exemplary of third-world development. Indeed, party officials proclaimed, "the leadership of the Communist Party of Kampuchea has become an especially valuable model for the peoples of the world, for the world [revolutionary] movement, and for the international communist movement."[103]

The political and economic transformations that followed military revolution in Democratic Kampuchea place the CPK in line with other anticolonial movements that imposed state-led development programs from the 1940s onward. In general, state capitalist forms of governance attempt to restructure agro-export societies through national industrialization, create internal markets through agrarian reform that limit or eliminate the political power of property owner classes, nationalize the control of natural resources, and harness labor to national development projects.[104] In this way, the CPK followed lockstep along the path charted by the Non-Aligned Movement. To be determined was the extent that CPK officials put in practice the lofty ideals enshrined in the Declaration of the New International Economic Order or the Colombo Declaration or, conversely, set in motion an economic program antithetical to these hoped for goals of productive and distribution justice.

"We Are Building Socialism in the Cooperatives"

In 1975 senior officials of the Communist Party of Kampuchea confronted a question that dogged Marxist revolutionaries throughout the twentieth century: What is the economic structure of postrevolutionary society?[1] Marx is decidedly unprogrammatic in his answer. For Marx, history consists of the changes brought about by human beings in the process of producing their existence. History, in other words, does not simply happen; nor is history predetermined. Rather, history *happens* through the activity of real people interacting with each other.[2] As Marx famously writes, "Men make their own history." However, Marx quickly qualifies this, remarking, "They do not make it just as they please; they do not make it under circumstances chosen by themselves, but under circumstances directly encountered, given, and transmitted from the past."[3]

According to Marx, the economic structure of society following revolution will necessarily be constrained by those structural conditions and social relations in existence *prior* to the revolution. There is, effectively, a historical continuity, that is, a transitional period between one mode of production and the next. This is not to suggest too fine a dichotomy but instead a dialectic transition. In this way, material conditions do not predetermine what will happened in history; they indicate rather the constraints—and possibilities—of what is possible.[4] So too the transformation of society following revolution. Marx postulates, "What we have to deal with here is a communist society, not as it has developed on its own foundations, but, on the contrary, as it emerges from capitalist society; which is thus in every respect, economically, morally and intellectually, still stamped with the birthmarks of the old society from whose womb it emerges."[5] In other words, prerevolutionary modes of production necessarily condition the social organization of postrevolutionary society.

As Marx describes in the *Grundrisse*, "The new forces of production and relations of production do not develop out of nothing, nor drop from the sky, nor from the womb of the self-positing Idea; but from within an in antithesis to the existing development of production and the inherited, traditional relations of property."[6] This explains why Marx premised that communism advances with the maturity of capitalism. Only with the maturation of capitalism and the corresponding deepening of alienation among the proletariat were conditions pregnant with revolution.[7] Senior leaders of the Communist Party of Kampuchea—in contradistinction to Marx's reading of history—premised their revolution as making a radical break, a social rupture, within the *longue durée* of Cambodian history. The Four-Year Plan, for example, affirms, "We are not preparing ourselves as a step toward socialism. In fact, our society is already a socialist society." The plan continues, "We leap from a people's democratic revolution to a socialist revolution, and quickly build socialism. We don't need a long period of time for the transformation."[8]

Once in power the CPK leadership identified (and probably anticipated) a lack of proper political consciousness among its members as a key obstacle to overcome. Party leaders recognized that most peasants joined the Khmer Rouge in support of the deposed prince and in response to the incessant bombing by the United States, and they understood that the rank-and-file cadre ideologically were ill informed, in large part because party officials downplayed their communist credentials and political training was minimal throughout the civil war. As such, during a zone assembly held August 20–24, 1975, members of the Standing Committee concluded, "The important problem is to sort out the political situation of the people, and do whatever is necessary to make the people stable in a monolithic bloc of solidarity with the revolutionary state power." To this end, as the CPK assumed its vanguard role in an attempt to build socialism—but also to establish the conditions necessary for their planned communal society—as it was necessary to fundamentally alter the existing socioeconomic organization of Cambodia. For the Khmer Rouge, they most certainly perceived the razing of towns and hamlets and the subsequent forced relocation of men, women, and children onto collectives as a blow against the evils of feudalism and capitalism; it was, effectively, a strike against private property and thus a path toward communism. However, forced collectivization and forced ex-urbanization provided also the material conditions required for economic development. Indeed, for the senior leadership of the CPK, the establishment of agricultural cooperatives was paramount. "Concretely, it is imperative to strengthen and expand the cooperatives," CPK leaders concluded at the August 20–24, 1975 zone assembly. It was necessary to employ "the strength of the cooperatives as the core, making them the hard core for the absorption of the new people. The new people must be satellites of the cooperatives politically and economically. This is our orientation. The people will be firm only when the cooperatives are solid." The text continues, "The cooperatives must be further strengthened and expanded. . . . In order to be able to effectively defend the country, the issue of people's living standards in the cooperatives must be resolved. We are striving to sort things out for the new people, too, to make them satisfied with the Revolution and make them see that this regime is one that belongs to them, so that they no longer desire to go anywhere else." [9]

CPK officials made similar pronouncements at a later zone assembly, held June 3–7, 1976. "There are always contradictions when we are making a socialist revolution," the speaker (perhaps Pol Pot) declared; "we cannot escape them." Accordingly, party leaders required appropriate measures, and consequently it was important to "grasp hold of the cooperatives." Significantly, the speaker explained that cooperatives provided the framework to build socialism, for in the collectivization of peasants it was possible "to make people understand the very important political line of the Party." The spokesperson directed, "Grasp hold of their consciousness, make things clear to them. The Party's every task and plan must be explained to them until they understand and things become clear. Dikes, canals, three tons—all is to build and defend the country. . . . If they understand clearly, they are happy, they do their own fighting, they have their children join the army or the work brigades to raise dikes and dig canals." [10] Ironically, the brutal policies associated with the collectivization of the peasantry unexpectedly and unintentionally created the social circumstances that Marx most loathed, as senior leaders of the CPK set Cambodia on a path whereby the dictates of a system of production for exchange subsumed an entire society. Indeed, as CPK authorities worked to eliminate *individual* private property, they effectively founded an autocratic society whereby all property was held by a ruling class, the CPK itself.

Class struggle, for Marx, was always about the struggle to overcome alienation. On the factory floor, for example, a revolutionary political consciousness among the proletariat begins with self-realization, but this result comes about only through worker solidarity. Absent the conditions of alienation, a self-realized proletariat is impossible. In prerevolutionary Cambodia, the material conditions of the peasantry—while precarious—were not alienating. Farmers mostly owned their land and the means of production, and although subject to usury, they were far from being estranged. In this chapter, I trace the transformation of precapitalist Khmer farming practices into an agricultural sector dominated by state-managed cooperatives.

The Allure of Agricultural Collectivization

As detailed in chapter 2, senior officials of the CPK drafted the Party's Four-Year Plan between July 21 and August 2, 1976. Prominent in the plan were two mutually reinforcing objectives. The first proposed that the party would "serve the people's livelihood, and to raise the people's standard of living quickly, both in terms of supplies and in other material goods." A second objective was "to seek, gather, save, and increase capital from agriculture" to expand rapidly Cambodia's agricultural, industrial, and defense sectors. To achieve industrial self-sufficiency, specifically, the CPK announced that it would "only have to earn [foreign] capital from agriculture."[11] For the Khmer Rouge these economic objectives would translate into "a relentless enhancement and expansion of cooperatives."[12]

CPK officials understood the promotion of the people's livelihood and the accumulation of capital as dialectic. In a commentary published before the unveiling of the Four-Year Plan, party leaders explained, "The promotion of people's living standards is not a separate duty but is strictly related with all Party's political lines, in particular, it is one of the most important keys to national defense and reconstruction within the Party's collectivism." The commentary continues, "Political sense cannot be separated from economic sense," meaning that "when collectivism is obviously efficient and serving the people's interests[,] then the people, workers and peasants will voluntarily support the cooperatives and unions."[13] Here we begin to gain a sense of why communist governments, such as the CPK, pursued, with seemingly unbridled exuberance, political and economic programs centered on the collectivization of agricultural workers.[14] And yet this is a question infrequently asked of the Khmer Rouge. Too often, scholars take at face value the necessity of collectivization among communist governments. Implicit in these accounts is a sentiment that the forced assemblage of workers onto large-scale farms is uniquely and definitively Marxist. Marx, however, was ambivalent about the possibility of collectives in the fomentation of revolution; and he was less assured of the viability of collectives as economic engines in postrevolutionary society. To grasp fully the salience of cooperatives in the history of Marxism, it is necessary to understand first the role of the peasantry for Marx.[15]

Recall that Marx (and Engels) stressed the revolutionary role of an industrial proletariat in more advanced capitalist states. For Marx the proletariat was key to overcome capitalism, for only the proletariat—the alienated industrial workers—would realize their exploitation and affect change through collective action. For those societies lacking a sizable proletarian population, Marx was ambiguous at best with respect to the revolutionary potential of the peasantry.[16] His hesitation centered on the contradictory position of the peasant. Peasants personified both the bourgeois and the proletariat. As owner of the means of production, that is, of land and tools, the peasant was a capitalist; as one who physically tilled the land, the peasant was a laborer. This contradiction posed a nagging theoretical problem for Marx: in the advent of revolution, with which side would the peasant align?

Absent theoretical clarity, Marx turned to real-world examples. In his studies of England, for example, Marx concluded that under feudalism the expropriation of the peasantry formed a necessary precondition for capitalism. Dispossessed of their lands, English peasants gravitated toward the growing cities and formed the bulk of the rising proletarian class. In the transition from feudalism to capitalism, at least in England, the peasantry thus assumed an important role because, on the one hand, there were proportionately fewer peasants and, on the other hand, many of the proletariat were former peasants. That the remaining peasants did not assume a more active role, in part because, as members of the petite bourgeoisie, they retained a stake in the private ownership of their farms.[17] Conversely, in his analysis of contemporary conditions in Russia, Marx was even less optimistic. Several commentators at the time, notably Vera Zasulich, questioned if village communes (*mir*) could serve as necessary incubators of revolution.[18] Marx took seriously this possibility but ultimately concluded they could serve no role either in the overthrow of the czar of in the establishment of socialism. That said, overall, Marx was supportive of efforts to work across class divides, including a possible peasant-proletarian alliance. However, in the advent of revolution, it would be the proletariat, not the peasantry, that took the lead.

This is not to deny, either, the salience of agricultural collectives for Marx. From an organizational standpoint, Marx recognized that economies of scale and size are extremely important in agriculture, and that large-scale farms are in better position to take advantage of new advances in agricultural technology and mechanical inventions. Simply put, Marx perceived in the small-scale, fragmented pattern of peasant agriculture a barrier to cooperative production, the division of labor, and the development of productive forces.[19] That is, the dispersed form of *farming* prohibited both capital accumulation and the solidarity necessary for individual self-realization. For these reasons, the consolidation of farms into agricultural units was a necessary precondition for socialist transformation. However, neither Marx's theoretical or empirical analyses say much about when or how, or even why, collectivization should take place in a country aspiring to be socialist. Indeed, nowhere did Marx discuss in concrete terms what the final organizational form of collectivized agriculture would be.[20] Nevertheless, subsequent inheritors of Marxism, notably in Russia and Germany, argued incessantly over the advantages and disadvantages of collectivization. Many Marxists, for example, countered that economies in agriculture were not so great and any benefits accruing from the consolidation of small farms depended upon the particular crop and intensity of agriculture. Other theorists, including Karl Kautsky, maintained that while large farms are more productive in general, several counteracting tendencies operate against their formation, thus identifying key organizational problems inherent to collectivization. Still others, such as Georgi Plekhanov, opposed the confiscation of land, believing that farms would be more productive under private ownership. Indeed, the German social democrat Eduard David argued that collectivization was a bad idea at any time.[21]

If there was any consensus among those Marxists who debated the necessity of collectivization, it was that details matter. Paramount, of course, was the economic relationship between agriculture and industry and, by extension, between the rural hinterland and urban centers. Equally important were myriad political and social considerations, including but not limited to the acquisition of land, potential compensation to landowners, rates of taxation, and the overall form of labor. In practice, Marxist theorists isolated one or two key factors upon which to base their arguments, all of which bore scant resemblance to anything Marx ever proposed. Nor were individual inheritors of Marx consistent in their claims and arguments. In the Soviet Union especially, Marxists, including Lenin, changed their minds depending on concrete realities and on the ever-changing political winds. Indeed, from the late 1920s onward, the fortunes of many Soviet Marxists rose and fell according to their alignment with Stalin.[22]

Immediately following the revolution, Lenin and the Bolsheviks postponed the goal of large-scale cooperative agriculture and adopted instead a platform based on the parceling and redistribution of land.[23] Eight months after the Bolshevik seizure of power, however, civil war engulfed Russia. Lasting nearly three years, the unfolding violence occasioned the introduction of an economic policy known as "war communism."[24] As Adam Kaufman writes, the deteriorating economic situation coupled with the instinct of self-preservation forced the Bolsheviks to take drastic economic measures. In order to feed the army and to supply it with weapons and other types of war material, the Bolsheviks militarized and nationalized all resources of the nation. This included the confiscation of grain surpluses, the elimination of market exchange, and the disappearance of money.[25] Consequently, throughout the war communism period the Soviet regime and the peasants clashed on the policy of state monopoly, compulsory delivery, and state procurement.[26] For Soviet Marxists, these measures "looked like a great step forward on the road to a classless, socialist economy." This was a "road on which wages, profits, credit and all other institutions and categories of the commodity-capitalist system would be discarded and dropped by the wayside and where, in their stead, Soviet and party economic regulations would replace the spontaneous laws of a market economy."[27]

It soon became apparent, especially to Lenin, that a frontal assault on Russia's economy was ill timed. The problem with war communism, Lenin explained, was that the Soviet government had attempted to move too quickly to communist production and distribution. Far from an effective sustainable economic program, war communism was (for Lenin) a necessary but temporary response to a wartime crisis.[28] In 1921, consequently, Russian planners introduced the New Economic Policy (NEP). Effectively, the NEP replaced compulsory grain deliveries by agricultural tax in kind and reestablished market agriculture, thereby freeing the peasants both to sell surpluses and to buy industrial products.[29] The NEP was clearly a retreat from the previous position of a direct attack on the bases of the capitalist system, as the program entailed a partial restoration of a commodity-capitalist order in Russia.[30] Indeed, in practice, the NEP marked a variant of state capitalism previously espoused by Lenin. Lenin came to see the importance of trading cooperatives, not peasant communes, as the centerpiece of state policy through the transition to socialism in the rural sector. For Lenin a limited revival of market mechanisms in the agricultural sector was necessary to obtain much needed grain, but this could happen only by winning the support of the peasants.[31] Although this implied the abandonment of orthodox Marxism, Lenin promoted a return to market mechanisms as a necessary stage in the transition to communism.[32]

The NEP served to reorganize and revitalize the economy in the wake of the civil war. However, the NEP could not resolve the twin problems of underinvestment in industry and the unreliability of peasant grain deliveries. In addition, party militants began to fear that the transition to communism was not progressing satisfactorily. Many Soviet Marxists feared that the power of the private sector and the influence of bourgeois ideology were expanding at the expense of socialism.[33] Consequently, a growing number of party members (especially those loyal to Stalin) backed the abandonment of the NEP in favor of "primitive socialist accumulation."

In 1920 Vladimir Smirnov and Nikolai Bukharin, respected leaders of the Bolshevik Party, forwarded *primitive socialist accumulation* as a necessary process analogous to Marx's account of *primitive capitalist accumulation*.[34] In *Capital* and the *Grundrisse*, Marx identifies a fundamental paradox of—and limitation to—classical economics, in that the process of capital accumulation presupposes the existence of some preaccumulated capital available for investment. Classical economists, however, such as Adam Smith, were unable (or unwilling) to specify the origins of capital. For Marx, therefore, primitive (or original) accumulation is a concept that designates the processes that generate the preconditions of the ongoing accumulation of capital; it designates that phase of growth in which the capitalist elements of the economy develop at the expense of the precapitalist sector.[35] In short, for Marx primitive accumulation constitutes the "original sin" of capitalist production.

More precisely, primitive capitalist accumulation represents the brutal separation of the immediate producers, the peasantry, from their means of production. As a *structural* transformation, therefore, primitive capitalist accumulation marks the dispossession of land commonly held by the producers and two basic conditions inform this transformation. First, laborers must be unable to secure their own means of production, and second, laborers must have no alternative but to offer their labor power to those who own the means of production. The social processes of primitive accumulation vary though, conditioned in part by specific histories and geographies of displacement and dispossession. These include the commodification and privatization of land; the forceful expulsion of peasant populations; the conversion of various forms of property rights into exclusive private property rights; the commodification of labor power and the suppression of traditional forms of production and consumption; the appropriation of natural resources; and the monetization of exchange and taxation.[36]

A key takeaway is the diverse pathways by which capital comes into existence. It is not the case that waged labor or the elimination of individually owned private property signify exclusively the introduction of capitalism. As Harry Cleaver explains, "In some cases the creation of waged labor was entirely marginal. Capital often either reinforced existing forms of social control and production (e.g. indirect rule) or transformed existing societies into new forms that did not use wage labor yet were well integrated into capital."[37] Jim Glassman agrees: "the process of proletarianization seems much more a contingent outcome of specific class struggles than a predetermined trajectory of capitalist development." Glassman elaborates that "in some contexts, capitalist can benefit not only from garnering cheap resources but from turning precapitalist workers into wage laborers in the process. In such contexts, however, workers themselves may struggle against this process of proletarization with greater or lesser effect. In other contexts capitalists can benefit from maintaining a large non-proletarianized labor force that contributes indirectly to capitalists' ability to formally exploit wage labor." [38]

Marx understood also that those people subjected to dispossession and displacement associated with primitive accumulation did not readily accept their fate. History illustrates that resistance was—and remains—ever present in opposition to the expansion of capital. In the *Grundrisse* Marx explains, "They must be forced to work within the conditions posited by capital. The propertyless are more inclined to become vagabonds and robbers and beggars than workers." [39] Consequently, a bourgeois legal system—"bloody legislation"— was imposed that effectively criminalized those people forcibly dispossessed and displaced from their land and livelihoods. To this end, Marx describes the history of capitalism as being "written in the annals of mankind in letters of blood and fire." [40] As Cleaver concludes, "the struggle between the emerging classes was about whether capital would be able to impose the commodity-form of class relations, that is, whether it had the power to drive peasants and tribal peoples from the land, to destroy their handicrafts and culture in order to create a new class of workers." [41]

Marxist theoreticians in Russia were well versed in Marx's historical studies of the English transition from feudalism to capitalism, and many Russian Marxists cautioned that these methods—the expropriation of the peasantry, enclosures of agricultural lands, and the exploitation of foreign colonies— were not open to Soviet Russia. [42] As Paul Le Blanc summarizes, "In the face of the multiple and murderous catastrophes of a brutal and brutalizing civil war, a rapid succession of foreign invasions, a vicious economic blockade, and the collapse of industry and agriculture, the radical soviet democracy of 1917 was destroyed." [43] For these reasons, in the hands of Smirnov and Bukharin, primitive *capitalist* accumulation became primitive *socialist* accumulation, a programmatic thesis to for the accumulation of necessary capital in a country beset by civil war. Crucially, Smirnov and Bukharin both understood the main problem of primary socialist accumulation facing Russia as the conscription of labor power from the presocialist sector, that is, the rural, agricultural areas, into the nationalized economy. In effect, this provided some justification for the mobilization efforts under war communism. In roundabout fashion, primitive socialist accumulation served a similar function as that premised by Marx, namely an incipient transformation of the peasantry into proletarians. During the NEP, however, the compulsory deployment of workers gave way to more moderate instruments and discussion of primitive socialist accumulation dropped off.[44]

The NEP represented a novel form of economic production and several Russian theorists, notably Evgeny Preobrazhensky, tried to make sense of the system. Among Russia's leading economists, Preobrazhensky adhered most closely to Marx's writings than any other.[45] The problem for Preobrazhensky was simple: If the Bolshevik regime was to survive and socialism prosper in Soviet Russia, then the Party had to realize two conditions. On the one hand, Russia had to achieve an absolute increase in total output each year in order to provide for its people, and, on the other hand, the state (socialist) sector had to grow more rapidly than the private (agrarian) sector.[46] The move away from the NEP required a process of primitive socialist accumulation, albeit in a decidedly different form from that of Smirnov or Bukharin. Whereas Smirnov and Bukharin considered the problem of Russian economic growth as the transfer of labor power, Preobrazhensky framed the problem as the transfer of products. For Preobrazhensky, sustained industrial growth required the construction of new factories and equipment, in short, that investments in fixed capital had to increase before an expanded output of manufacturing goods was possible. The challenge was to obtain the necessary capital for investment in industry. Foreign sources were not possible for the Soviets. Capital accumulation, therefore, had to come from within. The solution lay in the vast agricultural lands: Soviet state-run industries could only expand by drawing in surplus product from the private economy, that is, the peasantry.[47] Cooperatives, therefore, posed obstacles to the effective planning of a state-run economy. According to Preobrazhensky, "since cooperatives can exist in a capitalist society without in any way threatening its existence, this shows quite plainly that the cooperative in itself contains no active principle of transformation in the direction of socialized production relations."[48] For this reason, he premised Soviet planners should permit cooperatives only under state direction, a conclusion shared and expanded later by Stalin both in the form of collectivization and in the liquidation of communes.[49]

Other Russian Marxists, including Bukharin, called out an obvious drawback to these measures. If peasants received less compensation for the products, why would they produce beyond their immediate needs? In other words, asymmetric pricing acted as a disincentive to increased production: Farmers would simply grow enough for their own subsistence and refuse to sell at artificial prices set by the government. This posed a significant dilemma, in that Russian planners concluded agriculture was the primary path toward capital accumulation. Looking to the future, Bukharin agreed that under communism, there would be absolute freedom; during the transition period, however, compulsion was necessary, simply because the proletariat in semifeudal Russia did not yet constitute a homogenous group, that is, a class. For Bukharin compulsory discipline in all its forms—"from shootings to labor service"—was required to make workers conform to the standards of the vanguard.[50]

The introduction of primitive socialist accumulation as a weapon in the arsenal of Soviet planning marks an important departure in Marxist political economy in that primitive socialist became a necessary means to an end. Under Stalin and those who followed, the draconian practices that developed under primitive socialist accumulation became ends in their own right. This followed from the conclusion of Stalin and those around him that socialist revolutions in other countries would not come to the aid of the Soviet Republic; hence, Russian planners would build socialism in a single country.[51]

From 1929 onward, state-imposed collectivization became the centerpiece of Soviet agrarian policy, indeed, of the entire political economy constructed by the Soviet state with far-reaching societal implications.[52] Programmatically, economic planning at the national level is impractical, if not impossible, if myriad small-scale private farmers make production decisions. Rather, planning is possible only if all sectors of the economy come under centralized control. To that end, collectivization would permit the government the necessary social and political control to carry out directly a coordinated and coherent policy of economic development.[53] Notably, that which became "Stalinism" flowed inexorably from these premises. As Le Blanc writes, "Stalin's 'revolution from above' pushed through the forced collectivization of land and a rapid industrialization that remorselessly squeezed the working class, choked intellectual and cultural life, and killed millions of peasants, culminating in purge trials, mass executions, and a ghastly network of prison camps brutally exploiting its victims' labor."[54]

Stalin's ruthless collectivization program provided an important example for younger generations of Marxists, especially throughout the third world.[55] As James White identifies, the Bolshevik revolution was a turning point in the history of Marxism. From this point onward, Marxists everywhere looked on the Russian communist party as the organization that knew how to make a socialist revolution and saw it as the organization to emulate.[56] Soviet-style collectivization, to this end, became the model for agrarian development in many parts of the world and the centerpiece for class and accumulation strategies that were to underlie rapid industrialization.[57] Third-world Marxists saw that the Soviet Union had collectivized its agriculture and in the process embarked on a rapid investment program that transformed a "backward" country into one of the world's two superpowers.

Programmatically, the Soviets' apparent economic success was plain for all to see, and consequently many revolutionaries believed that collectivized agriculture was the key to economic development in a socialist setting. As Pryor concludes, the importance of the power of example set by the Soviet Union cannot be overemphasized. It meant that Marxist revolutionaries adopted an economic solution born of a specific set of circumstances in countries where those circumstances did not necessarily hold. It also meant that Marxists the world over subscribed to a faith in the extreme centralization of their respective political economies.[58] Consequently, Russia's direct experience with revolution and the collectivization of agriculture served as model. Revolutionaries certainly drew inspiration from the lofty polemics espoused by Marx and Engels in *The Communist Manifesto*, and revolutionaries justified their actions on the words of a man lionized by the Soviet Politburo. In the twentieth century, communist governments from Asia to Africa to South America championed agricultural collectives *in spite of* their allegiance to Marx.

Mao's People's Republic of China illustrates the adoption and modification of Soviet collectivization. The Chinese Communist Party pursued an urban-based Bolshevik revolutionary strategy before, in 1927, shifting to a rural-based and supposedly peasant-led strategy. Importantly, a moderate approach to land reform in the "base areas" facilitated recruitment to the fledgling CCP. When the CCP came to power in 1949, however, its leadership wholeheartedly embraced Soviet theory and policy on building communism, notably, the belief that the abolishment of private property resulted in the elimination of classes, thus marking the onset of socialism.[59] In Vietnam also, members of the ruling communist party saw the need to reorganize agricultural production in order for their country to prosper under a socialist political economy.[60] Much like their counterparts in China, state planners in Vietnam reasoned that the collective labor in cooperatives would more likely generate economies of scale than traditional household-based agricultural production.[61] In addition, the formation of cooperatives would enable greater control over the production, consumption, and trade of agricultural products; importantly, party officials could redirect a significant proportion of earnings from agriculture toward the building factories and other components of the socialist economy.[62]

For senior CPK members, their revolution was exceptional. As one senior leader explains, "we did not copy anyone. We analyzed our society concretely, and we raised our line according to our concrete situation."[63] As scholars, we must read this statement with exceptional scrutiny, for Khmer Rouge rhetoric is prone to hyperbole. Thus, while the CPK did not openly and obviously model its revolution or postrevolutionary society after any specific predecessor, it did confront many of the problems associated with other communist parties. The repeated references to "building socialism" and "self-reliance" peppered throughout CPK documents, for example, bear witness to this. As such, when in 1973 CPK leaders initiated a program of rural collectivization, they joined the ranks of other communist revolutionaries who followed the path blazed by Soviet planners.[64] In the following two sections, I document and evaluate the transformation of traditional Khmer farming practices and the formation of agrarian capitalism within Democratic Kampuchea. My argument is that the particular form of rural collectivization imposed by party leaders marked a radical—and unexpected—break in Cambodia's political economy, namely the subsumption of farm-based labor by capital. I begin with a discussion of traditional Khmer rice farming practices.

Traditional Farming Practices in Cambodia

Agrarian transformations involve changes not only in the cultivation and harvesting of crops but also in society. That is, rather than just sectoral adjustments and adaptations in the form of, for example, technological innovations, agrarian transformations entail a dialectic interplay of material conditions and social organization, of concrete practice and human consciousness. Agrarian transformations, accordingly, are not simply the replacement of draft animals with tractors or the introduction of new seeds; instead, agrarian transformations directly affect the entirety of society, a radical reconfiguration of social and spatial practices. To this end, it is helpful to distinguish, following Henry Bernstein, between *farming* and *agriculture*.[65] *Farming* is what farmers do and have done through millennia: cultivate the soil, raise livestock, or some combination of the two, typically within a system of established fields and demarcated pastures. Especially important are local knowledges: the dynamic and complex bodies of expertise, that is, practices and skills developed and sustained by peoples, households, and communities with shared histories and experiences.[66] As a social, material practice, farmers have always had to manage the natural conditions of their activities, with all the relevant risks and uncertainties, including the vagaries of weather and climate, the potential degradation of soils, and the danger of pests and disease.[67] With the introduction of new techniques, for example, farmers adapt these in response to their direct knowledge of local conditions, and plan accordingly the selection of seeds, of when to plant and to harvest, and of specific tools necessary to carry out these activities. Farming, in short, happens with the aid of generation upon generation of experimentation and accumulation of knowledge.

In agrarian societies before the advent of capitalism, farming was what most people did.[68] However, with the commodification of society, spurred often but not always by colonialism, farming in many parts of the world gave way to *agriculture*. Unlike farming, agriculture prefigures the market exchange of agrarian commodities. Decisions centered predominantly on subsistence needs give way, accordingly, to demands of the transactional exchange for surplus accumulation. The agrarian past is unevenly but eventually undermined by the increasing scale of agricultural production and trade, based on ever-wider and deeper integration with upstream and downstream industries of an emerging capitalist agricultural sector.[69] In the process, as agriculture subsumes traditional farming practices, societies likewise undergo profound alterations.

Before the Khmer Rouge came to power, traditional Khmer society centered on the nuclear family, as families worked together as a unit, responsible for both household production and consumption.[70] Women and men contributed to agricultural and other income-generating activities, though gendered divisions of labor existed. Men would typically plow the fields, transport goods, and maintain localized irrigation schemes, while women would prepare seed rice, sow and transplant the seedlings, and harvest the crops.[71] Typically, families cultivated vegetables and herbs in small gardens around their homes; families also commonly kept fruit trees and palms. Most households raised livestock, such as chickens, ducks, and pigs, while families that were more prosperous perhaps maintained a stable of draft animals, including oxen and water buffalo. Women were mostly responsible for the cultivation of vegetable gardens and the raising of livestock. Depending on one's home environment, families could supplement their resources by fishing and hunting (both normally male activities) and manufacturing (often by the elderly) small household items, such as baskets, for immediate use.

Families commonly lived in small hamlets or villages, usually inhabited by several hundred people. These assumed three basic spatial forms: linear, with houses spaced relatively close to another along a road or waterway; compact, with houses clustered in a roughly circular form, surrounded by farmlands; and dispersed, with houses scattered at some distance from one another.[72] Regardless of form, hamlets constituted the primary political-administrative unit, with village chiefs serving as local arbiter. Also important, however, was the intricate network of social relations, composed of kin and neighbors, and the corresponding loyalties and obligations that followed.[73] Within Khmer society, matrilocal marital residence was customary, as young married couples would live with or near the bride's mother. This arrangement served both social and economic functions, as the newly married couple would be able to provide for the woman's parents in their old age while the grandparents could also help raise the children.[74]

Social interactions beyond the confines of one's hamlet were often quite limited. This is not to say that households in rural villages were isolated; rather, outside contact was often purposeful. Social interactions, understandably, were strongest with neighboring villages. Ordinarily, men and women made at least one or two visits to nearby communities each day. Visits ranged from the banal, such as the exchange of news or gossip, to the pragmatic, for example, to buy and sell food and other necessary goods, to the deeply personal, to attend one another's important life-course ceremonies or to participate in religious functions. Specialists, such as midwives and carpenters, would frequently travel between villages to ply their trades. Household members might also visit larger hamlets and towns, on a more infrequent basis, perhaps once or twice a week, to purchase products not available locally or to visit commune chiefs for consultation over legal-administrative concerns, to report births and deaths, to obtain marriage or divorce certificates, or to adjudicate disputes that are more serious. Less common were visits to regional market towns, such as Battambang, Sisiphon, and Stung Treng, and travels to Cambodia's capital city, Phnom Penh, which were exceptionally rare for most peasants. Indeed, unless they lived relatively close to the capital, transportation costs, both in terms of money and time, were prohibitive for any regular interaction.[75]

The gradual dissolution of the natural economy occurred under French colonial rule. Change was both socially and spatially uneven, as Cambodia remained fundamentally an agrarian society with industrialization only minimally developed under the French. Arguably, the most far-reaching transformation entailed changes in land ownership. Before the arrival of the French, the Khmer king was the traditional owner of land and water. Farmers could, however, claim the right to land access and use by clearing forests and cultivating the land. If a farmer stopped cultivating the land for three consecutive years, de facto possession was lost and the land was available for use by others. This practice, known as appropriation "by the plow," was common and accepted as long as settlement did not infringe on the rights of others. If disputes did arise, village chiefs were the first line of adjudication.[76] Broadly, though, high-ranking officials, personally assigned by the king, exercised the most power with respect to property. Most influential were the myriad provincial or district governors, responsible for the collection of taxes.[77]

French colonial administrators dramatically transformed property ownership by the plow and initiated the commodification of land and labor. Their impetus was to establish the conditions necessary for the export of rice and other commodities, such as rubber, to accumulate capital for projects both in Indochina and in France. This required, on the one hand, the introduction of technical changes in production and the existence of a ready supply of workers, but also, on the other hand, legal changes in landownership. To this end, the French introduced the concept of *private* land ownership, coupled with the elimination of *communal* land property rights, in an effort to stimulate rice production and to secure lands suitable for French exploitation. Specifically, the modernization of land property rights consisted of a change from a possession right to an ownership right. Here, the difference is subtle but significant. Possession suggests that the right to the use of land entails certain conditions, including, as we have seen, a continued presence and utilization of the land as recognized by village and commune authorities. Ownership rights, however, are definitive and inalienable. The transformation of possession to ownership rights under the French, therefore, operated on the premise that the latter provides more security and incentives to farmers and investors to use the land more efficiently and thus constitutes an important step toward the commodification of land.[78] Consequently, the constitution of land as property by the French colonial administration awarded 139,559 hectares in 8,532 land grants to settlers; this transference created favorable conditions for the development of an incipient capitalist economy, for it signaled a different form of land redistribution. Large landholdings (albeit often fragmented) tended to expand, albeit gradually, at the expense of small household farms.[79]

Other practices introduced by the French contributed to the subsumption of labor to capital. A new tax system was instituted, a policy that obliged peasants to pay a certain percentage of their production in cash; accordingly, peasants were compelled to engage in the incipient market economy by selling part of the production. This cash economy created usury credit systems and resulted in widespread indebtedness among peasants.[80] In time, those peasants dispossessed of lands formed the bulwark of Cambodia's waged workforce, a process enforced by a repressive colonial apparatus. In 1924, for example, French officials outlawed both vagrancy and begging, having redefined these as crimes against the public order. Subject to imprisonment, landless peasants had few options other than to solicit waged employment.[81]

On the eve of civil war, two contradictory trends characterized Cambodia's rural landscape. On the one hand, the area of land under cultivation increased appreciably throughout the twentieth century. On the other hand, this expansion of farmland coincided with both the material fragmentation and social concentration of land. Overall, the agrarian sector comprised mostly small- and medium-sized family farms. Indeed, the majority of farmers were small landowners, owning upwards of five hectares. Most pressing for these farmers, however, was the fragmentation of land, an ongoing problem that existed prior to but was exacerbated by French colonialism. A farmer, for example, might hold *in total* five hectares of rice paddy. These five hectares, materially, consisted of several individual plots, perhaps less than one hectare in size each, spread over quite some distance. In practice, small landowners typically possessed their own agricultural tools and draft animals but lacked operating capital. Poor harvests, consequently, could portend financial ruin. Medium landowners fared marginally better in society and for much of the twentieth century comprised the largest sector of the rural population. These households characteristically owned between five and ten hectares of land, their own tools and animals, and enough capital to rent additional paddy. Least numerous were large landholders, that is, those families owning ten or more hectares. In general, these property owners did not work the land themselves but instead contracted others to perform the necessary work. On the one hand, the more prosperous landholders could utilize waged labor provided by landless peasants or, on the other hand, enter into tenancy or sharecropping relations with more destitute peasants (including small landowners).

Tenancy entails the renting of land in return for a fixed payment, in currency or in kind, determined in advance. Typically, the tenant provides the draft animals, farming equipment, seed, manure, and so forth. On the plus side, tenant farmers often held a degree of autonomy in that they could determine when and what to plant. However, the tenant also carried the entire burden of a potential bad harvest. A prolonged drought or unexpected late-season deluge could rapidly plunge the farmer into debt. Under sharecropping arrangements, landholders oversee the direct management of the harvest and provide land, livestock, and farming tools at interest.[82]

Life for all but the wealthiest farmers was precarious. Vulnerability, however, followed from indebtedness and usury. Tenants and sharecroppers found themselves stuck in never-ending cycles of seasonal indebtedness, having to borrow money, repay interest, and borrow again the next season. Even small landholders, especially in the wake of poor harvests, found themselves having to borrow money or purchase necessary supplies on credit. Usury assumed many forms in Cambodia, although two were most common. In the first instance, farmers would sell their land to repay debts incurred. However, the farmer retained the right to repurchase lands sold. If they farmer was unable to repurchase the land within a specified period, the buyer maintains possession, to be resold or leased to other landless peasants. A second form entailed the borrowing of money by farmers through the pawning of land. In this case, farmers had to pay back debts incurred at exorbitantly high interest rates; farmers who were unable to meet these financial obligations lost the land to the moneylender.[83]

Few farmers were immune to the threat of seasonal debt. Indeed, from the 1950s onward, approximately 75 percent of the Khmer peasantry was in significant debt. However, the fact that a majority of Khmer peasants owned some land did give them important ties with the land and their village society.[84] Khmer peasants owned their own land, and while they were somewhat receptive to some improvements, such as the elimination of exorbitant usury rates, they were averse to giving up their farms. Simply put, the Khmer peasantry was decidedly less receptive to collectivization programs than their counterparts in China and Vietnam were. In both China and Vietnam, land was overwhelmingly concentrated in the hands of a few property owners. In China, for example, landlords and wealthy peasant households accounted for 10 percent of the population but owned 56 percent of the land while, at the other extreme, 68 percent of rural smallholders, tenants, and hired laborers owned just 14 percent.[85] In northern Vietnam, about 5 percent of the rural households owned one-third of the agricultural land; peasants and laborers, comprising 62 percent of the rural population, owned just 13 percent. Conditions were worse in southern Vietnam. Here, less than 3 percent of the landowners controlled 45 percent of the cultivated land while 72 percent of the owners possessed just 12 percent; nearly 75 percent of rural households in Cochinchina owned no land and worked mainly as tenants and laborers for middle-sized and large property owners.

Building Socialism in Democratic Kampuchea

After their victory of April 17, 1975, Khmer Rouge forces began forcibly evacuating Phnom Penh. Upwards of three million people—more than half of whom were peasants who had fled the fighting during five years of civil war—were sent to the fields and forests of the countryside.

Many were forced to walk; truck or train transported others. It was apparent that little planning went into the specific details of evacuation—there was scant coordination of such a massive operation and the resultant death toll, while not accurately known, was substantial.

The evacuation of urban areas was in fact a long-standing objective of the Khmer Rouge. As early as 1971, for example, Khmer Rouge forces began to systematically burn villages and hamlets under their control.[86] In 1973 Khmer Rouge soldiers seized half of Kampong Cham City, taking fifteen thousand townspeople into the countryside with them, and in March 1974, just weeks before the fall of Phnom Penh, Khmer Rouge forces emptied the former capital of Oudong. In the process, Khmer Rouge cadre forced more than twenty thousand former residents into the countryside before razing the city.[87]

For many scholars, the evacuation and destruction of cities by the Khmer Rouge, according to conventional explanations, constitutes an "anti-urban" bias among the CPK leadership and, accordingly, we should view the practice of ex-urbanization as a form of *urbicide*, that is, the deliberate destruction (killing) of the material built environment.[88] Here, violence directed toward cities is neither secondary nor collateral to the targeting of civilians and military personnel; rather, the violence constitutes a practice of intentional annihilation of the cities themselves, for cities (and their inhabitants) are targeted because they denote a particular (and presumed "immoral") way of life.[89] According to this explanation, to accomplish its own "Super Great Leap Forward," the Khmer Rouge believed it necessary to completely erase—to wipe clean—any barriers to the revolution; this included most obviously the villages, towns, and cities. As Kevin McIntyre concludes, "in the swidden politics of the Khmer Rouge, Phnom Penh . . . and other cities and towns were slashed and sometimes burned to clear the brush for the new growth of Cambodian society."[90]

Under the Pol Pot regime, Khmer Rouge cadre did target and destroy urban areas, and forcibly relocate urban residents, and Khmer Rouge propaganda did foster the perception that urban violence was part of a moral campaign designed to "clean up and eliminate the filth of the rotten old society."[91] However, the material reality is somewhat more complex. Contrary to conventional accounts, I maintain that the evacuation of urban areas constitutes a form of primitive capitalist accumulation.[92] To achieve industrial self-sufficiency, the CPK decreed that they would "only have to earn [foreign] capital from agriculture."[93] In practice, therefore, the CPK sought to extend production through deforestation and large-scale irrigation schemes.[94] The CPK subsequently coupled this objective with the "relentless enhancement and expansion of cooperatives."[95] Hence, immediately preceding and following victory in 1975, the CPK intensified its effort to bring together its citizenry in the form of camps in order to achieve its economic objectives, namely the rapid increase in agricultural crops for export. Initially, however, there was scant coordination in the establishment of agricultural collectives—a problem that translated into the chaotic nature of the evacuation of Phnom Penh but also the uprooting of peasants from their villages and hamlets.[96]

Surviving documents indicate that the CPK's decision to organize peasant cooperatives *at a national level* occurred on May 20, 1973, and related directly to the ongoing war effort, namely "to launch military attacks against the enemies." In addition, cooperatives screened and selected youths to send to the frontline battlefields and facilitated the support of base units by caring for the injured and transporting ammunition and other supplies. Crucially, these first cooperatives provided a necessary political lesson for new recruits. Accordingly, through the formation of cooperatives, the "Party was able to strengthen and extend its army[,] quickly emboldening its consciousness, politics and manpower." Cooperatives thus "were able to provide materials and supports to the livelihood and consciousness of families of the revolutionary soldiers and cadres." [97] In effect, from 1973 onward, life in the liberated zones became increasingly harsh and rigid as Khmer Rouge cadre forcibly abolished landownership in the primary liberated areas, enforced complete collectivization, and demonetized the economy. Efforts to level the population included confiscation of goods, relocation of villages to new areas, dormitory living in some areas, mandatory and standardized hairstyles for Muslim women, requirements that all people wear black clothing with no jewelry, and the institution of rigid work schedules from sunup to sundown. Survivors recall that deprivation of food and water, arbitrary arrests and imprisonment, and executions were common.[98]

Ex-urbanization for the CPK leadership facilitated the larger objective of eliminating private ownership of land and of the forced collectivization of the population. Prior to liberation, property owners and usurers—from the vantage point of the Khmer Rouge—controlled and dominated the rural economies: the "feudal-land owner and capitalist classes owned [the economy]; they collected rice and other products freely [and sold] these commodities to the enemies and other foreigners." Now, after military victory, CPK officials viewed peasant cooperatives as the "cornerstone in ensuring the great victory of the Great Socialist Revolution and the socialist construction at present and in future." [99] Thus, for the CPK, the collectivization of the peasantry was necessary "to increase production . . . and contribute to defending and building the country." [100] As concentrations of forced laborers, cooperatives facilitated the transformation of Democratic Kampuchea's physical environment and, subsequently contributed to the production and distribution of agricultural commodities. In the words of the CPK: "Cooperatives were on the offensive by solving a hundred thousand difficulties. The cooperatives resolved problems such as shortage of labor forces, cattle, plowshares, plows, rakes, hoes, knives, axes, the means of production, etc." [101] Notably, for the CPK, the word *cooperative* applied exclusively to agricultural groupings, including, whenever possible, persons with blacksmithing, weaving, and other skills to make a unit self-sufficient. Persons working factories and fishing or in rubber or salt production were not considered to be in cooperatives; they were known simply as factory workers and so forth or as a group of factory or rubber workers. [102]

CPK officials registered little doubt in their overall approach to agricultural collectivization. Indeed, as evidenced in various speeches, meeting minutes, and published commentaries, senior officials of the CPK were remarkably sanguine. Within cooperatives, the CPK leadership reasoned, "No one needs to think and worry anymore about their living and working. No one needs to borrow from someone else for living like during the time they lived in the private regime." [103] Within a communist society, officials avowed, "the Party is in charge of promoting every aspect" of raising the people's livelihood and living standards. From the vantage point of the party, "We have distributed rice, clothing, salt, fish past, plates, cooking pots, shelter and medicines to the people." [104] Indeed, of the primacy of cooperatives, party leaders were convinced, concluding, "The power of the cooperatives is very mighty and indomitable." [105]

Initially, two broad patterns of agricultural organization emerged: mutual aid teams and solidarity groups. In the first system, families retained individual responsibility for all agricultural tasks—with the exception of harvesting, which was communal. Khmer Rouge cadres controlled all rice harvested, returning some to the villages while distributing the remainder elsewhere as needed to support the war effort. [106] Although private landownership continued, peasants were encouraged to join cooperatives. [107] The second system consisted of more formalized cooperatives, characterized by communal landownership by interfamily groups, communal labor, and rice distribution; trade within and between cooperatives was largely through barter. Pol Pot referred to these cooperatives, which entailed the grouping of ten to twelve families, as *collective mass organizations*. In places that had been liberated early in the war—usually areas where the Khmer Rouge enjoyed broad support—rebel leaders most frequently implemented the first, family-based strategy. In territories captured later in the war, especially those areas with strong republican support, the Khmer Rouge imposed the second, communal strategy. This often constituted a more abrupt break with the past and required greater force to achieve. [108]

In their effort to accumulate capital rapidly, party leaders grew worrisome about wastefulness and idolatry, complaining, "The wastefulness and lack of saving of utilities and consumption exist everywhere."[109] As such, Khmer Rouge cadre adopted the slogan "Work more, gain more, but spend less."[110] Party leaders encouraged its citizens to "strive to conserve more, conserve rice, conserve salt, conserve clothing, and so on."[111] In terms of governmental disbursements, officials were to be "thrifty," for the loss of "a nail, a piece of plywood, or even a piece of firewood" was important.[112] The most precious of all resources, however, was worker productivity. As Khmer Rouge officials bemoaned, "When they have free time and rest from work, sometimes they play badminton, play ping pong, or sit in circles talking uselessly." From the perspective of the Khmer Rouge, these idle workers were "capitalists and mandarin" who should be replaced with workers who embodied a more appropriate work ethic. Thus, senior officials commanded, "When you have free time from work, when you rest from work, do not remain idle. It is imperative to seize the opportunity to increase production, carrying water to water the crops, and caring for the crops."[113] This required, in turn, effective time management: "Even one day, one hour, one minute or one second, do not let the time go by uselessly, or use it to think about any difficult and personal issues."[114]

Senior CPK officials understood also that conditions had not been prime for revolution in the orthodox Marxian interpretation of class struggle. There was no appreciable population of dispossessed and displaced peasants, and there was certainly no sizable proletariat. Indebtedness was a major problem, but villagers for the most part adapted and endured. Senior leaders of the CPK feared revisionist attitudes of the peasantry, that is, any sentiment of dwindling support for the revolution itself. Furthermore, during the civil war men and women flocked to the Khmer Rouge not out of ideological conviction but did so in response to the ouster of their beloved prince, Sihanouk, or in response to the unremitting and brutal bombing campaign waged by the United States. Thus, the CPK leadership acknowledged that these contradictions remained and that it was necessary to educate both "male and female combatants . . . so that they [would] not slip or tremble."[115] Indeed, well into the revolution senior party members lamented that while the old relations of production were smashed, new relations of production under way, and the collective system strengthening and spreading, "inadequacies in the field of politics and consciousness" remained and "socialist consciousness and the collective relationship [were] still inadequate."[116] Moving forward, however, for party officials, a strong "socialist consciousness" would become the "rippling sinews of the collectivity" and the establishment of cooperatives "the most seething movement in the new revolutionary era."[117] Hence, to eliminate any improper ideas, it was necessary for the senior leadership of the CPK to demonstrate that "the true nature of socialist revolution is the true nature of class struggle between the proletarian class and the capitalist class." According to CPK officials, "The essential reality of private ownership is the essential reality of the capitalist class, the core content or the makeup of the capitalist class. The capitalists stand upon the foundation of private ownership to live and to work. Private ownership is the soul of the capitalist class. Without private ownership, the capitalist class loses it soul."[118] They explained, "In current Kampuchean society there is still class struggle between the proletarian class and the various oppressor classes, between the collective ownership of the proletarian class and the private ownership of all the various other classes."

Ideologically, a proper political consciousness was one devoid of capitalist thinking, that is, notions of private ownership and individuality. "Any ideas of saving money or putting away property are withering away. The Party's proletarian stand is being ever more strengthened and expanded," a commentary published in *Revolutionary Flag* explained. It continued, "Our collectivist system must be further strengthened and expanded in order to guarantee that or revolution is assured, so that there will be no revisionism."[119] In material terms, cooperatives would ultimately demonstrate the success or failure of building socialism. "Having thin capital in the cooperatives," party members explained, "arises from socialist revolutionary [thought] not having penetrated deeply into those cooperatives." Effectively, failure stemmed from improper leadership and consciousness at the local level, decidedly not from the party itself. "The world view and outlook of the Party is the proletarian world view and outlook. . . . Any cadre, any member who has a world view adhering to private property has many complications and cannot lead well."[120]

From the vantage point of the Khmer Rouge, therefore, it was imperative to sunder prior social relations centered on individuality. In this way, party officials hoped "to strengthen and expand the collective position, to constantly stand on this position and to strengthen and expand ourselves upon this stance, the collective spirit, the collective stance, to organize the collective, to strengthen and expand the collective, to constantly improve the collective."[121] A December 20, 1976, report on activities of the party center, for example, describes the ongoing efforts to build political consciousness. The report reads, "We have nourished political consciousness, proletarian patriotism and proletarian internationalism. We have also nourished dialectical materialism as a basis. . . . Proletarian patriotic consciousness and proletarian internationalism can transform people's nature into something new. As for the problem of nurturing a Marxist-Leninist viewpoint, we should allow this to seep in according to our chosen methods."[122]

Ultimately, though, the cultivation of a proper political consciousness would materialize from direct, physical labor coupled with direct, physical force. For the CPK leadership, the "building of socialism" was dialectic; it required of its people both the generation of surplus value—to physically rebuild the country—and the transformation of a proper political consciousness through the actual laboring involved. "What we want to show here," party officials explained, "is that practical work is not separate from cadre-building work. In the past, we have no linked practical work with cadre-building work."[123]

The processes of displacement, dispossession, and collectivization drastically altered traditional peasant life. As May Ebihara documents, communal organization and the dispersal of family members and kinfolk cleaved the solidarity of the family as a primary social unit of economic cooperation and emotional bonds and suppressed familial sentiments.[124] Over time, amid growing discontent, cooperatives assumed a greater security function. Increasingly, party cadre perceived peasant cooperatives as both the source and resolution of political conflict. Officials admitted, "all kinds of conflicts have emerged in the cooperatives." Notably, "attacks" were manifest "between capitalism and socialism, between the notions of privatism and collectivism, between the Party's socialist revolutionary line and socialist construction on all fronts and the anti-socialist revolutionary line and anti-socialist construction." More precisely, Khmer Rouge cadre identified specific attacks "against eating, clothing and daily life" and "against the labor force, dike building, canal digging, dry-season rice farming, wet-season rice farming and on how to achieve the Party's goal of producing 3 tons of rice per hectare."[125] In a word: everything.

"Only when we are resolute in sweeping out all categories of concealed enemies boring from within," an article appearing in *Revolutionary Flag* warned, "can we defend the country strongly." Crucially, cooperatives were both centers of potential enemy infiltration and centers of retribution and attack. Khmer Rouge cadre discovered what they perceived to be widespread "betrayal of the nation, betrayal of the people and betrayal of the revolution." For senior party members, treachery and perfidy was manifest in deliberate acts of sabotage. "They [the enemies from within] have starved the people and made them thirsty," the aforementioned article explains, and "caused [the peasants] to have nothing to wear and no place to stay. They wreck water, wreck seed rice, wreck rice seedlings, wreck compost, wreck draft animals, wreck plows and harrows, wreck digging tools, wreck spoons, plates and pots, wreck everything, do whatever can be done as long as it makes our people hunger and have nothing to eat."[126] In the cooperatives, especially, according to party members, "the enemy is conducting activities to wreck the revolution: They destroy the wicker baskets used to carry dirt; they destroy cattle; they destroy hoes. If we are unable to grasp this, we do not know, we do not understand. The hoes keep on breaking, we say they were not well-made; but the enemy is destroying them and we are unable to grasp that, we take no timely measures, we just think about requesting additional hoes."[127] The wretched conditions resulted not from poor planning, poor quality tools, or simple accidents, party leaders decried, but from traitorous elements. Hence, "The concealed enemies boring from within wreck the line of resolving the people's standard of living of our party in order to bring the people intro contradiction with the Party, at which time it is then easy for them to propagandize and split off the people from the party and take the people away by winning them over."[128]

Cooperatives, therefore, constituted a key battleground to identify and eliminate networks of traitors. "If one wants to discover the concrete truth," party officials advised, it is "necessary to go down to the lower-level bases," that is, the cooperatives.[129] "Cooperatives administered by bad class elements are without rice to eat," Khmer Rouge leaders explained, while "Cooperatives that are put together right and administered by good classes have good internal solidarity and produce enough to eat and to have a large surplus for provision to the state." In their fight against perceived traitors, senior CPK leaders vowed to take no quarter. "All of our cadres and combatants must clearly understand the role of cooperatives," party officials acknowledged. With "foes and adversaries" running rampant throughout the country, it was necessary "to watch them in concrete tests."[130] CPK authorities stressed, "They enemy will surely seek out every means to destroy our rice. They may destroy it in the fields. They might destroy it in the short houses. Be vigilant that they do not steal it and hide it. . . . This a strenuous class struggle goes on every single day; it is a contradiction in the society that we must get a grasp on and put measures in place to guard and protect against to the maximum."[131]

Vigilance was required at all levels of society, with cadres and combatants to "be vigilant over education, politics, consciousness and organization for cooperative members." Specific practices included "daily meetings, exchanges of experiences, explanations, education and instruction at production sites, within families, in homes, and through other short course trainings."[132] However, party officials made clear that "training alone is not enough. There must be organizational measures." To this end, the peasants were "to be judged in the movement, not by study in school." Accordingly, "Each zone must be examined like this. Each sector must be examined like this. Each district must be examined like this. Each cooperative must be examined like this. The army and ministries and offices must be examined like this. . . . There must be constant shock assaults."

"We have the potential to reform," party leaders said of the nonconformists. However, they added an ominous caveat: "Some of them will not reform."[133] For the Khmer Rouge, it was all very simple. "When the views and stances are correct, the measures taken are fundamentally correct." This meant that if people obeyed their dictates and implemented the programs set from above, rice would grow and water would flow. Abundance would be at hand. Thus, it was imperative "to take organizational measures to purge our state power, to make it clean, firm, and strong."[134] If not, according to the upper echelons, the "risky ones must be purged."[135] In the end, rice for the Khmer Rouge leadership was foundational to all it hoped to achieve. As such, the Khmer Rouge transformed rice from something peasants grew and ate to a national resource on which hinged the security of the nation, the revolution, and the party itself—a sentiment captured in the Khmer Rouge slogan, "Don't let one grain of rice be damaged."[136]

Conclusions

Throughout Democratic Kampuchea, workers labored and produced under the ever-present watch of a party that ruled in the name of the state for the express purpose of capital accumulation. The CPK effectively owned, controlled, and distributed at its discretion the resources and outputs extracted and produced by hundreds of thousands of men, women, and children at the point of a gun. The party subjected peasants to a greater degree of authorial control than most had previously experienced, whether under the imperialist French or the monarch Sihanouk.[137] Arrest reports provide grim insight. In April 1978, for example, Khmer Rouge cadre arrested Van Em and his wife, Mak Sam, in Angk Ta Saom commune. According to the arrest report, the couple allegedly said, "We are now living in a regime with no freedom at all. In addition, the leaders are illiterate and stupid. They just follow the orders from their upper echelons." Also in this report, another arrestee, A-Van Em, supposedly complained of living under the current regime since, in the old regime, sufficient food was available. "Now we are living in hardship," A-Van Em purportedly said, "We work hard but have little to eat, so I do not want to live here anymore."[138]

Too often, scholars simply note that so-called Marxist regimes forcibly assemble their workers into large communes and cooperatives without an adequate explanation of why. Scholars forward abstract labels, such as "Stalinism" or "Maoism," as independent variables, seemingly pregnant with explanation value. Senior leaders of the CPK, we learn, imposed collectivist strategies because *they were Maoists* (or Marxists, or Marxist-Leninists). Such linguistic fixing, however, provides little understanding and, in fact, serves only to obfuscate the complex history of collectivization as theorized and practiced by self-described socialists or communists. Far from exhibiting a blind faith in Marxism or some other label, senior leaders of the CPK forwarded a program of collectivization for very specific reasons in response to very real conditions inherent to postrevolutionary Cambodia. Here, I do take at face value the repeated claims that the Khmer Rouge did not copy anyone. Rather, my assessment is that, confronted with conditions similar to those in post-revolutionary Russia, CPK authorities adopted similar strategies.

The Russian Revolution was unprecedented in the history of socialism. Until that moment in 1917, no other communist party had successfully engineered a revolution and taken control of a country. Remarkably, this first socialist revolution broke the capitalist chain not at the strongest but rather at the weakest link.[139] In so doing, however, the Bolsheviks found themselves isolated. There were no other "communist" governments to turn to for assistance in the form of economic, political, or military aid. Indeed, Russian revolutionaries had to jumpstart a moribund economy, destroyed by years of civil war, under the onslaught of foreign adversaries determined to remove forcibly from power the Bolsheviks.[140] The immediate conditions of postrevolutionary Russia occasioned the turn toward coercion and authoritarian centralization, both anathema to orthodox Marxism. In fact, other than a boundless faith in economics of scale, subsequent plans to establish rural collectives had few direct links with the agrarian doctrines of Marx. Most important was the growing acceptance of coercive force to bring about agrarian change. Imposed collectivization, the cornerstone of Soviet agrarian policy and a model for third-world revolutions, constitutes the negation of the soundest elements of Marx's vision of socialist transformation.[141]

Those so-called Marxists who followed in the wake of Russia's revolution faced vastly different conditions. Chinese communists, for example, could look to the Soviets for both theoretical guidance and material support, and, in turn, Vietnamese communists could look to both the Soviet Union and China. In so doing, throughout much of the twentieth century, collectivization became widely regarded by third-world revolutionaries, including the Khmer Rouge, as the central feature of socialist rural development.[142] Specifically, in Democratic Kampuchea, the introduction of agricultural cooperatives effectively transformed traditional Khmer *farming* practices into a variant of agrarian capitalism. There is of course no "pure" agrarian capitalism, just as there is no "pure" communism. Studies of both a historical and contemporary nature illustrate the many variations agrarian capitalism can and has assumed. In particular, these studies demonstrate the general forms of labor used, the specific labor systems under which laborers work, the processes by which large assemblages of laborers are brought together, and the ways in which these collectivities function. Nevertheless, there is a tendency to circumscribe the analysis of labor under capitalism, notably to premise the individual wage earner as the sole basis of accumulation."[143] In this way, scholars register many *capital-positing activities* as anything other than capitalist.

Under the Khmer Rouge, the *economic transformation* brought about through forced collectivization was the impetus for profound *social* and *spatial* transformations that permeated Democratic Kampuchea. Functionally, the CPK did not initiate a Preobrazhensky-styled program of primitive socialist accumulation, that is, a capital-positing program whereby taxes and quota mechanisms would redistribute resources from the agricultural sector to finance industrialization. Instead, the CPK adopted a Stalinist program of forced collectivization to accumulate capital rapidly to invest in industry. In so doing, the senior leadership of the CPK produced a key contradiction that reverberated throughout its time in power. Simply put, the Khmer Rouge inserted farmers more fully into the global economy than did either the French colonialists or the Sihanouk administration, as production was destined not for village consumption but for foreign markets.

In practice, peasant cooperatives bore little resemblance to the bromides of Khmer Rouge propaganda. Farmers, including those classified as both base and new people, remained divorced from the means of production, and decision-making remained firmly entrenched among only the most loyal and dedicated Khmer Rouge cadre. Moreover, life under the Khmer Rouge was valued on a preference for one's capacity to labor and, consequently, to generate value at the level of the collective. This is seen, for example, in numerous slogans forwarded by the Khmer Rouge: "Angkar only favors those who are indefatigable"; "The slothful are spineless, the sluggish are lazy"; and "We absolutely must remove the lazy; it is useless to keep them, else they will cause trouble. We have to send them to hell."[144]

Nonetheless, from the vantage point of the CPK, peasant cooperatives remained a panacea to build socialism. As detailed in Khmer Rouge propaganda, "our rural landscape is changing very quickly—not on a monthly, but daily basis. Most obvious changes are attested by new dikes and canal systems, whose construction rhymes with the defining revolutionary step forward from traditional agriculture to modern agriculture." Concurrently, the document continues, "the profile of the people is changing. These changes include those living in rural areas and those who had left cities. The changes include fever-ish advancement in dike building and canal digging for the purposes of wet- and dry-season rice farming. These movement has pried open a new stance, a new world view, new technology and new forces, encompassing change of vision, change of culture, change of societal relations and change to all aspects of daily life." [145] Effectively, the CPK practice of consolidating all landholdings into enormous collectives was an important step in the transition to a capital-ist system predicated on the production for exchange. In this way, it is clear that the Khmer Rouge did not remotely begin to "leap over" capitalism but instead stomped its way into capitalism. To paraphrase Marx, the forced col-lectivization and ex-urbanization policies constituted the original sins of the Khmer Rouge.

CHAPTER 4

"Currency Is a Most Poisonous Tool"

The practice of forced collectivization and the state confiscation of rice introduced by senior leaders of the Communist Party of Kampuchea alienated the men, women, and children who endured years of hardship and violence throughout the country. In the aftermath of the Pol Pot regime, villagers spoke with bewilderment, anger, and hatred of the many ways in which their traditional way of life was overturned.[1] Before the revolution, villagers had determined their own work schedules, with time for rest in even the busiest seasons and periods of relative leisure during the year. Now, armed soldiers drove them to perform unrelenting labor that was arduous and exhausting; with the relentless pace of work broken only by brief breaks for hasty meals of insufficient rations. Indeed, survivors recall being in a constant state of hunger despite the stockpiles of foodstuffs. As May Ebihara documents, villagers lamented, "You could see food but you weren't allowed to eat it," and "there were piles of rice . . . but it was taken away in trucks."[2] Under the watchful eye of the Khmer Rouge, people labored under harsh conditions, subject always to summary punishment and possible death, to grow rice and other crops they would never eat.

CPK leaders were aware of the ever-present specter of famine. Early on, senior officials of the CPK government called for the continued monitoring of agricultural and food rationing throughout Democratic Kampuchea.[3] In March 1976, for example, members of the upper echelons ordered local cadres to send weekly reports to the party center "in order to adhere closely to plan and to resolve problems in a timely fashion, in the direction decided upon of three tons per hectare."[4] The purpose, in short, was to ensure compliance with agricultural production quotas established by the Central Committee.[5] Subsequent documents vividly detail the deteriorating conditions experienced throughout the country.

By way of illustration, during a meeting of division and regimental secretaries and logistic chiefs held on September 19, 1976, food shortages were all too apparent. Comrade Muth reports, "The rice harvest was exactly two tons over an area of 2,000 hectares, short by 61,000 bushels." However, he continues, "Calculating through 15 November, the new rice which has arrived will be exhausted," that "food supplies . . . will be exhausted in January," and that "secondary crops . . . have mostly rotted." Comrade Sokh warned also that while "369 hectares of heavy rice have been transplanted," there remained "a possibility that transplanting will not be completed by 10 October." He notes, "Of 15 hectares of ripe light rice, only one hectare has been harvested, but the rats have eaten a lot." In response, Son Sen counseled that cadre "must push achieving 90 to 100 percent of the plans" and that work units "must go on strong offensives."

Efforts to promote agrarian "offensives" required a combination of efforts, including the protection of harvests and the expansion of new fields. With respect to the former, Son Sen explains, cadre "must concentrate on storage, weeding, maintaining fertilizer, adding and caring for water" and that "field rats must be attacked and eradicated to protect the harvest." For the latter, units must expand fertile land wherever possible and to constructer more water reservoirs. Overall, however, it was vital to study "food supply statistics, because this is a strategic matter in building socialism." Indeed, according to Son Sen, "Not making statistics comes from the brothers and sisters not yet having the stance of thoroughness in making statistics, and also from ownership ideology, hiding statistics for their personal units. [We] must organize people to be responsible for recording statistics." For Son Sen, effectively leadership required hands-on experience: We "must go down close to lead, not just to meetings. [We] must go down to the rice paddies, to the rice, to the water pumps. Go down to see and to listen to reports to be able to summarize experiences clearly." [6]

Faced with acute food shortages, untold numbers of men, women, and children furtively cultivated private gardens or secretively gathered fruits, vegetables, and other foodstuffs. If caught, however, they met swift punishment, often in the form of arrest, detainment, or immediate execution. On September 16, 1976, for example, a division chief reported that a man named Neak Loeung stole a haversack of rice. Khmer Rouge soldiers seized the man, but later when he tried to escape, cadres "shot him dead and did not get to interrogate him about anything." [7]

In the ensuing months, as reports of famine and illness became more common, CPK leaders increasingly blamed these problems on "internal enemies" or mistakes of local officials in implementing CPK policy. [8] An article appearing in the November 1975 issue of *Revolutionary Flag*, for example, explained, "While our people were almost starving, some of our revolutionary male [and] female youths at certain offices, units, and ministries were living well, eating well, wearing flashy clothes, wasting things and having plenty. . . . At some places, they did not follow and apply the Party food ration. They instead cooked rice excessively because they saw that there was plenty of rice in the warehouse." The article threatens, "These past wrong activities are very painful for all of our revolutionary male [and] female youths, so we must determine to eliminate them decisively so that they will not take place again in our view, stance, and application." [9] Likewise, in a speech reprinted in the September 1977 issue warns, Pol Pot warns, "There are life-and-death contradictions owing to the presence of enemy agents, who belong to the various spy networks of the imperialists and international reaction and who secretly implant themselves to carry out subversive activities against our revolution." The article concludes: "Contradictions with these elements must be solved by the measures proper for enemies: separate, educate and win over the elements which can be won over; neutralize the elements which are wavering, preventing them from doing any damage to the revolution; and, finally, isolate and eradicate only the smallest possible number of those elements who are cruel and persist in acting against the revolution and the people, and collaborate with foreign enemies to destroy their own people and their own revolution." [10]

Scholars do not know with any certainty how many people in Democratic Kampuchea died because of famine-related conditions. Randle DeFalco suggests somewhere between 500,000 and 1.5 million lives were lost through a combination of starvation and disease, with many accounts opting for a mid-range figure of approximately 700,000. Importantly, while the actual death toll remains uncertain, scholars generally consider the cause of the famine as rather straightforward. In their effort to secure foreign capital, Khmer Rouge cadres confiscated and exported substantial amounts of rice in exchange for capital; in turn, the party funneled foreign earnings derived from the export of rice into Democrat Kampuchea's nascent industrial sector. The Khmer peasantry, forced to labor under harsh conditions, received inadequate food rations—often a watery rice gruel. Deprived of adequate nutrition, exhausted from working long hours under adverse conditions, and denied access to effective medical care, hundreds of thousands of men, women, and children succumbed to premature death. In short, as DeFalco concludes, "This hubristic mixture of impossible rice production quotas, forced labor, violence and denial created severe famine conditions for virtually the entire civilian population, resulting in extreme suffering and mass mortality." [11]

That famine materialized in Democratic Kampuchea because of CPK policy and practice is beyond doubt. DeFalco is correct in his conclusion that "specific CPK policies enacted by a small group of prominent leaders in Phnom Penh triggered, maintained and deepened famine conditions." Less understood, however, are the specifications of these policies, that is, how precisely the export of rice and the elimination of currency contributed to famine, for it is *not* the case, as DeFalco suggests, that "the CPK's pursuit of "pure" socialism led to famine." [12] Missing from conventional accounts is the crucial substitution of money with food rations, a CPK policy decision that dramatically affected the production and distribution of rice but, equally important, profoundly altered the class composition of Khmer society. As Bill Maurer writes, money is at once "a social relation, a symbolic system, and a material reality." [13] Taking Maurer's observation of money as a starting point, I reposition the material reality of the food ration as both a social relation and symbolic system. In doing so, I theorize how the abolition of money and markets made possible the subsumption of labor by capitalism and, in the process, gave birth to agrarian capitalism in Democratic Kampuchea.

The Abolition of Money and Markets

On September 19, 1975, senior officials of the CPK made the fateful decision to abolish currency. The impact of this choice would prove momentous for the tragedy to unfold and contributed significantly to the widespread violence that gripped Democratic Kampuchea. Scholars heretofore acknowledge the salience of the abolition of money but too often fail to contextualize properly the decision. Sheridan Prasso, for example, writes, "The Khmer Rouge . . . set out to impose the strictest Marxist doctrine yet implemented in the Communist world." Prasso explains, "Money and private property, according to Karl Marx, promote the individual over the community. Thus, Khmer Rouge leader Pol Pot, who had studied Marx's writings while a student in Paris in the 1950s, ordered that money, markets, and private property be abolished." He concludes, "In Pol Pot's Cambodia . . . all barter, private commercial activity, private ownership, means of exchange, and stores of value were prohibited and punishable by death. Personal possessions were also prohibited, with the exception of a change of clothing and a personal set of eating utensils brought to the collective at mealtimes." [14]

Aside from making several sweeping generalizations not supported with documentary evidence, Prasso mistakenly describes the decisions rendered by CPK leaders but more importantly fails to consider both the form and function of money. Pol Pot did not unilaterally decide to abolish money, nor did he or other CPK leaders make the decision in haste. As civil war was still ongoing, key Khmer Rouge leaders, including Pol Pot, prepared for the eventual introduction of their own currency, to replace that of the Lon Nol government. In December 1973, for example, Ieng Sary brought sample notes from Beijing for Pol Pot's approval, in anticipation that the Khmer Rouge would gradually phase out government currency. In the interim, CPK leaders imposed a temporary system of barter until they could introduce their new, revolutionary money later in 1974. Debate did arise, however, as to whether Khmer Rouge currency should be introduced in piecemeal fashion, as areas were "liberated," or at one time, after victory was achieved. In the end, members of the Central Committee determined that they would put into circulation their new currency only after Khmer Rouge forces liberated the entirety of the country.[15]

With victory achieved in April 1975, senior CPK leaders confronted the enormity of jumpstarting a devastated economy. Ben Kiernan reconstructs some of the events that followed.[16] Beginning on May 20, 1975, CPK leadership summoned all military and civilian officials of the new regime to a special meeting held in Phnom Penh. The assembly, with more than a thousand participants in attendance, lasted five days; the purpose was for district and region secretaries to receive the plan determined by the Central Committee and to return to their bases of operation to implement the plan. As Kiernan describes the meeting, this was the center's first major attempt to run its political writ throughout Cambodia.[17] Unfortunately, though, there is no definitive record of the meeting. According to Kiernan, no documents from the meeting have (apparently) survived, and indeed, few of those in attendance survived. Consequently, Kiernan draws his conclusion from firsthand interviews conducted with five Khmer Rouge cadre, four of whom personally attended the May meeting.[18] Khmer Rouge cadre discussed numerous topics and rendered several key decisions, including the evacuation of cities be permanent and the establishment of medium-level cooperatives; in addition, leaders probably foreshadowed communal eating but did call for the implementation of this order.[19] Of particular importance is that members of the Central Committee apparently called for the abolition of currency and the prohibition of markets. Nuon Chea reportedly said that building socialism in Democratic Kampuchea consisted of two parts, agriculture and industry, and that agriculture would be modernized in ten to fifteen years through the application of scientific methods— an assertion that recurs frequently in CPK documents.[20] Notably, Nuon Chea spoke of eliminating markets and of not allowing money to circulate in the country, for the existence of money and markets would restore private property, an anathema to the CPK's Marxist-Leninist principles.[21] As explained in a party publication, "We do not use currency. Currency is a most poisonous tool. It entices us at all times to return to private ownership. With currency we always want to buy this or buy that. Now no one thinks of spending money." [22]

Decisions rendered at the May 1975 were not without disagreement. Longtime revolutionary Hou Yuon, for example, allegedly balked at the idea of eliminating markets and money. He explained that Cambodia, having just emerged from years of war, was desperately short of capital and facilities. In addition, the rapid collectivization of the population was both impractical and infeasible. No doubt, Hou Yuon's vocal reservations contributed to his removal from senior leadership and, eventually, his execution. [23] However, it appears likely that other senior officials harbored similar reservations. Indeed, sometime around May or June, CPK officials designated Non Suon, a Khmer Rouge cadre longtime revolutionary, as chair of the national bank. That summer, Khmer Rouge cadre sent posters showing CPK currency to the various administrative areas, along with actual notes for use, pending final approval from Phnom Penh. [24]

Whether CPK leaders reversed their earlier decision to abolish currency or never fully committed to its abolition is unclear. As the months passed, efforts were underway to reintroduce currency, even if in limited fashion. In August Pich Chheang replaced Non Suon and initiated a training program for sixty peasant youths, who were to run the bank's branches in the regions. Moreover, as a trial run, Pich Chheang introduced the new currency in September in his home area, Region 41 of the Northern Zone. [25] Together, these activities reveal considerable uncertainty on the part of the CPK leadership. Indeed, repeated reversal of the CPK's monetary policy highlights very significant differences of opinion among members of the Central Committee. It was not until September 1975 that a more permanent decision came about.

Between May and September of 1975, Pol Pot and other officials traveled throughout the country to study firsthand conditions on the ground. These efforts culminated with a meeting held on September 19 to determine, in part, whether the CPK would authorize the use of currency. One month earlier, Chhit Chhoeun (alias Ta Mok), secretary of the Southwest Zone and member of the Central Committee, expressed his reservations about the use of currency. As a practical matter, Mok apparently favored a barter system, arguing that some regions were rich in rice and others revealed their own distinct advantages. Consequently, the simple exchange of products between administrative zones appeared most viable. Mok, however, disapproved strongly of the reintroduction of money and markets on ideological grounds. The presence of money, Mok warned, contributed to corruption among the people; this, by extension, posed a security risk, in that peasants were susceptible to bribes from enemy agents. Pol Pot found Mok's arguments persuasive.[26] Speaking before the Central Committee, Pol Pot identified several practical reasons to not introduce currency, notably that most Khmer were inexperienced in the use of currency and that the party was unable to prevent theft and counterfeiting. Most pressing, however, were ideological reasons.[27] As Pol Pot explained, "Up to now, the fact we do not use money has greatly reduced private property and thus has promoted the overall trend towards the collective. If we start using money again, it will bring back sentiments of private property and drive the individual away from the collective. Money is an instrument [that] creates privilege and power. Those who possess it can use it to bribe cadres . . . [and] to undermine our system. If we allow sentiments of private property to develop, little by little people's thoughts will turn only to ways of amassing private property." Pol Pot concluded, "Money constitutes a danger, both now and in the future. We must not be in a hurry to use it. . . . We need to think more deeply about this matter."[28]

The meeting of September 19, 1975, marked the culmination of lengthy debate and discussion regarding the abolition of money and markets. Even so, as Pol Pot's words indicate, the decision was far from final. Former Khmer Rouge cadre Thiounn Prasith, for example, testifies that the elimination of currency was always a temporary measure.[29] Lat Suoy likewise recalls that by 1978 rumors circulated widely that the party was going to put into circulation bank notes and economic activities within the cooperatives reorganized accordingly.[30] Pol Pot himself reported told journalists from Yugoslavia that "we have ceased to use money up to now . . . [but] we do not take the present system as a permanent one."[31] In part, the impetus toward the reintroduction of currency was a practical matter. As Philip Short writes, "When Democratic Kampuchean delegations travelled abroad, they had to carry with them suitcases full of U.S. dollars." In addition, as members of the CPK established trade ties with non-communist countries, especially with Japan and throughout Southeast Asia and Europe, arguments in favor of a national currency became stronger. To this end, Pol Pot and Ieng Sary evidently decided in late 1978 to reauthorize the use of money.[32]

The decision to eliminate money and markets was always and necessarily fraught with contradictions. As Kiernan quips, the choice to prohibit monetary exchanges may have consigned money to join "the dustbin of history," but it failed to eliminate "the profit motive."[33] In fact, the pressing need to accumulate capital rapidly had not diminished; instead, the abolition of currency, whether temporarily or permanently, introduced several obstacles the CPK had to confront, notably the seemingly intractable "agrarian question." In the aftermath of revolution in both Russia and China, for example, Marxist-trained economists pinned their hopes on agriculture to provide the necessary capital to invest in industry. One key practice, accordingly, was to tax peasant farmers heavily. In Democratic Kampuchea, however, the abolition of money ruled out this option. Accordingly, CPK officials had little recourse but the exploitation of the peasantry through forced labor. Paradoxically, the subsequent practice of primitive capitalist accumulation paved the way for the greater subsumption of labor by capital in Democratic Kampuchea. Simply put, and in a grave irony, the decision to abolish money and markets ushered in the advent of state capitalism.

Money, Labor, and Surplus Value

When senior leaders of the CPK abolished money and markets, they hoped to strike a blow against the exploitation inherent to capitalism. For these leaders, in fact, the suspension of currency marked the dawning of a socialist future, one that would witness the elimination of private property and individualism. Instead, their decision marked a new day in the unfolding life of capitalism and revealed with brutal clarity the immorality of an economic system of exchange oriented toward profit rather than human need. Effectively, while CPK policy eliminated money in its material form, it also kept intact the exploitative relations inherent in capitalism and codified the separation of Cambodia's direct producers from the fruits of their labor. For as Marx well understood, capitalism is about relations rather than things.

Within capitalism, money serves various functions, including money as medium of exchange, money as means of payment, money as store of value, and money as unit of account.[34] In the first chapter of *Capital*, Marx's objective is in part to explain the origin of the money form. He writes, "We have to trace the development of the expression of value contained in the value-relation of commodities from its simplest, almost imperceptible outline to the dazzling money-form. When this has been done, the mystery of money will immediately disappear."[35] To begin, however, Marx focuses not on money per se but instead on the exchange of commodities, describing the simple barter system, in this case, the exchange of one commodity, twenty yards of linen, with another, such as a coat. Following Marx, the "relative form of value and the equivalent form are two inseparable moments, which belong to and mutually condition each other; but, at the same time, they are mutually exclusive or opposed extremes." In other words, the relative form of one commodity, such as linen, presupposes that some other commodity confronts it in equivalent form; it is not possible, as Marx illustrates, to express the value of linen in the form of linen, nor can we express the value of a coat in the form of a coat.[36]

The salience of this observation is revealed fully when one considers Mok's argument to abolish currency and, subsequently, to promote a barter system throughout Democratic Kampuchea. In principle, it is possible that district A, for example, could provide a given amount of rice to district B in exchange for, say, a given amount of fish. In addition, it is notionally possible that Democratic Kampuchea could export a certain amount of rice to China and in return receive a number of tractors. Difficulties are readily apparent, however, in the determination of equivalences. Do we attempt to calculate how many sacks of rice are comparable to bushels of fish or tractors? Conversely, do we exchange commodities based solely on need, that is, district A requires twenty bushels of fish and district B requires one hundred sacks of rice and so party officials facilitate this exchange? Again, in principle, this form of barter could function, albeit not without long-term problems. More problematic is that the barter system does not permit the accumulation of capital. Especially at the international level, CPK leaders sought to increase revenue through the export of commodities, namely rice but also rubber and other agricultural products.

Historically, an increasing complexity of exchange relations produces an expanded form of value that crystallizes in a "universal equivalent," that is, a commodity that plays the exclusive role of a "money commodity."[37] Money, of course, has no value in and of itself. Instead, money is simply the representation of value and may appear materially as gold, silver, paper, or even cowry shells. The point is, a market system requires a money commodity of some sort to function effectively, but a money commodity can only come into being through the rise of market exchange.[38] In other words, the realization of *surplus* value, profit, requires the mediation of money within a market: thus, the rise of the money form makes value.

In Democratic Kampuchea, CPK leaders suspended a domestic monetary economy; however, the drive for capital accumulation required that they participate *as capitalists* in the global economy. In essence, Khmer Rouge officials introduced a cumbersome hybrid economy whereby at the international level value appeared in money form, while at the domestic level value appeared in the form of food rations. The linkage between the two systems proved irreconcilable, however, with famine appearing as the most distinctive but not exclusive material manifestation. To understand fully the fatal contradictions initiated by CPK officials, we must first consider the circulation of capital in general.

Marx writes, "Because all commodities, as values, are objectified human labor, and therefore in themselves commensurable, their values can be communally measured in one and the same specific commodity, and this commodity can be converted into the common measure of their values, that is, into money." Consequently, the "process of exchange is . . . accomplished through two metamorphoses of opposite yet complimentary character—the conversion of the commodity into money, and the re-conversion of the money into a commodity" and assumes the form "Commodity-Money-Commodity," or simply C-M-C. The first transformation, C-M, represents the conversion of a commodity into money (i.e., the act of selling), while the second transformation, M-C, represents the conversion of money into a commodity (i.e., the act of buying). Hence, this single process is two-sided: from one pole, that of the commodity-owner, it is a sale, and from the other pole, that of the money-owner, it is a purchase.[39] However, as Harvey observes, this raises the question: where can surplus value come from when the laws of exchange, M-C and then C-M, mandate an exchange of equivalents?[40]

For this reason, Marx concentrates on the role of money (as opposed to the commodity) in the circulation process.[41] This is expressed as M-C-M and constitutes the transformation of money into commodities and the reconversion of commodities into money.[42] Whereas the first circulation (C-M-C) results in the exchange of commodities (albeit mediated through money), under the second circulation (M-C-M) there is an exchange of money for money via commodities. Here, Marx finds the crucial component of capitalism in that "the circulatory process of M-C-M would be absurd and empty if the intention were, by using this roundabout route, to exchange two equal sums of money." Marx explains, "In the simple circulation of commodities [C-M-C] the two extremes have the same economic form. They are both commodities, and commodities of equal value. But they are also qualitatively different use-values, as for example corn and clothes." However, within the second circulation, "both extremes have the same economic form. They are both money, and therefore are not qualitatively different use values, for money is precisely the converted form of commodities." Consequently, the "process M-C-M does not . . . owe its content to any qualitative difference between its extremes, for they are both money, but solely to quantitative changes."[43] As Harvey writes, "M-C-M only makes sense if it results in an increment of value," this being surplus value and rewritten as M-C-M.[44]

This brings us back to the fundamental question of where surplus value originates. Harvey explains that if we are to observe the laws of exchange, then we must find a commodity that has the capacity to increase its value;

that commodity, for Marx, is labor power.[45] Marx argues that the *value of labor power* (wages) is equal not to what a worker can produce, such as a coat, but instead to the labor time necessary to make up what it costs to keep the laborer and his or her family alive. In other words, "The value of labor-power is the value of the means of subsistence necessary for the maintenance of its owner."[46] As Harvey elaborates, the "value of labor-power is fixed . . . by the value of all of those commodities that are needed to reproduce the laborer in a given state of life."[47]

Under capitalism, Marx contends, the exploitation of labor capacity generates surplus value and does so in two basic forms: absolute surplus value and relative surplus value. When capitalists purchase labor power—the capacity to work—they do so on two conditions: first, that the laborer works under the control of the capitalist to whom his or her labor belongs, and second, that the product is the property of the capitalist and not that of the worker.[48] Conventionally, a capitalist "buys" the commodity labor power from a worker for a given period of time, and in return the worker receives in wages the value of the labor power that ostensibly is equal to the value of the material necessities (e.g., food, water, shelter) necessary for the worker to reproduce himself or herself as a worker. However, the period of work time established by the contract will always be longer than this necessary labor time. Otherwise, as Fracchia explains, "there would be no gain for the capitalist and thus no reason to bother with the whole affair."[49] Consequently, Marx introduces the concept of necessary labor time, which is the time required to reproduce the laborer and his or her family; this is, as indicated above, the value of labor power and is used to determine wages. Workers, for example, may produce enough value in six hours to offset their reproduction. Capitalists, however, purchase labor power for a full day's work, say, ten hours. The remaining four hours, Marx argues, appear as *absolute* surplus labor time. The prolongation of the working day, according to Marx, "forms the general foundation of the capitalist system" and, by extension, any system of production for exchange. As Marx explains: "The fact that half a day's labor is necessary to keep the worker alive during 24 hours does not in any way prevent him from working a whole day. Therefore the value of labor power and the value which that labor-power valorizes . . . in the labor process, are two entirely different magnitudes; and this difference was what the capitalist had in mind when he was purchasing the labor-power."[50] In other words, workers produce enough value to cover the costs of their wages in just a part of the working day; the labor performed for the remainder of the day, therefore, does not have to be paid for—it is "surplus labor," which produces "absolute surplus value."[51]

Marx and Engels well understood that under capitalism, living laborers "live only so long as they find work, and [they] find work only so long as their labor increases capital."[52] This vital condition and subsequent enforcement, according to Marx, signifies the *formal* subsumption of labor by capital.[53] In the simplest terms, formal subsumption refers to labor processes in which the workers retain some autonomy in shaping the material character, organization, and management of production. In other words, formal subsumption takes the labor processes largely as it exists, and the production of surplus value comes strictly from that portion of the working day that a worker works in excess of the working time required to recoup his or her wages.[54] However, for Marx, it was not "necessary" labor time that was the root of labor power's value; rather it was *socially necessary labor time*. Defined as "the labor-time required to produce any use-value under the conditions of production normal for a given society and with the average degree of skilled and intensity of labor prevalent in that society," a consideration of socially necessary labor time transfers the level of argument from individual capitalists to society as a whole.[55] This is possible because the "production of relative surplus value depends critically upon all capitalists, since none alone produces a significant proportion of the commodities required for the reproduction of the working class."[56]

An increase in overall productivity increases the average number of commodities produced per unit of time; it thereby decreases the amount of socially necessary labor time required for the production of a single commodity and, hence, the value of each commodity.[57] With an increase in the productivity of labor, for example, through refinements of the division of labor or the introduction of machinery, the value of labor power falls and the portion of the working day necessary for the reproduction of that value shortens. Capital thus "has an immanent drive, and a constant tendency, towards increasing the productivity of labor, in order to cheapen commodities and, by cheapening commodities, to cheapen the worker himself."[58]

Socially necessary labor time is fundamental to the extraction of relative surplus value. The value of labor—at an abstract level—is represented by the value obtained by workers against the sale of their labor power; this typically corresponds, as indicated, to the labor time socially necessary to produce the wage goods regularly purchased on average by the working class.[59] As usually understood, competition among individual capitalists impels each of them toward the use of a labor process that is at least as efficient as the social average. Individual capitalists that can produce more efficiently achieve greater relative surplus value; those capitalists with inefficient production methods will not. This implies, as Harvey writes, a perpetual incentive for individual capitalists to increase the rate of accumulation through increasing exploitation in the labor process relative to the social average rate of exploitation. Hence, any capitalist who invests in constant capital or some other labor-related innovation may gain a temporary advantage over his or her competitors and thus extract greater profits. Harvey clarifies that capitalists employing superior production techniques can gain excess surplus value by trading at a price set by the social average when their production costs per unit are well below the social average. This advantage is ephemeral, however, because competitors will subsequently adopt similar production techniques or go out of business.[60]

There were, of course, no individual capitalists in Democratic Kampuchea, and any discussion of real subsumption appears immediately suspect. I counter, though, that state capitalism effectively functions along lines similar to those theorized by Marx. It is possible, for example, to view each zone, sector, district, or cooperative as an individual capitalist enterprise. Consequently, when CPK officials established *competition* between these divisions, the laboring activities operated much as independent factories might. Within the first year of the regime, by way of illustration, the Central Committee established the Red Flag Award, bestowed on those units that demonstrated meritorious commitment to the defense of the party and state and of the building of socialism. Subsequently, for example, in June 1977, the Central Committee of the CPK honored three districts—Prasot (Eastern Zone), Kampong Tralach (Western Zone), and Tram Kak (Southwest Zone)—for exemplary success in the fields of production, self-reliance, and collectivism. In awarding this distinction, CPK officials premised that "other districts and bases" would follow suit and "bring about more improvement."[61] In other words, the reorganization of laboring activities within specific governing units mimicked the activities of individual capitalists.

It is no accident that Marx describes capitalists as "personifications of economic relations."[62] As Heinrich explains, a person is a "capitalist" only when he or she is "capital personified," meaning that his or her activity follows the logic of capital, that is, capitalist commodity production. Under such conditions, economic production is geared toward the valorization of (surplus) value and not toward the satisfaction of needs. Consequently, it is not necessary that this person be the *owner* of capital.[63] Throughout Democratic Kampuchea, local cadre—compelled to compete with other cadre in the production of rice for exchange—operated as capital personified and existed merely as representatives of commodities.[64]

Socially necessary labor time is therefore fundamental to the extraction of relative surplus value, even in variants such as state capitalism. This is apparent, for example, in the introduction of the cooperative as much as the establishment of the assembly line, whereby the production process decomposes into different partial operations. Significantly, the production of relative surplus value alters the form of production, and a specifically capitalist form of production comes into being. At this point, the extraction of relative surplus value constitutes the *real* subsumption of labor by capital. Notably, the relations established under the formal subsumption of labor do not disappear; indeed, the direct subordination of the labor process to capital remains. Rather, on this foundation "there now arises a technologically and otherwise specific mode of production—that is, capitalist production—which transforms the nature of the labor process and its actual conditions. Only when that happens do we witness the real subsumption of labor under capital." [65] Real subsumption, in addition, involves an intensification of the labor process in which workers surrender most, if not all, of their autonomy. [66] Under conditions of real subsumption, labor power is "directly incorporated into the production process of capital as a living factor; it becomes one of its components, a variable component, which partly maintains and partly reproduces the capital values invested." Marx writes that the division of labor in manufacturing is not merely a particular method of creating relative surplus value. Not only does it increase the socially productive power of labor for the benefit of the capitalist instead of the worker; it also transforms the individual worker as new conditions for the domination of capital over labor are established. [67] These transformations, Boyd and Prudham explain, result in a progressive loss of control and autonomy for workers and in so doing changes the logic of surplus value production. [68]

Abstract and Concrete Labor in Democratic Kampuchea

Senior leaders of the CPK identified the necessity of both capital accumulation and foreign trade. With the abolition of money, these objectives appear problematic if not impossible. So how precisely did the CPK initiate a system of exchange that results in an increase in surplus value? We know that within the simple model of circulation, C-M-C, commodities are exchanged for money, and in turn money is used to purchase additional commodities. Did the CPK simply export commodities (such as rice) to China, for example, and in turn receive an equivalent amount of goods in return? Under this system, money is largely fictitious and resembles more a system of barter, along the lines of C-C.

One is tempted to conclude that "surplus" capital was simply derived from increased rice production; that is, the "surplus" identified by the CPK was not "surplus" from a Marxist understanding but merely additional rice to be exchange with foreign governments in return for other material goods. This account is far from satisfactory, however, and in fact, documentary evidence suggests a different explanation. Indeed, an analysis of the CPK's Four-Year Plan provides insight into the economic calculus adopted by senior officials and explains better the logic of CPK agricultural policy. This is not to suggest that the economic policies pursued by CPK leadership were either appropriate or effective. Indeed, as starvation deepened throughout Democratic Kampuchea, the failings of the CPK policy became all too apparent.

Workers under the Khmer Rouge were unfree laborers, that is, workers dispossessed and displaced from the land and livelihood, compelled to accumulate capital for the state. However, the coercive element of CPK policy and practice obscures the fundamental social relations introduced throughout Democratic Kampuchea. This assertion is not to minimize the brutality and violence evinced by the Khmer Rouge in its enforcement of draconian policies. Unquestionably, horrific violence marks the Khmer Rouge regime and several hundreds of thousands of corpses remain as silent witness to the depravity with which CPK policies were enforced. However, we must be sensitive to the functionality of Democratic Kampuchea's political economy and give equal attention to the social structures imposed by the CPK, for it is my argument that coercion informs the imposition of state capitalism, and, in turn the imposition of state capitalism requires ongoing coercion. In other words, there is a dialectic relationship between direct and structural violence, and we need be mindful of the oppositional tensions inherent to the relationship between the two.

To a certain degree, farming practices under the Khmer Rouge remained much as they had before the revolution. The day-to-day activities of clearing lands, planting seeds, and harvesting rice were largely unchanged. Notably different, however, was the fact that peasant farmers no longer cultivated their lands for personal or household subsistence but rather for exchange on the global market. From this vantage point, CPK policies indicate the formal subsumption of labor by capital. Consequently, CPK officials attained increased rice surpluses not so much through the introduction of new procedures but instead simply by the extension of the working day. As Michael Heinrich explains, a lengthening of the workday does not just occur when the number of daily working hours is increased but also when those hours are used more efficiently, for example, through the shortening of break times.[69] Under the CPK's Four-Year Plan, senior leaders transformed the traditional rhythms Khmer farming into a regimented agricultural system. Workers were to receive "three rest days per month" or "one rest day in every ten." Pregnant women were allocated two months' rest (in confinement) and for "those under hospitalization," party officials would determine the duration of rest according to the "concrete situation." CPK leaders, in addition, mandated that workers would use their leisure time in a productive fashion, explaining, "Resting at home is nominated and arranged as time for tending small gardens, cleaning up, hygiene, and light study of culture and politics." [70]

Effectively, the practice of forced labor and long working hours facilitated the cultivation of absolute surplus value. However, "an increase in the level of intensity of labor (that is, a speed-up of the labor process) has the same effect as a lengthening of labor-time." [71] To this end, Khmer Rouge cadre remained ever vigilant in the *pace* of worker performed. Local cadre assigned men, women, and children daily quotas, and armed soldiers stood guard as enforcers. For those laborers who failed to meet expectations, punishment was often swift and severe. Chhaom, a survivor of the genocide, recalls that daily life was very difficult. [72] Only fourteen years old at the time, Chhaom was initially assigned to a children's unit and later transferred him to a mobile unit comprised of adults. In both units, however, Chhaom began work at 5:00 a.m., as Khmer Rouge rang a bell signaling people to assemble. Chhaom explains that the Khmer Rouge used different signals to regulate daily life; for example, the call for lunch consisted of three rings of the bell. Hence, regimentation marked daily life for Chhaom, with all activities oriented toward agricultural production. Only the changing seasons affected his quotidian routine. During the dry season, as a member of the children's unit, Chhaom collected cow dung and human waste to use as fertilizer for the fields. Working alongside upwards of twenty other children, Chhaom had only a woven basket to collect the waste. He recalls that animal waste was most plentiful and easiest to collect; human waste was different. The Khmer Rouge provided no toilets and so people defecated anywhere, though usually around large bushes or trees. Around noontime, Chhaom and the other children assembled in the communal dining hall for lunch, which consisted usually of a plate of rice. Secretively, Chhaom supplemented his meager rations with frogs and insects he found in the fields—a punishable offense. After lunch, Chhaom returned to the collection of waste, working late into the day. In late 1977 or early 1978, party officials transferred Chhaom to a mobile working group tasked to dig canals. Khmer Rouge cadre assigned each person a daily quota to excavate three cubic meters of earth. Chhaom explains that Khmer Rouge soldiers executed workers who failed to meet their quota.

The experiences of Chhaom illustrate clearly several features of the formal subsumption of labor by capital, notably the lengthening and intensification of the working day. Also in evidence, however, is the restructuring of social relations and the reconfiguration of the traditional Khmer division of agrarian labor. Traditionally, both women and men engaged in farming practices. Men typically plowed the fields while women prepared nursery beds, transplanted seedlings, and harvested the crops. Daily life centered on the nuclear family, as families worked together. Under the Khmer Rouge, not only were daily routines altered, so too did the Khmer Rouge sunder the fundamental social relations of family life and, in the process, radically transform society. More precisely, I argue, the dissolution of the family effectively facilitated the transformation of traditional Khmer farming into a system of commodified agriculture.

Scholars have written at length on the separation of families under the Khmer Rouge. On the one hand, this practice served to increase the productivity of labor and, on the other hand, effectively transferred loyalty from parents to Angkar. As Kalyanee Mam explains, "Before the [Khmer Rouge] regime, families worked together as an economic unit. Each family owned the modes of production as well as the fruits of their labor. Families were also social units that offered emotional support." After the revolution, however, cooperatives displaced the traditional family structure.[73] May Ebihara expounds, "The solidarity of the family as a primary social unit of economic cooperative and emotional bonds was shattered by communal organization into labor teams segregated on the basis of age and gender, dispersal of family members and kinfolk into different work groups and communes, and suppression of familial sentiments."[74]

Throughout Democratic Kampuchea, local cadres separated family members into various working units. In practice, local cadre significantly influenced the concrete form labor arrangements assumed. As Mam explains, "depending on the area or village one belonged to, some families were allowed to live together after a day or working separately." Significant also was one's classification, for example, as "base" person or "new" person. In general, family separation was less common and less egregious for party members and base people than it was for new people. In general, CPK officials classified laborers as either *kemlang ping* (full strength) or *kemlang ksaoy* (weak strength), with the former consisting of adults and the latter comprising small children and the elderly. Local cadre further subdivided workers. Khmer Rouge cadres further segregated full-strength working units into two subgroups, identified as *kemlang* 1 and *kemlang* 2. The first subgroup comprised young, able-bodied, single men and women who worked in mobile work brigades (*kong chhlat*) segregated by sex: males belonged to *kong boroh* and females belonged to *kong neary*. The second consisted also of young, able-bodied workers but included those who were married. These workers generally worked closer to their home village or cooperative. Full-strength workers, regardless of classification, performed the heaviest work details, including clearing forests, plowing fields, planting, transplanting, and harvesting rice, and digging or carrying dirt for irrigation projects.[75] Elderly workers, that is, those aged fifty years and older, formed work teams known as *senah chun*. Khmer Rouge cadres divided these teams also according to sex, with men belonging to *senah chun boroh* and women to *senah chun neary*. Productive tasks for these working units included sewing, gardening, collecting small pieces of firewood, and the care of infants and young children. Depending on the conditions and the attitudes of the cooperative chief, some elderly workers might be required to labor in the rice fields or engage in other, more strenuous work. Lastly, cadre assigned children fourteen years of age or younger to work groups known as *kong komar*, with boys and girls separated into *kong komara* and *kong khomarei*, respectively. Children were responsible for watching after cows and water buffalo, light digging in gardens and fields, collecting firewood, and gathering cow dung for fertilizer.[76]

The dissolution of the family was effectively a means of dissolving the traditional family farm. Lengthening of labor time and increasing productivity are two fundamental means for raising the rate of valorization of capital, and the senior CPK leadership introduced both as capitalist practice steadily subsumed Khmer farming practices through the introduction of segregated divisions of labor and greater control over the timing of farming-related activities.[77] There are, however, physical limits to the production of absolute surplus value, limits I argue the Khmer Rouge overcame by the generation of a form of *relative* surplus value. This requires some explanation.

To begin, workers in capitalist enterprises undertake concrete labor to produce commodities; this concrete labor, in turn, contributes to the formation of both value and exchange value.[78] More precisely, capitalist production begins with a large number of workers, brought together under the command of a capitalist, work together for the production of the same type of commodity. Hence, the establishment of cooperatives, and the explicit goal of producing rice *as a commodity to generate exchange value*, marked the transformation of traditional Khmer farming by agrarian capitalism. Notably, the cooperation of many workers brings about, even without a change in the technical conditions of production, a reduction in value of products. Heinrich identifies two reasons for this. The first is that workers use many means of production in common, so that they contribute a smaller share of value to the product. For example, one hundred laborers in a cooperative may produce ten times as much rice as ten workers, but they will not require ten times as many buildings to house them. Second, a new power emerges from cooperation, in that ten people arranged in a work-chain, such as during the excavation of a canal or the planting of seedlings, can work considerably faster than if each individual performs separately.[79] In so doing, concrete labor aggregates as abstract labor—the homogenous expenditure of labor effort. As such, the value of a commodity, such as rice, depends not on the hours of concrete labor per unit produced but instead on the hours of socially necessary abstract labor time required to produce it. Likewise, the exchange value is similarly determined based on the amalgamation of all productive labor in a given period and its allocation according to the quantity of homogenous labor the commodity represents in equivalent exchange.[80]

Conventionally, under conditions of capitalist production, the reduction in value of products means that workers require less wages to reproduce themselves. For example, suppose workers live on rice alone, and the cost of rice falls in half because of increases in productivity.[81] Capitalists are able to reduce wages by a quarter but at the same time, workers are still able to purchase more rice. In principle, capitalists gain the collective form of relative surplus value and workers enjoy a modest improvement in their standard of living. How, though, could this relationship materialize in Democratic Kampuchea? As indicated earlier, senior officials suspended the circulation of currency and, by extension, wages. The answer is deceptively simple. CPK officials replaced monetary wages with food rations.

In capitalist societies, the products of concrete labor count as abstract social labor; hence, exchange does not concern quality or type of concrete labor but only quantity of abstract labor.[82] In Democratic Kampuchea, in like fashion, CPK officials established their economic calculations based on abstract social labor. As detailed in their Four-Year Plan, for example, party leaders determined that "from 1977, the ration for the people will average . . . 312 kilograms of rice per person per year throughout the country."[83] Based on this ration, that is, the socially necessary amount of food required to reproduce labor, party members determined the amount of surplus value expected from the export of rice. By way of illustration, the "Plan for Rice Production throughout the Country during the Period 1977–1980" appears as table 3 in the Four-Year Plan. Here, CPK officials anticipate the production of 5.5 million tons of rice in 1977, with production increasing to 7.7 million tons in 1980. A footnote explains that "total production for fields harvested twice per year is figured as 6 tons per hectare; ordinary fields harvested once per year is estimated at 3 tons per hectare." Table 5 presents figures on capital expenditures and capital earned from the export of rice. Thus, of the target 5.5 million tons of rice produced in 1977, the CPK determined that an equivalency of

3.2 million tons of rice would be expended as capital (e.g., food rations, seeds, and "welfare"). Of the estimated 2.3 million tons of "surplus" rice, 1.3 million tons were to be exported. Based on an exchange rate of US$200 per ton of rice, the CPK concluded that it would earn—in 1977—more than US$277 million. Subsequently, a ratio of 7:3 was calculated, whereby 70 percent of surplus would be spent for the "base" in order to build the zones, regions, and other units, while the remaining 30 percent was set aside for the state to defend and build the country.[84] According to CPK calculations, earnings from rice were to increase each year between 1977 and 1980, with earning in 1980 anticipated at more than US$424 million.

Subsequently, for each administrative zone, party officials made separate calculations to determine the balance between surplus production and food rations. In the Western Zone, for example, a senior party official explained how such calculations would be determined: "If the Zone has 600,000 people, they must eat 150,000 tons of [rice]. But we want more than this in order to locate much additional oil, to get ever more rice mills, threshing machines, water pumps, and means of transportation, both as an auxiliary manual force and to give strength to our forces of production. So we must not get just 150,000 tons of [rice]. We must get 300,000, 400,000, 500,000 tons just to break even and be able to build socialism."[85] Effectively, these abstract calculations formed the cornerstone of the CPK's overall economic policy. This required, in turn, a detailed understanding of all inputs and outputs, a requirement acknowledged by party leaders. Indeed, senior CPK members clarified, "Upper echelon need to know the amount [of rice] so it can easily make arrangements, for one thing for solving the livelihood of the people, but for another to think about sale and exchange as well. We must arrange for the brothers and sisters to think, to plan, because we are not just producing for families, we have reached a stage of major production and cannot think just about small production."[86]

The rapid expansion of agriculture required an abstract system based on the standardization of labor and a matching implementation of food rations. As detailed in the Four-Year Plan, party leaders developed a system to distribute food rations based on labor capacity.[87] Those workers classified in the No. 1 system would be allocated three cans of rice per day; those in the No. 2 system, two and a half cans; No. 3, two cans; and No. 4, one and a half cans). This numeric system refers to the type of labor involved; those people performing the heaviest manual labor, in principle, were to receive the highest rations. The elderly or the sick, who performed the lightest tasks, received the smallest rations. In addition, all workers would receive two side dishes (soup and dried food). Detailed work schedules were also devised—although not necessarily implemented—that determined how many days of work were required for so-ciety as a whole. In this way, party planners calculated an amount of surplus value based on the *socially necessary labor time* required to plant and harvest rice. By extension, local cadre calculated work quotas specific to their coopera-tive or administrative unit, such the amount of soil to excavate or the acreage of forest to clear. Notably, CPK officials projected rice production to increase each year but planned to hold food rations constant. In other words, party leaders fixed the cost to reproduce labor from year to year, that is, officials expected workers to be more productive from one year to the next but live on the same food ration from year to year.

It is necessary, at this point, to consider more precisely the *value* of labor power as conceived by the CPK. Marx well understood that "the owner of labor-power is mortal." Accordingly, workers require a certain amount of wages to re-produce themselves—that is, simply to live. However, workers, even under the best conditions, eventually die. For this reason, Marx concludes, "the of means of subsistence necessary for the production of labor-power must include the means necessary for the worker's replacements, i.e. his children, in order that this race of peculiar commodity-owners may perpetuate its presence on the market."[88] According to Marx, "The extent of 'necessary means of subsistence' differs among the various countries and historical periods, and depends upon what is normally counted among the necessary requirements of life."[89] In other words, "the determination of the value of labor-power contains a historical and moral element."[90] What was this moral element for the Khmer Rouge?

Throughout Democratic Kampuchea, the dissolution of the traditional Khmer family coincided with the transformation of traditional Khmer farm-ing practices and formed a key component of the CPK's overall approach to national economic development. As explained in an article published in *Revolutionary Youth*, "We consider matters of family as being inseparable from matters of the entire nation and people." The article continues, "When our nation is unmercifully oppressed, exploited, and placed under hardship by the imperialists-feudalists, our families are also exploited. Therefore, in order that our families may know true happiness, peace, and prosperity, our entire nation and people must first be liberated and freed from every type of exploitation by the reactionary imperialists-feudalists-capitalists." This required vigilance in selecting spouses, the proper education and "building" of spouses after mar-riage, and subsequently the proper building of families. Together, these mea-sures would "strengthen and expand the cooperativization movement."[91]

The Khmer Rouge, in addition, prohibited by deadly means all other means of subsistence—a practice that was, from its perspective, both legal and moral.

Party slogans warned, "Hands off the people's property! Not a single grain of rice, a single chili, a single needle!"[92] With few exceptions, notably for "base" people or more trusted cadre, Khmer Rouge cadre prevented people from cultivating personal gardens or foraging for food. In effect, through the establishment of supervised cooperatives, everyone in time became dependent upon the party to satisfy even their most basic of provisions. Likewise, throughout 1976 and 1977, Khmer Rouge cadre imposed communal eating throughout the cooperatives. This practice served a variety of functions. On the one hand, collective dining was a means of ensuring discipline and loyalty to the party. On the other hand, communal eating facilitated the distribution and consumption of food; this was a crucial element for those cadres responsible for providing set amounts of surplus to the party. Concurrently, official CPK policy forbade private cooking or eating, stating that everything in the country was the property of the revolution; consequently, all fruits, vegetables, and animals found in the wild belonged to the party. Workers risked imprisonment, torture, or execution for simply taking a fish from a pond or a coconut from a tree.[93]

Fundamentally, the CPK assumed all responsibility for the provision of reproductive costs. According to the Four-Year Plan, the party would provide all "material necessities for the People," allocated "on a co-operative, family, and individual basis." These would include clothing, mosquito nets, blankets, pillows, water pitchers, glasses, plates, spoons, writing books, spectacles, raincoats, scissors, and so on.[94] In practice, CPK officials provided few of these goods. This should not blind us, however, from the key insight that Khmer Rouge cadres sought to depreciate the costs of the "necessary means of subsistence" in order to minimize the value of labor power. Accordingly, workers required less wages, that is, food rations, to reproduce themselves.

Properly speaking, we need to view the food ration not as a *thing* but instead as representative of a social relation. It signified a relation between party members, that is, those who control the means of production and its allocation, and the workers, those who do not. By extension, the fetishism of the food ration as a thing conceals and diverts our attention from the material circumstances of its origination and circulation. Simply put, the food ration originated in the material conditions of CPK economic policies, notably the suspension of currency. Indeed, without the suspension of money, there would be little need for food rations. Workers, for example, could have received wages (as in a fully formed capitalist economy) or chits, that is, some form of coupon or voucher that workers could exchange for food and other necessities. What happens, however, if food rations replace currency but the fundamental relationship between those who own the means of production and those denied remains constant?

Money is a representation of value; by extension, food rations similarly appear as representations of value. However, money and food rations are not equivalent, in that food rations circulate and exchange differently than wages. Food rations, to begin, represent capital in two distinct ways. On the one hand, rations constitute an investment on behalf of the capitalists, in that rations serve as a form of wages, that is, something exchanged in return for labor. On the other hand, the literal consumption of rations, in other words, the eating of the food ration by workers, siphons off potential surplus. There is less food available to exchange on the market. In addition, workers do not use food rations, unlike with wages, to purchase food commodities, hence there is no valorization occurring with biological consumption. Indeed, the opposite happens, as the consumption of food rations by workers imposes myriad contradictions whereby the reproduction of the worker results in the cessation of capital circulating. These follow from the fact that the category of worker comprises a unity of opposites.

In most capitalist societies, workers are consumers in different, mutually reinforcing ways. Workers, for example, are biological consumers, in that workers consume nutrients for biological reproduction. In addition, though, and specific to the capitalist mode of production, workers consume commodities, that is, they purchase goods and services. Both forms of consumption are necessary for the continuation of capitalism: the former reproduces the class of workers and the second valorizes capital. Normally, workers purchase (consume) commodities to be eaten (consumed) in exchange for capital; in other words, they pay for commodities with wages obtained through their employment. As both producers and consumers, workers personify a contradiction unique to capitalism. Capitalists want to pay the minimum wage possible, in order to accrue greater profits; yet, if workers receive inadequate wages, they are less able to purchase more commodities, thus placing the valorization of capital at risk. Historically, capitalists have been able to circumvent this contraction in a variety of ways, notably by extending credit to workers. Under the economic system introduced in Democratic Kampuchea, however, the provision of higher rations (in the form of rice) would decrease the amount of capital (rice) the CPK had available for valorization in the global economy. Conversely, decreased rations facilitated the accumulation of greater profits. In short, under a system of agrarian capitalism imposed by CPK leadership, the food ration assumed the form of capital. Consequently, when senior personnel of the CPK suspended currency, they did not negate capital but merely substituted one form of capital (wages) with another (rations).

Conclusions

The key to understanding the (structural) violence of Democratic Kampuchea is the initiation of food rations (rice) as a means of exchange. Before 1975 the majority of Cambodia's peasants were not waged workers; indeed, most remained subsistence farmers or fisherfolk. There were few tenant farmers, sharecroppers, or others who were compelled to sell their labor capacity to survive. Debt of course was a major problem. After years of civil war and socialist revolution, the Khmer Rouge imposed a particular social relation that denied all workers access to the means of subsistence. In short, all citizens became dependent upon the party to provide food, water, clothing, and shelter. However, rather than offering a wage in monetary form for labor provided, the Khmer Rouge offered food rations. And this makes all the difference, for every spoonful of rice was simultaneously a bite out of profit.

The Khmer Rouge wanted to build postrevolutionary society through the export of rice, a policy that justified the pursuit of an ever-expanding agricultural surplus for export. To increase overall production, the Khmer Rouge sought to increase the area under cultivation, increase the overall productivity of agriculture, and limit domestic rice consumption. To increase cultivated area, labor was required to build paddy, irrigation works, and cultivate new fields. The plan to increase productivity involved the domestic production or importation of agricultural tools, fertilizers, pesticides, and herbicides. To produce these agricultural inputs domestically entailed additional forced labor, while importation depended once again on the rice surplus (and, by extension, forced labor). Finally, to reduce domestic rice consumption, the Khmer Rouge imposed a regulating system on the workforce. In these ways, the new political economy of Democratic Kampuchea placed the majority of the population between the teeth of two powerful forces: a demand for surplus rice and agricultural inputs that justified severe labor policies and an austere rationing system that subjected men, women, and children to starvation wages.

The Khmer Rouge in addition sought to simplify questions of class justice. Indeed, as conceived by senior leaders of the CPK, Democratic Kampuchea was a classless society, thus mitigating any serious concerns regarding either productive or distributive justice. With the vast majority of the population forced to live and work collectively, there were no palpable distinctions between "productive" and "non-productive" workers; instead, everyone was to work for the revolution, the party, and the state. Workers were to receive rations distributed according to needs, with necessity determined abstractly based on individual attributes and collective requirements. In other words, the hardest workers, performing the most vital tasks, received (in principle) greater shares of rations; those laborers deemed less capable, in turn, received fewer shares. At no point, however, did cooperatives function according to the democratic ideals hoped for by early Marxists, including Marx himself. Throughout Democratic Kampuchea, the direct producers—those laborers impelled to clear forests and cultivate fields, excavate canals and construct dams, and plant and harvest rice—did not participate in the collective control or direction of the labor process, nor did they have a say in the collective disposition of surplus generated through the export of rice and other commodities. Rather, all decisions were concentrated, ultimately, in the persona of senior CPK cadre.

These economic structures of violence contributed most especially to the direct violence that permeated Democratic Kampuchea. The fragility of CPK rule upon victory contributed on the one hand to the development of a massive security apparatus designed to seek out and "smash" perceived external and internal enemies. Surviving CPK documents describe Khmer Rouge cadre arresting people for stealing food or merely complaining about insufficient rations. CPK leaders also purged local officials who admitted that starvation was occurring in their areas. As the food crisis increased, the CPK blamed traitorous and inept low-level cadres for undermining the food production system and initiated a series of purges against suspected traitors and reactionary elements within the party.[95] In short, the deaths from exposure, starvation, and disease during the Cambodian genocide were not the side effects of poor research, poor planning, or poor implementation; instead, the economic strategies adopted by the CPK leadership resulted much as Marx would have expected, that is, with the violent death of laborers, consumed by the "werewolf-like hunger for surplus labor."[96]

Epilogue

Standing before Marx's grave in 1883, Engels delivered a short eulogy for his longtime friend and collaborator. In this speech, Engels lamented the loss of Marx, not personally but as an "immeasurable loss" for both "the militant proletariat of Europe and America" and for "historical science." Indeed, as explained by Engels, the work of Marx effectively blended political praxis and scientific knowledge. "For Marx was before all else a revolutionist," Engels continued, in that "his real mission in life was to contribute, in one way or another, to the overthrow of capitalist society and of the state institutions, which it had brought into being, to contribute to the liberation of the modern proletariat." To this end, science reigned supreme, in that "science was for Marx a historically dynamic, revolutionary force."[1]

Marx never provided an explicit, cogent theory of social revolution. Nevertheless, it is possible to reconstruct, holistically, the basic elements of revolutionary change as understood by Marx. In the decades before Marx and the appearance of *The Communist Manifesto*, the Jacobin tradition inherited from the French Revolution dominated calls for revolution throughout Europe. Accordingly, myriad socialists, communists, anarchists and other would-be revolutionaries premised social change as an action initiated and conducted by small groups of conspirators acting on behalf of "the people," who were to be liberated from above.[2] Marx, conversely, forwarded a radical reinterpretation of revolution, a praxis predicated on revolution from below, characterized by mass self-emancipation. In *The German Ideology*, Marx and Engels explain: "Both for the production on a mass scale of this communist consciousness, and for the success of the cause itself, the alteration of men on a mass scale is necessary, an alteration which can only take place in a practical movement, a revolution; the revolution is necessary, therefore not only because the ruling class cannot be overthrown in any other way, but also because the class overthrowing it can only in a revolution succeed in ridding itself of all the muck of ages and become fitted to found society anew."[3]

Socialism seemingly offered the best opportunity to maintain the earth for future generations and to provide the greatest prospect for the development of human freedom and potential. Still, Marx was not naïve. Nowhere is there any evidence to suggest that Marx believed that a sustainable relation to the earth would automatically materialize under socialism of any form. Rather, the writings of Marx reveal a deep and profound belief that only a radical transformation of the metabolic relation of human labor to nature could forestall environmental collapse and the alienation of humanity.[4]

And what of postrevolutionary society? As Michael Harrington writes, "one can seize power—but then it is necessary to run an entire, complex economy, and that cannot be done at the point of a gun."[5] Here, Marx says little about postcapitalist society in any coherent, explicit fashion. Most frequently, Marx speaks of a political transition period during which capitalist society is transformed in a revolutionary way into its opposite, that is, a transition from the "capitalist mode of production" to an "associated" mode of production.[6] Thus, Marx envisages only one society that succeeds capitalism, and this "noncapitalist" society constitutes "communist society" or the "socialist constitution of mankind."[7] Lenin, however, reads into Marx a steadfast distinction between socialism and communism and in so doing sets the tone for subsequent socialist revolutions in the twentieth century.[8] Lenin forwards this dualism based on statements that appear in Marx's *Critique of the Gotha Program*, wherein Marx writes, "between capitalist and communist society lies the period of the revolutionary transformation of the one into the other."[9] Socialism, by implication, must constitute this intermediate or transitional period between capitalism and communism. This inference, for Lenin, holds despite that nowhere else does Marx define socialism as either the transition to communism or the lower phase of communism. It is communism *tout court*.[10] Indeed, Marx invariably refers to socialism and communism interchangeably—a common practice in the nineteenth century—or he employs some variant, such as the phrase "cooperative society," which incidentally appears also in the *Critique of the Gotha Program*.[11]

At issue is Marx's references to a "first phase" and a later "higher phase" of communist society. Here, it is worth considering these phases in proper context. Marx writes that "what we have to deal with here is a communist society, not as it has developed on its own foundations, but, on the contrary, as it emerges from capitalist society; which is thus in every respect, economically, morally and intellectually, still stamped with the birthmarks of the old society from whose womb it emerges." In other words, Marx affirms his argument that any postcapitalist (communist) society emanates from capitalist society and cannot materialize fully formed "on its own foundations." Communist society, as it emerges, is marked with the "birthmarks of the old society," meaning that social inequalities remain. This follows from Marx's contention that judicial changes, such as the elimination of private property, do not ceteris paribus eliminate capitalism. These defects, Marx explains, "are inevitable in the first phase of communist society as it is when it has just emerged after prolonged birth pangs from capitalist society." By extension, Marx writes, "In a higher phase of communist society, after the enslaving subordination of individuals under division of labor, and therewith also the antithesis between mental and physical labor has vanished . . . ; after the productive forces have also increased with the all-round development of the individual, and all the springs of co-operative wealth flow more abundantly—only then can the narrow horizon of bourgeois right be fully left behind and society inscribe on its banners: from each according to his ability, to each according to his needs." [12]

For Marx the salient point is that both so-called phases are part and parcel of the same political transition period. Hence, the apparent transition from capitalism to the first phase of capitalism is qualitatively different from the transition from the first to the second phase of communism, in that the former involves a revolution in the social relations of production, whereas the latter does not. Specifically, the first and second phases do not entail different modes of production but instead refer to a prolonged transformation of capitalist social relations of production. [13] Here, Marx's dialectics are in full view, in that he is concerned with processes and relations as opposed to disparate things. In other words, material reality, including the transformation of social relations, is more than the epiphenomena we can count or classify. Capitalist society is not an object but the distillation of myriad, concrete relations; the same holds for communist society. The transformation of the former into the latter proceeds gradually, imperceptibly, as day transitions to night. Perhaps it is best to think of the so-called first phase as a twilight period, a transition under way but clearly not constituting a distinct period. Simply put, for Marx, the goal of socialism is to negate capitalism. [14] Revolutions are dialectic, not nihilistic; transitions, therefore, cannot be short-term events.

Unlike Marx's gradualist, dialectic understanding, Lenin postulates two transitions, the first transitioning from capitalism to socialism and the second from socialism to communism. [15] Significantly, for Lenin both socialism and communism constitute separate modes of production based on collective ownership of the means of production, such that profit, rent, and interest are not sources of personal income. However, under socialism workers continue to receive wages and exchange these wages for consumer goods, while under communism there is no market in consumer goods. Consumer goods are either free for the taking or rationed according to individual needs. In short, the difference between the two forms of communism is that under socialism there is exchange but no exploitation, whereas under fully formed communism there is neither exploitation nor exchange.[16]

Lenin effectively stands Marx on his head. For Marx socialism by definition constitutes a class society, a union of free individuals. Lenin speaks not of this but of a socialist *state*—an expression found nowhere in Marx. Lenin's concept of socialism greatly impoverishes the dialectic in Marx. By not presenting the first phase of communism as a transformation of social relations, Lenin reduces socialism to a specific property form, namely the *state* ownership of the means of production through the elimination of *individual* private ownership. Lenin's promotion of so-called social ownership, or ownership in the name of the workers, does not sunder the exploitative relationships of capitalism; rather, Lenin merely transfers the source of alienation away from individual capitalists toward the state, now occupied by members of the vanguard. Under Lenin, socialism becomes state capitalism.[17]

This was a necessary and strategic move on Lenin's behalf, in that conditions in Russia were far from optimal for a *Marxist* revolution. It bears mentioning that Lenin's Marxism "was a Russianized Marxism developed with Russian circumstances in mind."[18] Thus, Lenin modifies the writing of Marx based on his conclusion that Marxism *tout court* was inapplicable to the concrete conditions found in Russia. Indeed, many so-called Russian Marxists understood this fact by the late nineteenth and early twentieth centuries. Several of Marx's personal Russian acquaintances doubted the ready application of Marxism to Russia yet recognized its rhetorical significance to the revolutionary movement. In addition, many other Russians, notably Mikhail Bakunin and Sergey Lavrov, were unable to reconcile their own vision of Russia's future with Marx's supposed prediction that industrial capitalism must necessarily precede communism.[19] It is not surprising, therefore, that the socialism that emerged in Russia, including that forwarded by avowed "Marxists," turns out to be the exact opposite of the socialism which one finds in Marx's texts.

Ironically, the practice of twentieth-century "socialism" has been a vast exercise in the enslavement of the human individual whose emancipation was the ultimate goal of the socialist revolution as envisioned by Marx.[20] Subsequent followers of Marx expanded, modified, distorted, and perverted much of Marx's schematic of revolution so much that the so-called Marxist revolutions of the twentieth century bear scant resemblance to Marx's own position. Indeed, it is remarkable that "no existing so-called 'socialist' regime has ever allowed the implementation of what, according to Marx, constitutes the very condition of a socialist revolution, namely, that the emancipation of the working class is the task of the workers themselves."[21] Senior members of Democratic Kampuchea, to this end, identified their party as Marxist-Leninist. In our subsequent interpretations of CPK policy, however, we should heed the words of Trotsky, who in *Challenge of Left Opposition* writes, "Neither classes nor parties can be judged by what they say." Rather, we should judge according to the material practices.

The socialist revolution in Democratic Kampuchea was a peasant-dominant as opposed to a peasant-led revolution. Many members of the Cambodian communist movement, including Pol Pot, viewed themselves as—or at least claimed to be—a "dictatorship of the proletariat," that is, as exalted members of a vanguard. In the years following the revolution, for example, Pol Pot announced in a public speech that victory had been achieved through "the implementation of the Party's dictatorship of the proletariat in all areas of . . . revolutionary activity." Pol Pot explained, "We promote broad democracy among the people by a correct application of democratic centralism, so that this immense force will mobilize enthusiastically and rapidly for socialist revolution and construction, at great leaps and bounds forward." However, he cautioned that "we absolutely, without hesitation, apply the dictatorship of the proletariat to our enemies and to the tiny handful of reactionary elements who oppose the revolution, who seek to destroy it, who sell out to the foreign imperialists and reactionaries in order to ruin their own nation, their own people and their own revolution."[22]

Certainly, the CPK exalted the "peasant" in public rhetoric and idolized the "peasant" in song and poetry. In practice, though, members of the ruling party remained cautious, skeptical, and suspicious of the peasantry. Simply put, the CPK vanguard recognized that the rural-based rank-and-file cadre had joined the movement largely because of their unyielding support of the former monarch and their opposition to US bombing. The peasantry as a whole did not exhibit a proper political consciousness, and it was for this reason that the CPK upon seizing power needed to "build socialism" in all fields.

Members of the CPK were, from their perspective, attempting to produce a just society. This acknowledgment is not to discount the violence manifest in CPK policy and practice but to assess critically the particular social relations and material conditions both envisioned and enacted in the establishment of Democratic Kampuchea. Substantively, party leaders drew inspiration both from the Russian Revolution and from the Non-Aligned Movement. On the one hand, key elements of Lenin's explication of the state informed CPK governance. Scholars frequently describe Democratic Kampuchea as lacking in governance. Boraden Nhem, for example, describes the Khmer Rouge regime as an "empty government." [23] This description only holds, however, if one employs a restrictive definition of government. In Democratic Kampuchea, senior officials claimed adherence to the principles of Marxism-Leninism, and while their devotion was uneven, their understanding of governance was consistent with many of the ideas espoused by Marx and Lenin, among others. Marx, for example, premised that socialism would substitute social or collective control over the physical means of production for private property relations. In other words, the democratic association and organization of production by the associated producers themselves negated the continuation of the "state" as commonly understood.[24] Lenin expanded these ideas, arguing for the destruction of the bourgeois state apparatus and its replacement with a *temporary* workers' state. In time, even this would wither away as the building of socialism proceeded, in which the functions of control and management would pass from the hands of a bureaucratic apparatus into the hands of the workers as a whole.[25] As such, Nhem is correct to conclude that in Democratic Kampuchea, party leaders "tended to favor the establishment of a ministry only for some specific and ad hoc job." [26] However, we must understand this as indicative of a Marxist-Leninist conception of governance and not that of an "empty government" as defined by conventional standards.

On the other hand, CPK officials explicitly framed their postrevolutionary programs along the lines forwarded by the NAM. The Constitution of Democratic Kampuchea, drafted in 1975 and ratified in 1976, stated explicitly the CPK's adherence to the principles of the NAM. During the 1950s and 1960s, many former colonies, but especially those following the NAM, promoted a particular economic strategy known as import-substitution industrialization. Proponents of import-substitution industrialization argued that lesser-developed countries should initially substitute domestic production of previously imported, simple consumer goods and then substitute through domestic production for a wider range of more sophisticated manufactured items. In other words, advocates of import-substitution industrialization promoted an economic strategy predicated on self-sufficiency. Variously understood within broader theories of dependency or underdevelopment, the argument was this: For decades if not centuries the economies of colonies were held in check by unfair trade arrangements and production processes that consigned the colonies to positions of subservience within the global economy. Colonies and former colonies imported most of their manufactured goods in return for the export of primary products, such as sugar, bananas, coffee, tea, and cotton. Conversely, under import-substitution industrialization, governments of former colonies would be able to protect their domestic industries and by extension encourage the production of domestic consumer goods. Revenue saved from not having to import these goods could then be used to purchase other manufactured commodities that could not be produced given the country's overall level of industrial development. Such an approach is readily apparent in CPK documents. For example, minutes from a meeting held on May 8, 1976, state: "We will decrease importing items next year, including cotton and jute, because we are working hard to produce ours. We will import only some important items such as chemical fertilizer, plastic, acid, iron factory, and other raw materials." This strategy the CPK deemed most appropriate, in that solutions development proceeded not "by taking loans from the West or Eastern Europe," for in so doing the CPK would lose their "self-reliant stance."[27] This statement illustrates the CPK's adherence to the Non-Aligned Movement and its cautionary position in the global economy.

Once in power, party leaders confronted head-on their own variant of the agrarian question, that is, how to facilitate industrial development through the promotion of agriculture. Here, we should recognize that the problems faced and solutions proposed are far from unique and that CPK policy and practice is not separable from the wider history of socialist revolutions or, for that matter, of the advancement of capitalism. There is a complex history, for example, to the practice of collectivization; one that includes theorists such as Vladimir Smirnov, Nikolai Bukharin, and Evgeny Preobrazhensky. This analysis of agrarian transformations in Democratic Kampuchea requires a theoretical engagement with several Marxist concepts as understood and developed not only by Marx but also by subsequent Marxists in Russia, China, and elsewhere. This requires an effort to see the agricultural policies of the CPK not in isolation but instead to appreciate their connections with other attempts to respond to the malleable agrarian question. From this vantage point, CPK officials appear less exceptional, less irrational. Contemporaneous documents of the CPK detail clearly their awareness of these debates; it is incumbent that scholars of the Khmer Rouge do likewise.

A recognition of similarities allows for the identification of differences. Thus, while CPK leaders pursued a strategy based on the forced collectivization of the peasantry, their decision to abolish currency domestically did set them apart from other Marxist-inspired governments. Here, senior officials of the CPK erred in believing that simply abolishing commodity production, money, and wage labor was tantamount to socialist revolution. Most problematic was that these members of the CPK did not sunder the fundamental social relations of capitalist production. Party leaders were unable—indeed, unwilling—to eradicate capital, for surplus profits were necessary to modernize their economy. To this end, policies planned and implemented by the CPK deepened capitalist relations throughout society and led to the real subsumption of labor and nature to the dictates of capital. For the Khmer Rouge, the establishment of cooperatives became a panacea for all of their problems, both materially and ideologically. In Democratic Kampuchea, under the guidance of the CPK, the transformation from traditional farming to agriculture marked truly the coming of capitalism—that is, a system of production for exchange whereby material practices of dispossession and displacement separated the immediate producers from the means of production—to Cambodia. As such, far from being unique, the prescriptions forwarded by the CPK provide one more example of communist leaders pursuing the Holy Grail of a postrevolutionary utopia.

Red Harvests, ultimately, provides a political economy of the Cambodian genocide and thus contributes to a vibrant field of genocide scholarship that seeks to document and interpret how economic programs are productive of the conditions for genocide and mass violence.[28] In so doing, I reinterpret the Cambodian genocide as part and parcel of a state-guided effort to transform traditional farming practices into a capital-positing activity, that is, as a program of agrarian capitalism. The critical study of agrarian capitalism is a robust field that attempts to explain "the specificities, modalities, complexities, durations and contradictions of agrarian transitions, in the different places and times of capitalism."[29] Scholars of agrarian capitalism necessarily focus on those societies marked by definitive social relations that typify capitalism, that is, the commodification of land, labor, and property, and the accumulation of surplus value through the exploitation of waged workers. Conceptually, however, it is useful to think of agrarian capitalism as a trajectory of forms of subsumption of labor by capital based on the dispossession and control of labor by agrarian classes engaged in farming as a business. The flexibility of this approach, Banaji continues, is that it allows for the variety of backgrounds from which agrarian capitalists have, typically, been drawn, the diversity of enterprises they have operated (for example, plantations, estates, and farms), and a more profound understanding of the "commodification of labor power" as meaning more than just the predominance of day laborers paid in cash.[30] In response to Banaji's opening, *Red Harvests* brings together advances in agrarian studies and genocide through a case study of agrarian transformation within a so-called socialist state. As a former colony and newly independent state, party officials within Democratic Kampuchea joined countless other leaders of the Third World in an attempt to reorganize their society informed by Soviet-style

Marxism and the guiding principles of the Non-Aligned Movement. These officials promised salvation from oppression and exploitation but, through the evacuation of cities and the corralling of men, women, and children onto cooperatives, introduced conditions that led to widespread calamity. It is thus a story of the dialectics of state capitalism and agrarian transformation, a story very different from conventional accounts. CPK leaders sought to initiate a transformation of traditional, precapitalist farming practices to a socialist mode of production, but in so doing they more fully subsumed Khmer society to the dictates of capitalism. The context of the Cambodian genocide, in short, was the problem of agrarian-based capital accumulation.

Notes

Preface

1. Marx and Engels, *Communist Manifesto*, 35.
2. The number of people killed during the Cambodian genocide is unknown; in addition, scholars do not know how many people died from starvation-related conditions, disease, and exhaustion or from torture and execution. Compounding the problem is that scholars also cannot disaggregate from the approximately two million deaths those who died from the civil war (1970–75) of the US-led bombing campaign between 1965 and 1973. See Heuveline, "Between One and Three Million"; De Walque, "Selective Mortality"; Etcheson, *After the Killing Fields*; Owen and Kiernan, "Bombs over Cambodia"; and Heuveline, "Boundaries of Genocide."
3. Etcheson, *Rise and Demise of Democratic Kampuchea*; Kiernan, *How Pol Pot Came to Power*; Chandler, *Tragedy of Cambodian History*; Kiernan, *Pol Pot Regime*; Dy, *A History of Democratic Kampuchea*; and Nhem, *Khmer Rouge*.
4. Terminology is important. Salvatore Engel-Dimauro for example favors the term "state-socialism" over "state-capitalism"; Paresh Chattopadhyay, conversely, writes of "market socialism." See Chattopadhyay, *Marx's Associated Mode of Production*; Engel-Dimauro, "Enduring Relevance of State-Socialism."
5. See also Cliff, *State Capitalism in Russia*; Jerome and Buick, "Soviet State Capitalism"; Petras, "State Capitalism"; Turok, "Zambia's System of State Capitalism"; Cooper, "State Capitalism, Class Structure, and Social Transformation"; Buick and Crump, *State Capitalism*; and Matar, "Twilight of 'State Capitalism.' "
6. Engels, *Anti-Dühring*, 382.
7. Marx, *Capital*, vol. 2, 177.
8. Resnick and Wolff, "State Capitalism in the USSR," 48.
9. But see Kiernan, "Origins of Khmer Communism"; Kiernan, "Kampuchea and Stalinism," 232–50; Frieson, "Political Nature of Democratic Kampuchea"; Edwards, "Rise of the Khmer Rouge"; Heder, *Cambodian Communism*; Path and Kanavou, "Converts, not Ideologues"; and Harmann, "Scripting Mass Atrocity."
10. Ben Kiernan, in his *Pol Pot Regime*, likewise argues that, fundamentally, the Communist Party of Kampuchea was not Marxist but instead simply racist, nationalistic, and totalitarian. Elsewhere, however, he does suggest a more Stalinist foundation for the Khmer Rouge; see Kiernan, "Kampuchea and Stalinism," 232–50. For a rebuttal of the primacy of a "racist ideological" underpinning of the Khmer Rouge, see Heder, "Racism, Marxism, Labelling, and Genocide."
11. White, "What Is a Communist System," 249.
12. Jackson, "Ideology of Total Revolution," 241–50; Clegg, Pina e Cunha, and Rego,

"Theory and Practice of Utopia"; Pina e Cunha et al., "Organization (Angkar) as a State of Exception"; and Williams and Neilson, "They Will Rot the Society."

13. Straus, "Organic Purity," 50.
14. Document No. D30882, "Long Live the 17th Anniversary of the Communist Party of Kampuchea," archived at the Documentation Center of Cambodia, Phnom Penh.
15. Cherne, "Cambodia—Auschwitz of Asia," 22; Nhem, *Khmer Rouge*, 43.
16. Owens, "Collective Dynamics of Genocidal Violence," 412; Draguhn, "The Indochina Conflict," 102.
17. Lenin, "Right of Nations to Self-Determination," 556.
18. Taşdemir Yaşin, "Adventure of Capital," 379.
19. Here, my methodological debt to Terence Byres is readily apparent. See Byres, "Political Economy," 508.
20. Document No. E3/130 (00184022), "Communist Party of Kampuchea—Statute," archived by the Extraordinary Chambers in the Court of Cambodia, http://www.eccc .gov.kh/en.
21. See, for example, Cliff, *State Capitalism in Russia*; Fitzpatrick, *Everyday Stalinism*; Landsman, *Dictatorship and Demand*; Sanchez-Sibony, *Red Globalization*; and Brown and Johnson, *Maoism at the Grassroots*.
22. Banaji, "Fictions of Free Labor," 82.
23. Byres, "Agrarian Question," 4.
24. For helpful overviews, see Hammen, "Marx and the Agrarian Question"; Byres, "Agrarian Transition and the Agrarian Question"; McLaughlin, "Rethinking the Agrarian Question"; Akram-Lodhi, "The Agrarian Question, Past and Present"; Bernstein, "Is There an Agrarian Question"; Akram-Lodhi and Kay, "Surveying the Agrarian Question (Part 1)"; Akram-Lodhi and Kay, "Surveying the Agrarian Question (Part 2)"; and Moyo, Jha, and Yeros, "Classical Agrarian Question."
25. Here I follow James Scott in that the peasantry is taken to include small-holding as well as sharecropping and tenant cultivators who have some degree of control over the production process; it does not include migrant laborers, plantation workers, and waged landless day laborers. See Scott, "Hegemony and the Peasantry," 267.
26. Byres, "Agrarian Question," 7–8.
27. Scott, "Hegemony and the Peasantry," 269.
28. Byres, "Agrarian Question," 8.
29. Scott, "Hegemony and the Peasantry," 267.
30. Byres, "Agrarian Question," 15.
31. Byres, 5.
32. Resnick and Wolff, "Communism: Between Class and Classless"; Resnick and Wolff, "State Capitalism in the USSR"; Resnick and Wolff, "Between State and Private Capitalism"; Resnick and Wolff, *Class Theory and History*; and Satya Gabriel, Stephen A. Resnick, and Richard D. Wolff, "State Capitalism versus Communism: What Happened in the USSR and the PRC?" *Critical Sociology* 34, no. 4 (2008): 539–56.
33. Edelman and Wolford, "Introduction," 963.
34. Barker, "Class Struggle and Social Movements," 43.
35. Kristjanson-Gural, "Value, Cooperatives," 354.
36. Quinn, "Pattern and Scope of Violence"; Hinton, "Why Did You Kill?"; Vannak, *Khmer Rouge Division 703*; Ea, *Chain of Terror*; Hinton, *Why Did They Kill*.
37. Valentino, *Final Solutions*, 491.
38. Eagleton, *Why Marx Was Right*, 17.
39. Henning, *Philosophy after Marx*, 96.
40. White, "What Is a Communist System," 254.
41. Au, *Reclaiming Communist Philosophy*, 1.
42. Dean, *Governmentality*.

43. Document No. E3/196, "Statement of the Communist Party of Kampuchea to the Communist Workers' Party of Denmark, July 1978," archived at the Extraordinary Chambers in the Courts of Cambodia.
44. Horowitz, *Taking Lives*, 2; see also Bauman, *Modernity and the Holocaust*.
45. Barnes, "Functional Utility of Genocide." See also Chossudovsky, "Economic Genocide in Rwanda"; Verwimp, "Development Ideology"; Philip Verwimp, "Political Economy of Coffee"; and Kamola, "Global Coffee Economy."
46. Levene, "Chittagong Hill Tracts," 343.
47. Verwimp, "Political Economy of Coffee," 164.
48. Levene, "Chittagong Hill Tracts," 343.

Chapter 1. "Revolution Is the People's War"

1. Chapter title from a Khmer Rouge slogan, quoted in Locard, *Pol Pot's Little Red Book*, 153. Marx and Engels, *Communist Manifesto*, 50.
2. Quoted in Locard, *Pol Pot's Little Red Book*, 213.
3. Locard, 211–12.
4. Communist Party of Kampuchea, "Excerpted Report on the Leading Views," 24–25.
5. A comprehensive account of the decades preceding the foundation of Democratic Kampuchea is beyond the scope of my immediate task. See Vickery, *Cambodia, 1975–1982*; Kiernan, *How Pol Pot Came to Power*; Chandler, *Tragedy of Cambodian History*; Kiernan, *Pol Pot Regime*; Becker, *When the War Was Over*; Chandler, *A History of Cambodia*; and Tully, *A Short History of Cambodia*.
6. Choonara, *Unravelling Capitalism*, 12.
7. Marx, *A Contribution*, 20–21.
8. Berman, "Concept of 'Articulation,' " 408.
9. Allen, *Marx*, 128.
10. Marx, *Capital*, vol. 2, 120.
11. Fraser and Wilde, *Marx Dictionary*, 33. Fraser and Wilde clarify that the word *bestimmen* is frequently translated or understood as "determines," thus resulting in a misleading interpretation of Marx's metaphor.
12. Mitchell, "Historical Materialism and Marxism," 54.
13. Ollman, *Alienation*, 151, 134.
14. Barone, *Radical Political Economy*, 8. See also Molyneux, "The Working Class," 5–8.
15. Allen, *Marx*, 67, 63.
16. Marx, *A Contribution*, 21.
17. Marx and Engels, *Communist Manifesto*, 35.
18. Allen, *Marx*, 62, 67.
19. Karl Marx, "General Rules of the International Workingmen's Association, October 1864," Marxists.org, https://www.marxists.org/history/international/iwma/documents/1864/rules.htm.
20. Elizabeth Schulte, "A Story Written by the Working Class Itself," SocialistWorker.org, https://socialistworker.org/2018/10/09/a-story-written-by-the-working-class-itself.
21. Yates, "Nothing to Lose," 15.
22. Yates, 20.
23. Allen, *Marx*, 70.
24. Yates, "Nothing to Lose," 20.
25. Howard and King, *History of Marxian Economics*, 286.
26. Both Marx and Engels were greatly interested in the political and economic developments transpiring in Russia. Unfortunately, both were also were

frustratingly vague on all the problems of vital concern to the Russian revolutionary movement. See Pipes, "Russian Marxism"; and Eaton, "Marx and the Russians."

27. Howard and King, *History of Marxian Economics*, 286.
28. Harrison, "Primary Accumulation," 82.
29. Antonio Gramsci, "The Revolution against 'Capital,' " Marxists.org, https://www .marxists.org/archive/gramsci/1917/12/revolution-against-capital.htm.
30. Merrington, "Theory and Practice," 146.
31. Lenin, *Essential Works*, 153.
32. Gramsci, "Revolution against 'Capital.' "
33. Leon Trotsky, "Our Political Tasks," Marxists.org, https://www.marxists.org/archive /trotsky/1904/tasks/.
34. Marx and Engels, *German Ideology*, 57.
35. Karl Marx, "Theses on Feuerbach," Marxists.org, https://www.marxists.org/archive /marx/works/1845/theses/theses.htm.
36. Chattopadhyay, "Myth of Twentieth-Century Socialism," 38.
37. Heardon, *Tragedy of Vietnam*, 8.
38. Paige, *Agrarian Revolutions*, 283.
39. Paige, 281–83; Heardon, *Tragedy of Vietnam*, 8.
40. Paige, *Agrarian Revolutions*, 305.
41. Helmers, "Rice in the Cambodian Economy," 2–3. Beyond these two systems, there were other productive arrangements, including larger holdings owned by ethnic Vietnamese and Chinese landowners.
42. Nesbitt, "Rice in the Cambodian Economy," 2.
43. Duiker, *Communist Road to Power*, 10.
44. Chandler, *A History*, 161.
45. Chandler, "From 'Cambodge,' " 38.
46. Kiernan, "Introduction," 3–7.
47. Slocomb, *An Economic History*, 71.
48. Kiernan, "Origins of Khmer Communism," 162.
49. Manning, *Transitional Justice*, 42.
50. Elizabeth Becker details that many of the Issaraks refused to work with the communists and refused to join in a united front with them against the French. This would lead to a permanent split in Cambodia between communist and noncommunist independence movements. See Becker, *When the War Was Over*, 70.
51. Chandler, "From 'Cambodge,' " 39.
52. Manning, *Transitional Justice*, 42.
53. Becker, *When the War Was Over*, 71.
54. Chandler, "From 'Cambodge,' " 39.
55. Quoted in Becker, *When the War Was Over*, 71.
56. Heder, *Cambodian Communism*, 15.
57. Norodom Sihanuk was the son of Prince Norodom Suramarit, who was married to Monivong's daughter. See Chandler, *A History of Cambodia*, 166.
58. Shawcross, *Sideshow*, 47.
59. Manning, *Transitional Justice*, 42; Chandler, *Tragedy of Cambodia*, 65–66.
60. Chandler, *Tragedy of Cambodia*, 68.
61. Chandler, 68–72; Becker, *When the War Was Over*, 76.
62. Chandler, *Tragedy of Cambodia*, 108.
63. Chandler, *A History*, 187.
64. Chandler, *Tragedy of Cambodia*, 71; Kiernan, "Origins of Khmer Communism," 173.
65. The salience of the Geneva Conference is beyond doubt. It is worth considering, though, the broader implications of the conference, for it is readily clear that the five major participants—the United States, the Soviet Union, China, France, and the United

Kingdom—entered negotiations for reasons other than the status of either Korea or Vietnam, and certainly not out of any concern for Cambodia. For the Soviets, the meetings came at an auspicious moment. Stalin had just died and, with the appearance of the People's Republic of China, the Soviets were able to confront diplomatically the United States, Britain, and France with an ally of their own. Overall, however, apart from shoring up its security and an opportunistic hope to disrupt the Western alliance, the Soviet Union expressed little interest in Indochina and was thus somewhat indifferent to the particularities of any eventual settlement. The Chinese, conversely, saw an opening for recognition on the world stage and in the process an opportunity to demonstrate their credentials to their Soviet counterparts. Nevertheless, Chinese officials confronted two immediate challenges: economic growth and the need to reduce foreign commitments. The support of armed conflict in Korea and Vietnam exhausted China financially and militarily and they were unwilling to fund continuing military activities in Indochina. As such, and unbeknownst to the American delegation, China officials had already concluded that they would not throw hundreds of thousands of soldiers into future conflicts in Asia. Here, the Chinese communists gambled that Cold War would not lead to an expanded war between the superpowers.

As for the United States, delegates were opposed to the proposed conference and participated only reluctantly. Their trepidation stemmed from concerns related to the growing presence of China. However, policy-makers in the United States realized that they could not readily oppose Chinese involvement at a conference addressing conflict in Asia. Accordingly, American officials entered the conference with a palpable belligerency and conducted themselves with an intractability rooted in the belief that concession was tantamount to capitulation. In retrospect, it is easy to discern why the Geneva Conference marked the end of one war and the beginning of a new one. In brief, French delegates sought a negotiated settlement to end their disastrous war in Indochina. The United States hoped to establish an allied coalition committed to the defense of Southeast Asia and the resumption of conflict in Indochina. The United Kingdom desired a peaceful settlement and the prevention of increased US military aggression in the region, and both the Soviet Union and Communist China hoped to gain international stature while preventing the escalation of war in Asia. The hopes, objectives, or concerns—indeed, even the participation—of the Vietnamese, Cambodians, Koreans, or Laotians mattered very little to the five powers.

See Immerman, "United States and the Geneva Conference"; Qiang, "China and the Geneva Conference"; Ruane, "Containing America"; Zhang, "Constructing 'Peaceful Coexistence'"; Asselin, "Democratic Republic of Vietnam"; Chen, "Beginning of the End"; and Wang, "Neutralizing Indochina."

66. Ross, "Masters of the Khmer Rouge," 10. See also Porter, "Vietnamese Communist Policy toward Kampuchea," 69–70.
67. Heder, *Cambodian Communism*, 17–18.
68. Porter, "Vietnamese Communist Policy," 73.
69. Manning, *Transitional Justice*, 42.
70. Chandler, *Brother Number One*, 47; Tully, *A Short History of Cambodia*, 129.
71. Liefer, "Cambodia," 59.
72. Gordon, "Cambodia," 439.
73. Simmonds, "Laos and Cambodia," 580.
74. Seekins, "Historical Setting," 32–34.
75. Gordon, "Cambodia," 443.
76. Clymer, "Perils of Neutrality," 613.
77. Chandler, *A History of Cambodia*, 189. See also Slocomb, *An Economic History*, 76.
78. Heder, *Cambodian Communism*, 49.
79. Kiernan, "Origins of Khmer Communism," 174–75.

80. Becker, *When the War Was Over*, 56.
81. Kiernan, *Pol Pot Regime*, 13.
82. Becker, *When the War Was Over*, 81.
83. Short, *Pol Pot*, 137. See also Ross, "Masters of the Khmer Rouge," 46.
84. Ross, "Masters of the Khmer Rouge," 47–48.
85. Document D30882, "Long Live the 17th Anniversary of the Communist Party of Kampuchea," archived at the Documentation Center of Cambodia, Phnom Penh.
86. Ross, "Masters of the Khmer Rouge," 49–50. See also Short, *Pol Pot*, 146–47.
87. Heder, *Cambodian Communism*, 93.
88. Slocomb, *People's Republic of Kampuchea*, 10.
89. Heder, *Cambodian Communism*, 11.
90. Ross, "Masters of the Khmer Rouge," 51.
91. Slocomb, *People's Republic of Kampuchea*, 11.
92. Ross, "Masters of the Khmer Rouge," 57.
93. Quoted in Short, *Pol Pot*, 161. See also Ross, "Masters of the Khmer Rouge," 60.
94. Ross, "Masters of the Khmer Rouge," 60.
95. Chandler, *Brother Number One*, 76.
96. Manning, *Transitional Justice*, 43.
97. Kirk, "Cambodia's Economic Crisis," 240; Becker, *When the War Was Over*, 101.
98. Manning, *Transitional Justice*, 43.
99. Becker, *When the War Was Over*, 105; Short, *Pol Pot*, 167; Chandler, *Tragedy of Cambodia*, 165.
100. Manning, *Transitional Justice*, 43.
101. Ross, "Masters of the Khmer Rouge," 1.
102. Clymer, *Troubled Relations*, 99–100.
103. Operation Menu comprised six bombing campaigns, known as Breakfast, Lunch, Snack, Dinner, Supper, and Dessert. Each campaign targeted a specific base area located in Cambodia. See Kiernan, "American Bombardment of Kampuchea"; Owen and Kiernan, "Bombs over Cambodia"; and Kiernan and Owen, "Making More Enemies than We Kill."
104. Clymer, *Troubled Relations*, 99. Sihanouk's role and responsibility remain a source of contention. Clymer maintains that Sihanouk did not give his approval for military encroachment into Cambodia; he did, however, tolerate *limited* engagement. Sihanouk, for example, stomached certain demands of both the DRV and the US to operate within Cambodia's borders. However, as Clymer explains, these were specific and limited arrangements, agreed to only in a desperate hope to keep the violence away from Cambodia and to retain his country's independence and neutrality.
105. Chandler, *A History of Cambodia*, 208.
106. Gordon and Young, "Khmer Republic," 27.
107. Summers, "Cambodia," 255.
108. Nguyen, *Hanoi's War*, 170.
109. Kiernan, "Origins of Khmer Communism," 179.
110. Chandler, *Tragedy of Cambodian History*, 210.
111. Kiernan, "Origins of Khmer Communism," 179.
112. Manning, *Transitional Justice*, 44.
113. Kiernan, *How Pol Pot Came to Power*, 390. See also Manning, *Transitional Justice*, 44.
114. Chandler, "From 'Cambodge,' " 43.
115. Hunt, *Political Ideas*, 322, 323.
116. Chattopadhyay, "Which Socialism," 2791.
117. Chattopadhyay, "Passage to Socialism," 61.
118. Chattopadhyay, "Myth of Twentieth-Century Socialism," 30.
119. Tyner, *Killing of Cambodia*, 88.
120. Chandler, *Tragedy of Cambodian History*, 236–37.

121. Document No. E2/165, "The People's Representative Assembly of Kampuchea, 11–13 April 1976," archived by the Extraordinary Chambers in the Courts of Cambodia at http://www.eccc.gov.kh/en.
122. Document No. D30882, "Long Live the 17th Anniversary of the Communist Party of Kampuchea," archived at the Documentation Center of Cambodia, Phnom Penh.
123. Quoted in Slocomb, *People's Republic of Kampuchea*, 21.

Chapter 2. "Be Masters of Your Own Destiny!"

1.   Chapter title from a widely disseminated slogan of the Khmer Rouge, quoted in Locard, *Pol Pot's Little Red Book*, 80. Shaw, "From Comparative to International Genocide Studies," 646.
2.   Foucault, "Governmentality," 201–22; Foucault, "Subject and Power," 326–48; MacKinnon, "Managerialism, Governmentality and the State"; Raco and Imrie, "Governmentality and Rights"; Bulkeley, Watson, and Hudson, "Modes of Governing"; Foucault, *Security, Territory, Population*; Huxley, "Geographies of Governmentality," 185–204; Nadesan, *Governmentality, Biopower, and Everyday Life*; and Dean, *Governmentality*.
3.   Especially during the early years of revolution, disagreements among Russian Marxists were rampant, and it is not surprising that positions changed often. Indeed, as material conditions on the ground changed, so too did Russian officials change their opinions. See van Ree, "Socialism in One Country: A Reassessment"; van Ree, "Lenin's Conception of Socialism"; and van Ree, " 'Socialism in One Country' before Stalin."
4.   van Ree, "Socialism in One Country: A Reassessment," 83, 108, 97, 79, 113.
5.   Doğan, "Socialism and Nationalism," 285.
6.   See, for example, Escobar, "Discourse and Power in Development"; Smith, "Satanic Geographies of Globalization"; and Andrews and Bawa, "A Post-Development Hoax."
7.   Ahiakpor, "Success and Failure of Dependency Theory"; Hills, "Dependency Theory and Its Relevance Today," 169.
8.   Hills, "Dependency Theory," 170.
9.   Frank, *Capitalism and Underdevelopment*; Sunkel, "National Development Policy"; dos Santos, "Structure of Dependence"; Galtung, "Structural Theory of Imperialism"; Cardoso, "Consumption of Dependency Theory."
10.   Dos Santos, "Structure of Dependence," 235.
11.   Benjamin, "Bookend to Bandung," 40. Key figures included Paul Baran, Paul Sweezy, Immanuel Wallerstein, Ernesto Laclau, Robert Brenner, Giovani Arrighi, and Samir Amin, among others.
12.   Tomlinson, "What Was the Third World," 312.
13.   Benjamin, "Bookend to Bandung," 34.
14.   Scholars nowadays consider the term "third world" as antiquated, derogatory, and pejorative, a relic of Cold War imperialism. However, to dismiss the term outright is to miss the fact that Third Worldism served as a rallying cry for liberation movements throughout Asia, Africa, Latin America, and Oceania—including that of the Khmer Rouge. See, for example, Berger, "End of the 'Third World.' "
15.   Kalter, "From Global to Local," 119. See also Keyfitz, "Alfred Sauvy," 727–33; Tabah, "Alfred Sauvy."
16.   Kalter, "From Global to Local," 119.
17.   Fanon, *The Wretched of the Earth*, 238, 239.
18.   Kalter, "From Global to Local," 120.
19.   Doğan, "Socialism and Nationalism," 286.
20.   Burke, "The Compelling Dialogue of Freedom," 948.

21. Berger, "After the Third World," 12.
22. Lüthi, "Non-Aligned Movement," 98.
23. Berger, "After the Third World," 12.
24. Berger, "End of the 'Third World,'" 259.
25. Benjamin, "Bookend to Bandung," 35–36.
26. Berger, "After the Third World," 12.
27. Doğan, "Socialism and Nationalism," 287.
28. Lüthi, "Non-Aligned Movement," 99.
29. Berger, "After the Third World," 13; Doğan, "Socialism and Nationalism," 287.
30. Lüthi, "Non-Aligned Movement," 98.
31. Rakove, "Rise and Fall of Non-Aligned Mediation," 991.
32. Berger, "After the Third World," 10. See also Dinkel, "Third World Begins to Flex Its Muscles."
33. Doğan, "Socialism and Nationalism," 284, 285.
34. Institute of Foreign Affairs, *Summit Declarations of Non-Aligned Movement*, 84.
35. Institute of Foreign Affairs, 102.
36. Document No. D55874, archived at the Documentation Center of Cambodia, Phnom Penh.
37. Document No. D55874, archived at the Documentation Center of Cambodia, Phnom Penh.
38. For extensive discussions of S-21, see Chandler, *Voices from S-21*; and Tyner, *Politics of Lists*.
39. Document No. D55874, archived at the Documentation Center of Cambodia, Phnom Penh.
40. Document No. D55874, archived at the Documentation Center of Cambodia, Phnom Penh.
41. Document No. D55874, archived at the Documentation Center of Cambodia, Phnom Penh.
42. Isaacs, *Without Honor*, 224. See also Chomsky and Herman, *After the Cataclysm*.
43. Document No. D55874, archived at the Documentation Center of Cambodia, Phnom Penh.
44. Quinn, "Cambodia 1976," 49.
45. Quoted in Slocomb, *People's Republic of Kampuchea*, 21.
46. Frieson, "Political Nature of Democratic Kampuchea," 405.
47. Foucault, "Subject and Power," 341; Dean, *Governmentality*, 17, 18.
48. See, for example, Waller, *Democratic Centralism*; Johnston, "Democratic Centralism"; and Angle, "Decent Democratic Centralism/"
49. Johnston, "Democratic Centralism," 135.
50. Lenin, *Essential Works*, 288.
51. Throughout the twentieth century, both the discourse and practice of democratic centralism acquired various meanings, as Marxists in China and elsewhere adopted and adapted the term to elide with their own needs. In China, for example, the Chinese Communist Party accepted Marxism-Leninism as its political canon and thus made democratic centralism a key tenant of its policies and programs. Democratic centralism was also a key feature of the Democratic Republic of Vietnam and provided a rationale for the subsequent introduction of Soviet-styled state capitalism.
52. Brandenberger and Dubrovsky, "The People Need a Tsar," 874.
53. See also Kiernan, "Kampuchea and Stalinism," 232–50.
54. Chandler, "Constitution of Democratic Kampuchea," 507.
55. Document No. D55874, archived at the Documentation Center of Cambodia, Phnom Penh. It is noteworthy that Article 2 also specifies that "articles for everyday use remain the personal property of the individual." This demonstrates that as of

December 1975—at least in principle—individual private property was not yet abolished.

56. Chandler, "Constitution of Democratic Kampuchea," 513.
57. Chandler, 514. Chandler notes also that both the United States and Vietnam were intended audiences of the Constitution.
58. Chandler, 513.
59. Document No. D55874, archived at the Documentation Center of Cambodia, Phnom Penh.
60. Document No. D00674, "Communist Party of Kampuchea: Statute," archived at the Documentation Center of Cambodia, Phnom Penh. See also Office of the Co-Investigating Judges, Closing Order, 16.
61. Document No. D00674, "Communist Party of Kampuchea: Statute," archived at the Documentation Center of Cambodia, Phnom Penh.
62. Document No. D00674, "Communist Party of Kampuchea: Statute," archived at the Documentation Center of Cambodia, Phnom Penh.
63. Document No. D55874, archived at the Documentation Center of Cambodia, Phnom Penh.
64. Document No. D00674, "Communist Party of Kampuchea: Statute," archived at the Documentation Center of Cambodia, Phnom Penh; Office of the Co-Investigating Judges, Closing Order, 17.
65. von Beyme, "Comparative View of Democratic Centralism," 260.
66. Office of the Co-Prosecutors, Co-Prosecutors' Rule 66 Final Submission, 53.
67. Foucault, *Security, Territory, Population*, 108.
68. Documentary evidence indicates that the CPK Standing Committee decided as early as October 9, 1975, on these positions. See Office of the Co-Prosecutors, Co-Prosecutors' Rule 66 Final Submission, 51. For an overview of these ministries, see Mertha, *Brothers in Arms* 35–53.
69. Document No. D21227, archived in the Documentation Center of Cambodia, Phnom Penh, Cambodia, provides details on the establishment of these ministries. In practice, most of these ministries were inoperable and (apparently) existed on paper only. Nonetheless, their existence, however limited, provides insight into the particular governing logic envisioned by members of the CPK.
70. The respective ministers of these committees are Chey Soun, Cheng An, Koy Thuon, Ek Sophon, Mei Brang, and Ta Che. It is unclear as to how active any of these committees truly were; preliminary archival evidence suggests that the agriculture and commerce committees were most active. See Document No. D21227, archived in the Documentation Center of Cambodia, Phnom Penh, Cambodia.
71. Membership fluctuated because of repeated purges. Usually, membership consisted of more than thirty men and women. Apart from the Standing Committee members (who served on both committees), the Central Committee included Khieu Samphan, Koy Thuon, Ney Saran, and Ke Pok. The Central Committee also included a "Specialist Military Committee" involving Pol Pot, Nuon Chea, Son Sen, So Phim, and Ta Mok; Vorn Vet and Ke Pauk would later be added. See also Office of the Co-Investigating Judges, Closing Order, 18.
72. Office of the Co-Investigating Judges, Closing Order, 17.
73. Membership of the committee fluctuated because of internal purges initiated by Pol Pot toward other members suspected of traitorous activities.
74. Document No. E3/1612, "Meeting of the Standing Committee 9 October 1975," archived by the Extraordinary Chambers in the Courts of Cambodia at http://www.eccc.gov.kh/en.
75. Tyner, *Politics of Lists*.
76. Bulkeley, Watson, and Hudson, "Modes of Governing," 2737.

77. Communist Party of Kampuchea, "The Party's Four-Year Plan," 51.
78. Dean, *Governmentality*, 43.
79. Chandler, "Introduction," 42.
80. Communist Party of Kampuchea, "The Party's Four-Year Plan," 101, 102 and 104.
81. Communist Party of Kampuchea, "Excerpted Report on the Leading Views," 34.
82. Document No. E3/228, "Meeting of the Standing Committee 9 January 1976," archived by the Extraordinary Chambers in the Courts of Cambodia at http://www.eccc.gov.kh /en.
83. Communist Party of Kampuchea, "The Party's Four-Year Plan," 49.
84. Jackson, "Ideology of Total Revolution," 45.
85. Twining, "The Economy," 110.
86. Wu, "From Self-Reliance," 452.
87. Hope, "Self-Reliance," 455.
88. Wu, "From Self-Reliance," 452.
89. Document No. E3/1612, "Meeting of the Standing Committee 9 October 1975," archived by the Extraordinary Chambers in the Courts of Cambodia at http://www.eccc .gov.kh/en.
90. Hope, "Self-Reliance," 456.
91. Smith, "Underdevelopment of Development Literature"; Todaro, *Economic Development in the Third World*; Bruton, "A Reconsideration"; Potter et al., *Geographies of Development*.
92. Bruton, "A Reconsideration," 904.
93. Document No. D00698, "Cooperation with the Ministry of Commerce," archived at the Documentation Center of Cambodia, Phnom Penh.
94. Communist Party of Kampuchea, "The Party's Four-Year Plan," 46.
95. Communist Party of Kampuchea, "Report of Activities," 200. This statement reveals on the one hand a general indifference to use-value; anything can be commodified. On the other hand, it highlights a broader indifference to life itself. If we reconsider the well-repeated slogan of the Khmer Rouge—"to keep you is no gain, to lose you is no loss"—we gain a different understanding of CPK practice. The apparent indifference to life expressed by the Khmer Rouge results not from some abstract callousness on behalf of the party center but rather a materialist rationale predicated on capital accumulation. The overarching concern of the CPK was to reorient all policies toward this singular goal. This theme is developed in greater detail in chapter 8.
96. Communist Party of Kampuchea, "Report of Activities," 200.
97. Communist Party of Kampuchea, "Excerpted Report on the Leading Views," 27.
98. Communist Party of Kampuchea, "Preliminary Explanation," 131.
99. Communist Party of Kampuchea, "The Party's Four-Year Plan," 51.
100. Tomlinson, "What Was the Third World," 312.
101. Berger, "After the Third World," 10.
102. Document No. D55874, archived at the Documentation Center of Cambodia, Phnom Penh.
103. Document No. E3/5, "Revolutionary Flag, Issue 8, August 75," archived by the Extraordinary Chambers in the Courts of Cambodia at http://www.eccc.gov.kh/en.
104. Petras, "State Capitalism," 4.

Chapter 3. "We Are Building Socialism in the Cooperatives"

1. Chapter title from Document No. E3/4, "Revolutionary Flag Issue 7, July 1976," archived by the Extraordinary Chambers in the Courts of Cambodia at http://www.eccc .gov.kh/en. Lebowitz, *Socialist Imperative*, 62.
2. D'Amato, *Meaning of Marxism*, 36.

3. Marx, "Eighteenth Brumaire," 329.
4. D'Amato, *Meaning of Marxism*, 37.
5. Marx, *Critique of the Gotha Program*, 8.
6. Marx, *Grundrisse*, 278.
7. Sayers, "Alienation as a Critical Concept," 292.
8. Communist Party of Kampuchea, "The Party's Four-Year Plan," 45, 49.
9. Document E3/216, "Record of the Standing Committee's Visit to the Northwest Zone, 20–24 August 1975," archived by the Extraordinary Chambers in the Courts of Cambodia at http://www.eccc.gov.kh/en.
10. Communist Party of Kampuchea, "Excerpted Report on the Leading Views," 17.
11. CPK, "The Party's Four-Year Plan," 51, 96.
12. Document E3/748, "Some Important Excerpts from the First Nationwide Party Economic Congress November 1975," archived by the Extraordinary Chambers in the Courts of Cambodia at http://www.eccc.gov.kh/en.
13. Document No. E3/748, "Revolutionary Flag Special Issue, October–November 1975," archived by the Extraordinary Chambers in the Courts of Cambodia at http://www.eccc .gov.kh/en.
14. Selden, "Crisis of Collectivization," 4–11.
15. Hammen, "Marx and the Agrarian Question"; Duggett, "Marx on Peasants," 159–82; Chumar, "Peasant Question."
16. Duggett, "Marx on Peasants," 173.
17. Duggett, 167–68.
18. Edelman, "Late Marx and the Russian Road," 55–59; Figes, "Collective Farming," 89–97.
19. Selden, "Crisis of Collectivization," 5.
20. Pryor, *The Red and the Green*, 35–42.
21. Pryor, 38–44.
22. Pryor, 41–44; Millar, "Soviet Rapid Development"; Millar, "Mass Collectivization"; Nove, "Agricultural Surplus Hypothesis"; Day, "Preobrzhensky"; Millar, "Note on Primitive Accumulation"; Harrison, "Primary Accumulation"; Saith, "Primitive Accumulation"; and Burdekin, "Preobrazhensky's Theory."
23. Im, "Collectivization and Socialist Transition," 41.
24. Kaufman, "Origin," 243. See also Roberts, "War Communism"; Malle, *Economic Organization of War Communism*; and Boettke, "Political Economy of Utopia."
25. Kaufman, "Origin," 243.
26. Im, "Collectivization," 41; Selden, "Crisis of Collectivization," 6.
27. Kaufman, "Origin," 244.
28. Selden, "Crisis of Collectivization," 6.
29. Im, "Collectivization," 41.
30. Kaufman, "Origin," 250.
31. Selden, "Crisis of Collectivization," 6.
32. Day, "Preobrazhensky," 196.
33. Uldricks, "Russia and Europe," 82.
34. Evenitsky, "Preobrazhensky and the Political Economy"; Kaser, "The Soviet Ideology"; Buchanan, "Lenin and Bukharin"; and Harrison, "Soviet Primary Accumulation Processes."
35. Thomson, "Primitive Capitalist Accumulation," 313. See also Harrison, "Soviet Primary Accumulation," 387.
36. Harvey, *New Imperialism*, 145.
37. Cleaver, *Reading* Capital *Politically*, 85.
38. Glassman, "Primitive Accumulation," 616.
39. Marx, *Grundrisse*, 736.
40. Marx, *Capital*, vol. 1, 896, 875.

41. Cleaver, *Reading* Capital *Politically*, 86.
42. White, *Marx and Russia*, 190.
43. LeBlanc, *Marx, Lenin*, 114.
44. Harrison, "Soviet Primary Accumulation," 387.
45. Day, "Preobrazhensky," 199.
46. Millar, "Note on Primitive Accumulation," 388.
47. Burdekin, "Preobrazhensky's Theory," 296–98.
48. Preobrazhensky, *New Economics*, 219.
49. Kaser, "The Soviet Ideology," 72.
50. White, *Marx and Russia*, 183.
51. LeBlanc, *Marx, Lenin*, 120.
52. Selden, "Crisis of Collectivization," 6.
53. Pryor, *The Red and the Green*, 48.
54. LeBlanc, *Marx, Lenin*, 120, 119.
55. See, for example, Kerkvliet, "Wobbly Foundations"; Kerkvliet and Selden, "Agrarian Transformations"; and Raymond, "No Responsibility and No Rice."
56. White, *Marx and Russia*, 181.
57. Selden, "Crisis of Collectivization," 4.
58. Pryor, *The Red and the Green*, 52.
59. Vlachou, "Socialist Transformation of China," 11.
60. Kerkviliet, "Wobbly Foundations," 195.
61. Raymond, "No Responsibility and No Rice," 44.
62. Kerkviliet, "Wobbly Foundations," 232.
63. Communist Party of Kampuchea, "Abbreviated Lesson," 219.
64. Willmott, "Analytical Errors"; Yuon, "Peasantry of Kampuchea," 34–68; Nim, "Land Tenure," 69–86; Yuon, "Solving Rural Problems," 136–65.
65. Bernstein, *Class Dynamics*.
66. Beckford and Barker, "Role and Value of Local Knowledge," 118.
67. Bernstein, *Class Dynamics*, 62.
68. Bernstein, 64.
69. Friedmann, "Commentary," 680.
70. Mam, "Oral History of Family Life under the Khmer Rouge," 3. See also Ebihara, "Intervillage, Intertown,"; Ebihara, "Residence Patterns,"; Kiernan, "Introduction," 1–28; Ebihara, "Cambodian Village," 51–63; Chhor, "Destruction of Family Foundation"; Huy, "Khmer Rouge Wedding"; Ledgerwood and Vijghen, "Decision-Making in Rural Khmer Villages," 109–50; Karkaria, *Failure through Neglect*; Heuveline and Poch, "Do Marriages Forget Their Past"; Lee, *Rice Plus*; Brickell, "Gender Relations"; Derks, *Khmer Women on the Move*; Jain, "Forced Marriage as a Crime"; LeVine, *Love and Dread in Cambodia*; Guérin, "Khmer Peasants and Land Access"; Phuong, "Forced Marriage to Avoid Death"; Hoefinger, *Sex, Love and Money in Cambodia*; Diepart, *Fragmentation of Land Tenure Systems*; and Ebihara, *Svay*.
71. Lee, *Rice Plus*, 25–27.
72. Ebihara, *Svay*, 29.
73. Diepart and Sem, *Cambodian Peasantry*, 10.
74. Lee, *Rice Plus*, 23.
75. Ebihira, "Intervillage, Intertown," 364, 368.
76. Diepart, *Fragmentation of Land Tenure Systems*, 6.
77. Diepart and Sem, *Cambodian Peasantry*, 12.
78. Diepart, *Fragmentation of Land Tenure Systems*, 8.
79. Yuon, "Peasantry of Kampuchea," 37.
80. Diepart and Sem, *Cambodian Peasantry*, 13.

81. Guérin, "Khmer Peasants," 455–56.
82. Yuon, "Peasantry of Kampuchea," 39–40.
83. Yuon, 38.
84. Kiernan, "Introduction," 8, 10.
85. Kerkvliet and Selden, "Agrarian Transformations," 38.
86. Quinn, "Pattern and Scope of Violence," 191.
87. Kiernan, *How Pol Pot Came to Power*, 371 and 384.
88. Bishop and Clancey, "City-as-Target," 54–74; Shaw, "New Wars of the City," 141–53; Shaw, *What Is Genocide*; Coward, *Urbicide*; Fregonese, "Urbicide of Beirut"; Hewitt, "Proving Grounds"; Ramadan, "Destroying Nahr el-Bared."
89. Hewitt, "Proving Grounds."
90. McIntyre, "Geography as Destiny," 758.
91. McIntyre, 730.
92. Tyner, "Gender and Sexual Violence."
93. Communist Party of Kampuchea, "Preliminary Explanation," 96.
94. Tyner et al., "Khmer Rouge Irrigation Schemes."
95. Document E3/748, "Some Important Excerpts from the First Nationwide Party Economic Congress November 1975," archived by the Extraordinary Chambers in the Courts of Cambodia at http://www.eccc.gov.kh/en.
96. Tyner et al., "Phnom Penh during the Cambodian Genocide"; Rice and Tyner, "Rice Cities of the Khmer Rouge"; Tyner et al., "Evacuation of Phnom Penh"; and Curtis et al., "Adding Spatial Context."
97. Document No. E3/50, "Third Year Anniversary of the Organization of Peasant Cooperatives," archived by the Extraordinary Chambers in the Courts of Cambodia at http://www.eccc.gov.kh/en.
98. Carney, "The Unexpected Victory," 29, 30.
99. Document No. E3/50, "Third Year Anniversary of the Organization of Peasant Cooperatives," archived by the Extraordinary Chambers in the Courts of Cambodia at http://www.eccc.gov.kh/en.
100. Document No. E3/748, "Some Important Excerpts from the First Nationwide Party Economic Congress November 1975," archived by the Extraordinary Chambers in the Courts of Cambodia at http://www.eccc.gov.kh.en.
101. Document No. E3/50, "Third Year Anniversary of the Organization of Peasant Cooperatives," archived by the Extraordinary Chambers in the Courts of Cambodia at http://www.eccc.gov.kh/en.
102. Twining, "The Economy," 127.
103. Document No. E3/752, "Revolutionary Male and Female Youth Issue 3, March 1976," archived by the Extraordinary Chambers in the Courts of Cambodia at http://www.eccc.gov.kh/en.
104. Document No. E3/748, "Revolutionary Flag Special Issue, October–November 1975," archived by the Extraordinary Chambers in the Courts of Cambodia at http://www.eccc.gov.kh/en.
105. Document E3/216, "Record of the Standing Committee's Visit to the Northwest Zone, 20–24 August 1975," archived by the Extraordinary Chambers in the Courts of Cambodia at http://www.eccc.gov.kh/en.
106. Twining, "The Economy," 125.
107. Carney, "Unexpected Victory," 28.
108. Twining, "The Economy," 125–26.
109. Document No. E3/748, "Revolutionary Flag Special Issue, October–November 1975," archived by the Extraordinary Chambers in the Courts of Cambodia at http://www.eccc.gov.kh/en.

110. Document No. E3/752, "Revolutionary Male and Female Youth Issue 3, March 1976," archived by the Extraordinary Chambers in the Courts of Cambodia at http://www.eccc .gov.kh/en.

111. Document No. E3/760, "Revolutionary Flag Issue 6, June 1976," archived by the Extraordinary Chambers in the Courts of Cambodia at http://www.eccc.gov.kh/en.

112. Document No. E3/752, "Revolutionary Male and Female Youth Issue 3, March 1976," archived by the Extraordinary Chambers in the Courts of Cambodia at http://www.eccc .gov.kh/en.

113. Document No. E3/760, "Revolutionary Flag Issue 6, June 1976," archived by the Extraordinary Chambers in the Courts of Cambodia at http://www.eccc.gov.kh/en.

114. Document No. E3/752, "Revolutionary Male and Female Youth Issue 3, March 1976," archived by the Extraordinary Chambers in the Courts of Cambodia at http://www.eccc .gov.kh/en.

115. Communist Party of Kampuchea, "Abbreviated Lesson," 223.

116. Communist Party of Kampuchea, "Excerpted Report on the Leading Views," 19; Communist Party of Kampuchea, "Abbreviated Lesson," 222.

117. Communist Party of Kampuchea, "Excerpted Report on the Leading Views," 19; Document No. E3/729, "Revolutionary Youth Issue No. 10, October 1975," archived by the Extraordinary Chambers in the Courts of Cambodia at http://www.eccc.gov.kh/en.

118. Document No. E3/10, "Revolutionary Flag Special Issue, September–October 1976," archived by the Extraordinary Chambers in the Courts of Cambodia at http://www.eccc .gov.kh/en.

119. Document No. E3/170, "Revolutionary Flag Special Issue, October–November 1977," archived by the Extraordinary Chambers in the Courts of Cambodia at http://www.eccc .gov.kh/en.

120. Document No. E3/4, "Revolutionary Flag Issue 7, July 1976," archived by the Extraordinary Chambers in the Courts of Cambodia at http://www.eccc.gov.kh/en.

121. Document No. E3/10, "Revolutionary Flag Special Issue, September–October 1976," archived by the Extraordinary Chambers in the Courts of Cambodia at http://www.eccc .gov.kh/en.

122. Communist Party of Kampuchea, "Report of Activities," 202.

123. Document No. E3/170, "Revolutionary Flag Special Issue, October–November 1977," archived by the Extraordinary Chambers in the Courts of Cambodia at http://www.eccc .gov.kh/en.

124. Ebihara, "A Cambodian Village," 55.

125. Document No. E3/50, "Third Year Anniversary of the Organization of Peasant Cooperatives," archived by the Extraordinary Chambers in the Courts of Cambodia at http://www.eccc.gov.kh/en.

126. Document No. E3/746, "Revolutionary Flag Issue 7, July 1978," archived by the Extraordinary Chambers in the Courts of Cambodia at http://www.eccc.gov.kh/en.

127. Document No. E3/4, "Revolutionary Flag Issue 7, July 1976," archived by the Extraordinary Chambers in the Courts of Cambodia at http://www.eccc.gov.kh/en.

128. Document No. E3/746, "Revolutionary Flag Issue 7, July 1978," archived by the Extraordinary Chambers in the Courts of Cambodia at http://www.eccc.gov.kh/en.

129. Document No. E3/746, "Revolutionary Flag Issue 7, July 1978," archived by the Extraordinary Chambers in the Courts of Cambodia at http://www.eccc.gov.kh/en.

130. Document No. E3/170, "Revolutionary Flag Special Issue, October–November 1977," archived by the Extraordinary Chambers in the Courts of Cambodia at http://www.eccc .gov.kh/en.

131. Document No. E3/139, "Revolutionary Flag Issue 11, November 1976," archived by the Extraordinary Chambers in the Courts of Cambodia at http://www.eccc.gov.kh/en.

132. Document No. E3/50, "Third Year Anniversary of the Organization of Peasant Cooperatives," archived by the Extraordinary Chambers in the Courts of Cambodia at http://www.eccc.gov.kh/en.

133. Document No. E3/139, "Revolutionary Flag Issue 11, November 1976," archived by the Extraordinary Chambers in the Courts of Cambodia at http://www.eccc.gov.kh/en.

134. Document No. E3/10, "Revolutionary Flag Issue, September–October 1976," archived by the Extraordinary Chambers in the Courts of Cambodia at http://www.eccc.gov.kh /en.

135. Document No. E3/170, "Revolutionary Flag Special Issue, October–November 1977," archived by the Extraordinary Chambers in the Courts of Cambodia at http://www.eccc .gov.kh/en. See also Document No. E3/10, "Revolutionary Flag Special Issue, September–October 1976," archived by the Extraordinary Chambers in the Courts of Cambodia at http://www.eccc.gov.kh/en.

136. Document No. E3/139, "Revolutionary Flag Issue 11, November 1976," archived by the Extraordinary Chambers in the Courts of Cambodia at http://www.eccc.gov.kh/en.

137. See for example Uimonen, "Responses to Revolutionary Change."

138. Document No. E3/4092, "March 1978 Responses Beginning on [illegible] March 1978," archived by the Extraordinary Chambers in the Courts of Cambodia at http://www.eccc .gov.kh/en.

139. Saith, "Primitive Accumulation," 2.

140. Bacino, *Reconstructing Russia*; Willett, *Russian Sideshow*; and Foglesong, *America's Secret War*.

141. Selden, "Crisis of Collectivization," 6.

142. Selden, 4.

143. Banaji, *Theory as History*, 335, 145.

144. Locard, *Pol Pot's Little Red Book*, 187–88.

145. Document No. E3/50, "Third Year Anniversary of the Organization of Peasant Cooperatives," archived by the Extraordinary Chambers in the Courts of Cambodia at http://www.eccc.gov.kh/en.

Chapter 4. "Currency Is a Most Poisonous Tool"

1. Chapter title from Document No. E3/10, "Revolutionary Flag Special Issue September–October 1976," archived by the Extraordinary Chambers in the Courts of Cambodia at http://www.eccc.gov.kh/en. Ebihara, "Cambodian Village," 51–63; and Ledgerwood, Ebihara, and Mortland, "Introduction," 1–26.

2. Ebihara, "A Cambodian Village," 55–56.

3. DeFalco, "Accounting for Famine," 150. See also DeFalco, "Justice and Starvation."

4. Communist Party of Kampuchea, "Decisions of the Central Committee," 3.

5. DeFalco, "Voices of Genocide," 29–32; Tyner and Rice, "To Live and Let Die"; Tyner and Rice, "Cambodia's Political Economy"; and Hiebert, "Genocide, Revolution, and Starvation."

6. Document No. E3/810, "Minutes of Meeting of Secretaries and Logistics [Chiefs] of Divisions and Regiments," archived by the Extraordinary Chambers in the Courts of Cambodia at http://www.eccc.gov.kh/en. See also Communist Party of Kampuchea, "The Party's Four-Year Plan," 36–119.

7. Document No. E3/822, "Minutes of the Meeting [of] Comrade Tal of Division 290 and Division 170," archived by the Extraordinary Chambers in the Courts of Cambodia at http://www.eccc.gov.kh/en.

8. DeFalco, "Accounting for Famine," 147.

9. Document No. E3/750, "Revolutionary Male and Female Youths Number 11 November 1975," archived by the Extraordinary Chambers in the Courts of Cambodia at http://www.eccc.gov.kh/en.

10. Document No. E3/11, "Revolutionary Flag Special Issue September 1977," archived by the Extraordinary Chambers in the Courts of Cambodia at http://www.eccc.gov.kh/en.

11. DeFalco, "Justice and Starvation," 46, 53–54.

12. DeFalco, 83.

13. Maurer, "Anthropology of Money," 27.

14. Prasso, "Riel Value of Money," 2.

15. Short, *Pol Pot*, 256–57, 258.

16. Kiernan, *Pol Pot Regime*, 55. Kiernan's account in based on personal interviews conducted with surviving Khmer Rouge cadre, including Heng Samrin and Chea Sim.

17. Kiernan, 55.

18. These five sources are Sin Son, former political commissar of the Third Battalion of the First Eastern Division; Ret, a center battalion commander from the Northern Zone; May Ly, a CPK district committee member from Region 21; Chea Sim, CPK secretary of Ponhea Krek District; and Heng Samrin, a longtime revolutionary who, by war's end, was in command of the 126th Regiment of the Eastern Zone's First Division. See Kiernan, *Pol Pot Regime*, 55–57.

19. Kiernan, *Pol Pot Regime*, 58. The practice of Buddhism also was prohibited from this point forward.

20. Kiernan, 56. Kiernan cites his interview with Chea Sim.

21. Kiernan, 57.

22. Document No. E3/10, "Revolutionary Flag Special Issue September–October 1976," archived by the Extraordinary Chambers in the Courts of Cambodia at http://www.eccc.gov.kh/en.

23. Kiernan, *Pol Pot Regime*, 59.

24. Short, *Pol Pot*, 306.

25. Short, 306–7.

26. Short, 307.

27. Kiernan, *Pol Pot Regime*, 98.

28. Quoted in Short, *Pol Pot*, 307.

29. Document No. E3/96, "Written Testimony of Prasith Thiounn, 8 June 2009," archived by the Extraordinary Chambers in the Courts of Cambodia at http://www.eccc.gov.kh/en.

30. Document No. E1/329.1, "Transcript of Trial Proceedings, Case File No. 002/19-09-2007-ECCC/TC, 12 August 2015, Trial Day 310," archived by the Extraordinary Chambers in the Courts of Cambodia at http://www.eccc.gov.kh/en.

31. Quoted in Short, *Pol Pot*, 383.

32. Short, *Pol Pot*, 383.

33. Kiernan, *Pol Pot Regime*, 99.

34. Christophers, "Follow the Thing," 1070.

35. Marx, *Capital*, vol. 1, 139.

36. Marx, 139–40.

37. Harvey, *A Companion*, 31.

38. Harvey, 31.

39. Marx, *Capital*, vol. 1, 188, 200, 203.

40. Harvey, *A Companion*, 86.

41. Harvey, 87.

42. Marx, *Capital*, vol. 1, 248.

43. Marx, 248, 250, 251.

44. Harvey, *A Companion*, 85.

45. Harvey, 86.
46. Marx, *Capital*, vol. 1, 274.
47. Harvey, *A Companion*, 103.
48. Marx, *Capital*, vol. 1, 291–92.
49. Fracchia, "Capitalist Labour-Process," 43.
50. Marx, *Capital*, vol. 1, 645, 300.
51. D'Amato, *Meaning of Marxism*, 56.
52. Marx and Engels, *Communist Manifesto*, 42.
53. Read, *Micro-Politics of Capital*, 10.
54. Boyd and Prudham, "On the Themed Collection," 878.
55. Marx, *Capital*, vol. 1, 129.
56. Fine and Saad-Filho, *Marx's "Capital,"* 38.
57. Postone, *Time, Labor, and Social Domination*, 193.
58. Marx, *Capital*, vol. 1, 436–37.
59. Fine and Saad-Filho, *Marx's "Capital,"* 32.
60. Harvey, *Limits to Capital*, 29, 31.
61. Document No. E3/135, "Letter of Honorary Red Flag from Communist Party of Kampuchea's Central Committee," archived by the Extraordinary Chambers in the Courts of Cambodia at http://www.eccc.gov.kh/en.
62. Marx, *Capital*, vol. 1, 179.
63. Heinrich, *An Introduction*, 87–88.
64. Marx, *Capital*, vol. 1, 179.
65. Marx, 1024, 1034–35.
66. Boyd and Prudham, "On the Themed Collection," 878.
67. Marx, *Capital*, vol. 1, 1040, 486.
68. Boyd and Prudham, "On the Themed Collection," 878.
69. Heinrich, *An Introduction,* 104.
70. CPK, "Four-Year Plan," 112.
71. Heinrich, *An Introduction*, 104.
72. Chhaom is a pseudonym. Interview conducted by Sokvisal Kimsroy and Chhunly Chhay on September 3, 2018.
73. Mam, *Oral History*, 8.
74. Ebihara, "Cambodian Village," 55.
75. Mam, *An Oral History*, 9.
76. Mam, "Endurance of the Cambodian Family," 134–35.
77. Heinrich, *An Introduction*, 105.
78. Kristjanson-Gural, "Value, Cooperatives," 356.
79. Heinrich, *An Introduction*, 109.
80. Kristjanson-Gural, "Value, Cooperatives," 356.
81. This is example is modified from Harvey, *A Companion*, 169–70.
82. Fine and Saad-Filho, *Marx's "Capital,"* 17–18.
83. CPK, "Four-Year Plan," 51. This translates into approximately 0.85 kilograms per day.
84. CPK, 54, 56–57. It is unclear as to distribution of the remaining one million tons.
85. Communist Party of Kampuchea, "Excerpted Report on the Leading Views," 20.
86. Document No. E3/232, "Minutes of Meeting on Base Work 8 March 1976," archived by the Extraordinary Chambers in the Courts of Cambodia at http://www.eccc.gov.kh/en.
87. The cans used for measurement were most often Nestle condensed milk cans; each can could contain approximately two hundred grams of rice.
88. Marx, *Capital*, vol. 1, 275.
89. Harvey, *A Companion*, 94.
90. Marx, *Capital*, vol. 1, 275.
91. Document No. E3/775, "Revolutionary and Non-Revolutionary World Views Regarding

the Matter of Family Building," archived by the Extraordinary Chambers in the Courts of Cambodia at http://www.eccc.gov.kh/en.

92. Quoted in Locard, *Pol Pot's Little Red Book*, 82.
93. DeFalco, "Voice of Genocide," 30–31.
94. CPK, "Four-Year Plan," 111.
95. Hinton, *Why Did They Kill*. See also Tyner et al., "Emerging Data Sources."
96. Marx, *Capital*, vol. 1, 353.

Epilogue

1.   "Frederick Engel's Speech at the Grave of Karl Marx, Highgate Cemetery, London, March 17, 1883," Marxists.org, https://www.marxists.org/archive/marx/works/1883 /death/burial.htm.
2.   Smith, "Revolution," 36.
3.   Marx and Engels, *German Ideology*, 60.
4.   Foster, "Marx's Theory of Metabolic Rift," 386.
5.   Harrington, *Socialism*, 23.
6.   Marx, *Capital*, vol. 3, 572.
7.   Chattopadhyay, "Economic Content," 92.
8.   Chattopadhyay, 92. See also Chattopadhyay, "Which Socialism"; Chattopadhyay, "Capitalism as Socialism"; and Chattopadhyay, "Marx Made to Serve."
9.   Marx, *Critique of the Gotha Program*, 18.
10. Chattopadhyay, "Myth of Twentieth-Century Socialism," 24.
11. Marx, *Critique of the Gotha Program*, 8.
12. Marx, 10, 8.
13. Chattopadhyay, "Economic Content," 102.
14. Jossa, "Democratic Road to Socialism," 341.
15. Chattopadhyay, "Worlds Apart," 5631.
16. Arneson, "Marx on the Choice," 180.
17. Chattopadhyay, "Myth of Twentieth-Century Socialism," 32–33.
18. Ryan, "Revolution Is War," 250.
19. Eaton, "Marx and the Russians," 89 and 106.
20. Chattopadhyay, "Myth of Twentieth-Century Socialism," 42.
21. Chattopadhyay, "Which Socialism," 2792.
22. Document No. D30882, "Long Live the 17th Anniversary of the Communist Party of Kampuchea," 62, archived at the Documentation Center of Cambodia, Phnom Penh.
23. Nhem, *Khmer Rouge*, 46.
24. Elliot, "Karl Marx," 294–95, 318.
25. Rothenberg, "Lenin on the State," 424–25.
26. Nhem, *Khmer Rouge*, 48.
27. Document No. D00698, "Cooperation with the Ministry of Commerce," archived at the Documentation Center of Cambodia, Phnom Penh.
28. Kamola, "Global Coffee Economy," 576.
29. Bernstein, "Some Reflections on Agrarian Change," 456. See also Edelman and Wolford, "Introduction."
30. Banaji, "The Metamorphosis," 115.

Bibliography

Ahiakpor, James C. "The Success and Failure of Dependency Theory: The Experience of Ghana." *International Organization* 39, no. 3 (1985): 535–52.

Akram-Lodhi, A. Haroon. "The Agrarian Question, Past and Present." *Journal of Peasant Studies* 25, no. 4 (1998): 134–49.

Akram-Lodhi, A. Haroon, and Cristobal Kay. "Surveying the Agrarian Question (Part 1): Unearthing Foundations, Exploring Diversity." *Journal of Peasant Studies* 37, no. 1 (2010): 177–202.

———. "Surveying the Agrarian Question (Part 2): Current Debates and Beyond." *Journal of Peasant Studies* 37, no. 2 (2010): 255–84.

Allen, Kieran. *Marx: The Alternative to Capitalism.* London: Pluto Press, 2017.

Andrews, Nathan, and Sylvia Bawa. "A Post-Development Hoax? (Re)-Examining the Past, Present and Future of Development Studies." *Third World Quarterly* 35, no. 6 (2014): 922–38.

Angle, Stephen C. "Decent Democratic Centralism." *Political Theory* 33, no. 4 (2005): 518–46.

Arneson, Richard J. "Marx on the Choice between Socialism and Communism." *Ethics* 93, no. 1 (1982): 180–82.

Asselin, Pierre. "The Democratic Republic of Vietnam and the 1954 Geneva Conference: A Revisionist Critique." *Cold War History* 11, no. 2 (2011): 155–95.

Au, Wilson A.S. *Reclaiming Communist Philosophy: Marx, Lenin, Mao, and the Dialectics of Nature.* Charlotte, NC: Information Age Publishing, 2017.

Ayres, David. *Anatomy of a Crisis: Education, Development, and the State in Cambodia, 1953–1998.* Chiang Mai: Silkworm Books, 2003.

Bacino, Leo C. *Reconstructing Russia: US Policy in Revolutionary Russia, 1917–1922.* Kent, OH: Kent State University Press, 1999.

Banaji, Jairus. "The Fictions of Free Labor: Contract, Coercion, and So-Called Unfree Labor." *Historical Materialism* 11, no. 3 (2003): 69–85.

———. "Merchant Capitalism, Peasant Households and Industrial Accumulation: Integration of a Model." *Journal of Agrarian Change* 16, no. 3 (2016): 410–31.

———. "The Metamorphosis of Agrarian Capitalism." *Journal of Agrarian Change* 2, no. 1 (2002): 96–119.

———. *Theory as History: Essays on Modes of Production and Exploitation.* Leiden, The Netherlands: Brill, 2010.

Barker, Colin. "Class Struggle and Social Movements." In *Marxism and Social Movements*, edited by Colin Barker, Laurence Cox, John Krinsky, and Alf Gunvald Nilsen, 41–61. Chicago: Haymarket Books, 2014.

Barnes, Catherine. "The Functional Utility of Genocide: Towards a Framework for Understanding the Connection between Genocide and Regime Consolidation, Expansion and Maintenance." *Journal of Genocide Research* 7, no. 3 (2005): 309–330.

Barone, Charles A. *Radical Political Economy: A Concise Introduction.* New York: Routledge, 2015.

Bauman, Zygmunt. *Modernity and the Holocaust.* Ithaca, NY: Cornell University Press, 1991.

Becker, Elizabeth. *When the War Was Over: Cambodia and the Khmer Rouge Revolution.* New York: Public Affairs, 1998.

Beckford, Clinton, and David Barker. "The Role and Value of Local Knowledge in Jamaican Agriculture: Adaptation and Change in Small-Scale Farming." *Geographical Journal* 173, no. 2 (2007): 118–28.

Benjamin, Bret. "Bookend to Bandung: The New International Economic Order and the Antinomies of the Bandung Era." *Humanity: An International Journal of Human Rights, Humanitarianism, and Development* 6, no. 1 (2015): 33–46.

Berger, Mark T. "After the Third World: History, Destiny and the Fate of Third Worldism." *Third World Quarterly* 25, no. 1 (2004): 9–39.

———. "The End of the 'Third World'?" *Third World Quarterly* 15, no. 2 (1994): 257–75.

Berman, Bruce J. "The Concept of 'Articulation' and the Political Economy of Colonialism." *Canadian Journal of African Studies* 18, no. 2 (1984): 407–14.

Bernstein, Henry. "Agrarian Political Economy and Modern World Capitalism: The Contributions of Food Regime Analysis." *Journal of Peasant Studies* 43, no. 3 (2016): 611–47.

———. "Agrarian Questions Then and Now." *Journal of Peasant Studies* 20, no. 1–2 (1996): 22–59.

———. *Class Dynamics of Agrarian Change.* Sterling, VA: Kumarian Press, 2010.

———. "Farewells to the Peasantry." *Transformations* 52 (2003): 1–19.

———. "Is There an Agrarian Question in the 21st Century?" *Canadian Journal of Development Studies* 27, no. 4 (2006): 449–60.

———. "Some Reflections on Agrarian Change in China." *Journal of Agrarian Change* 15, no. 3 (2015): 454–77.

Bernstein, Henry, and Terence J. Byres. "From Peasant Studies to Agrarian Change." *Journal of Agrarian Change* 1, no. 1 (2001): 1–56.

Bin, Daniel. "So-Called Accumulation by Dispossession." *Critical Sociology* 44, no. 1 (2018): 75–88.

Bishop, Ryan, and Greg Clancey. "The City-as-Target, or Perpetuation and Death." In *Cities, War, and Terrorism: Towards an Urban Geopolitics*, edited by Stephen Graham, 54–74 Malden, MA: Blackwell, 2004.

Boettke, Peter. "The Political Economy of Utopia: Communism in Soviet Russia, 1918–1921." *Journal des Economistes et des Etudes Humaines* 1, no. 2 (1990): 91–138.

Boyd, William, and Scott Prudham. "On the Themed Collection: 'The Formal and Real Subsumption of Nature.' " *Society and Natural Resources* 30, no. 7 (2017): 877–84.

Brandenberger David L., and A. M. Dubrovsky. " 'The People Need a Tsar': The Emergence of National Bolshevism as Stalinist Ideology, 1931–1941." *Europe-Asia Studies* 50, no. 5 (1998): 873–92.

Brenner, Robert. "Agrarian Class Structure and Economic Development in Pre-Industrial Europe." *Past and Present* 70 (1976): 30–75.

Brickell, Katherine. "Gender Relations in the Khmer 'Home': Post-Conflict Perspectives." PhD dissertation, London School of Economics and Political Science, 2007.

Brown, Jeremy, and Matthew D. Johnson, eds. *Maoism at the Grassroots: Everyday Life in China's Era of High Socialism.* Cambridge, MA: Harvard University Press, 2015.

Bruton, Henry J. "A Reconsideration of Import Substitution" *Journal of Economic Literature* 36, no. 2 (1998): 903–36.

Buchanan, H. Ray. "Lenin and Bukharin on the Transition from Capitalism to Socialism: The Meshchersky Controversy." *Soviet Studies* 28, no. 1 (1976): 66–82.

Buick, Adam, and John Crump. *State Capitalism: The Wages System under New Management.* London: Macmillan, 1986.

Bulkeley, Harriet, Matt Watson, and Ray Hudson. "Modes of Governing Municipal Waste." *Environment and Planning A* 39, no. 11 (2007): 2733–53.

Burdekin, Richard C. K. "Preobrazhensky's Theory of Primitive Socialist Accumulation." *Journal of Contemporary Asia* 19, no. 3 (1989): 297–307.

Burke, Roland. " 'The Compelling Dialogue of Freedom': Human Rights at the Bandung Conference." *Human Rights Quarterly* 28, no. 4 (2006): 947–65.

Buttel, Frederick. "Some Reflections on Late Twentieth Century Agrarian Political Economy." *Sociologia Ruralis* 41, no. 2 (2001): 165–81.

Byres, Terence J. "The Agrarian Question, Forms of Capitalist Agrarian Transition and the State: An Essay with Reference to Asia." *Social Scientist* 14, nos. 11–12 (1986): 3–67.

———. "Agrarian Transition and the Agrarian Question." *Journal of Peasant Studies* 4, no. 3 (1977): 258–74.

———. "Political Economy, the Agrarian Question and the Comparative Method." *Economic and Political Weekly* 30, no. 10 (1995): 507–13.

———. "In Pursuit of Capitalist Agrarian Transition." *Journal of Agrarian Change* 16, no. 3 (2016): 432–51.

Byrne, David. "Radical Geography as Mere Political Economy: The Local Politics of Space." *Capital & Class* 19, no. 2 (1995): 117–38.

Cardoso, Fernando. "The Consumption of Dependency Theory in the United States." *Latin American Research Review* 12, no. 3 (1977): 7–24.

Caswell, Michelle. *Archiving the Unspeakable: Silence, Memory, and the Photographic Record in Cambodia.* Madison: University of Wisconsin Press, 2014.

Chandler, David. *Brother Number One: A Political Biography of Pol Pot.* Revised ed. Chiang Mai, Thailand: Silkworm Books, 1999.

———. "The Constitution of Democratic Kampuchea (Cambodia): The Semantics of Revolutionary Change." *Pacific Affairs* 49, no. 3 (1976): 506–15.

———. "From 'Cambodge' to 'Kampuchea': State and Revolution in Cambodia, 1863–1979." *Thesis Eleven* 50 (1997): 35–49.

———. *A History of Cambodia.* 3rd ed. Boulder, CO: Westview Press, 2000.

———. "Introduction." In *Pol Pot Plans the Future: Confidential Leadership Documents from Democratic Kampuchea, 1976–1977,* edited by David Chandler, Ben Kiernan, and Chanta Boua, 36–43. New Haven, CT: Yale University Southeast Asia Studies, 1988.

———. *The Tragedy of Cambodian History: Politics, War, and Revolution since 1945.* New Haven, CT: Yale University Press, 1991.

———. *Voices from S-21: Terror and History in Pol Pot's Secret Prison.* Berkeley: University of California Press, 1999.

Chattopadhyay, Paresh. "Capitalism as Socialism in the Early Soviet Doctrine: Lenin, Trotsky, Bukharin, Preobrazhensky." *Review of Radical Political Economics* 28, no. 3 (1996): 74–82.

———. "The Economic Content of Socialism Marx vs. Lenin." *Review of Radical Political Economics* 24, no. 3–4 (1992): 90–110.

———. "Marx Made to Serve Party-State." *Economic & Political Weekly* 45, no. 41 (2010): 35–38.

———. *Marx's Associated Mode of Production: A Critique of Marxism.* New York: Palgrave Macmillan, 2016.

———. "The Myth of Twentieth-Century and the Continuing Relevance of Karl Marx." *Socialism and Democracy* 24, no. 3 (2010): 23–45.

———. "Passage to Socialism: The Dialectic of Progress in Marx." *Historical Materialism* 14, no. 3 (2007): 45–84.

———. "Which Socialism Is in Question?" *Economic and Political Weekly* (1989): 2791–94.

———. "Worlds Apart: Socialism in Marx and in Early Bolshevism, A Provisional Overview." *Economic and Political Weekly* 40, no. 53 (2005): 5629–34.

Chen, Jian. "The Beginning of the End: 1956 as a Turning Point in Chinese and Cold War History." *Modern China Studies* 22, no. 1 (2015): 99–126.

Cherne, Leo. "Cambodia—Auschwitz of Asia." *Worldview* 21, nos. 7–8 (1978): 21–25.

Chhor, Siv Leng. "Destruction of Family Foundation in Kampuchea." *Searching for the Truth* 11 (2000): 22–23.

Chomsky, Noam, and Edward S. Herman. *After the Cataclysm: Postwar Indochina and the Reconstruction of Imperial Ideology.* Chicago, IL: Haymarket Books, 2014.

Choonara, Joseph. *Unravelling Capitalism: A Guide to Marxist Political Economy.* London: Bookmarks Publications, 2017.

Chossudovsky, Michel. "Economic Genocide in Rwanda." *Economic and Political Weekly* 31, no. 15 (1996): 938–41.

Christophers, Brett. "Follow the Thing: Money." *Environment and Planning D: Society and Space* 29, no. 6 (2011): 1068–1084.

Chumar, Nirmal K. "The Peasant Question from Marx to Lenin: The Russian Experience." *Economic and Political Weekly* 37, no. 20 (2002): 1927–38.

Cleaver, Harry. *Reading* Capital *Politically.* Leeds, UK: AK Press, 2000.

Clegg, Stewart, Miguel Pina e Cunha, and Arménio Rego. "The Theory and Practice of Utopia in a Total Institution: The Pineapple Panopticon." *Organization Studies* 33, no. 12 (2012): 1735–1757.

Cliff, Tony. *State Capitalism in Russia.* London: Pluto Press, 1955.

Clymer, Kenton J. "The Perils of Neutrality: The Break in U.S.-Cambodian Relations, 1965." *Diplomatic History* 23, no. 4 (1999): 609–31.

———. *Troubled Relations: The United States and Cambodia since 1870.* DeKalb: Northern Illinois University Press, 2007.

Communist Party of Kampuchea. "Abbreviated Lesson on the History of the Kampuchean Revolutionary Movement Led by the Communist Party of Kampuchea." In *Pol Pot Plans the Future: Confidential Leadership Documents from Democratic Kampuchea, 1976–1977,* edited by David Chandler, Ben Kiernan, and Chanthou Boua, 217–26. New Haven, CT: Yale Center for International and Area Studies, 1988.

———. "Decisions of the Central Committee on a Variety of Questions." In *Pol Pot Plans the Future: Confidential Leadership Documents from Democratic Kampuchea, 1976–1977,* edited by David Chandler, Ben Kiernan, and Chanthou Boua, 3–8. New Haven, CT: Yale Center for International and Area Studies, 1988.

———. "Excerpted Report on the Leading Views of the Comrade Representing the Party Organization at a Zone Assembly." In *Pol Pot Plans the Future: Confidential Leadership Documents from Democratic Kampuchea, 1976–1977,* edited by David Chandler, Ben Kiernan, and Chanthou Boua, 13–35 New Haven, CT: Yale University Southeast Asia Studies, 1988.

———. "The Party's Four-Year Plan to Build Socialism in All Fields, 1977–1980." In *Pol Pot Plans the Future: Confidential Leadership Documents from Democratic Kampuchea, 1976–1977,* edited by David Chandler, Ben Kiernan, and Chanthou Boua, 36–119. New Haven, CT: Yale University Southeast Asia Studies, 1988.

———. "Preliminary Explanation before Reading the Plan, by the Party Secretary." In *Pol Pot Plans the Future: Confidential Leadership Documents from Democratic Kampuchea, 1976–1977,* edited by David Chandler, Ben Kiernan, and Chanthou Boua, 120–63. New Haven, CT: Yale University Southeast Asia Studies, 1988.

———. "Report of Activities of the Party Center According to the Genral Political Tasks of 1976." In *Pol Pot Plans the Future: Confidential Leadership Documents from Democratic*

Kampuchea, 1976–1977, edited by David Chandler, Ben Kiernan, and Chanthou Boua, 182–212. New Haven, CT: Yale University Southeast Asia Studies, 1988.

Connolly, Chris. "The American Factor: Sino-American Rapprochement and Chinese Attitudes to the Vietnam War, 1968–72." *Cold War History* 5, no. 4 (2005): 501–27.

Cooper, Mark N. "State Capitalism, Class Structure, and Social Transformation in the Third World: The Case of Egypt." *International Journal of Middle East Studies* 15, no. 4 (1983): 451–69.

Coward, Martin. *Urbicide: The Politics of Urban Destruction.* New York: Routledge, 2008.

Cunha, Miguel Pina e, Stewart Clegg, Arménio Rego, and Michelle Lancione. "The Organization (*Angkar*) as a State of Exception: The Case of the S-21 Extermination Camp, Phnom Penh." *Journal of Political Power* 5, no. 2 (2012): 279–99.

Curtis, Andrew, James Tyner, Jayakrishnan Ajayakumar, Sokvisal Kimsroy, and Kok-Chhay Ly. "Adding Spatial Context to the April 17, 1975 Evacuation of Phnom Penh: How Spatial Video Geonarratives Can Geographically Enrich Genocide Testimony." *GeoHumanities* 5, no. 2 (2019): 386–404.

D'Amato, Paul. *The Meaning of Marxism.* Chicago: Haymarket Books, 2006.

Day, Richard B. "Preobrzhensky and the Theory of the Transition Period." *Soviet Studies* 27, no. 2 (1975): 196–219.

Dean, Mitchell. *Governmentality: Power and Rule in Modern Society.* 2nd ed. Thousand Oaks, CA: SAGE Publications, 2010.

DeFalco, Randle C. "Accounting for Famine at the Extraordinary Chambers in the Courts of Cambodia: The Crimes against Humanity of Extermination, Inhumane Acts and Persecution." *International Journal of Transitional Justice* 5, no. 1 (2011): 142–58.

———. "Justice and Starvation in Cambodia: The Khmer Rouge Famine." *Cambodia Law and Policy Journal* 2 (2014): 45–84.

———. "Voices of Genocide: Justice and the Khmer Rouge Famine." *Searching for the Truth* (First Quarter, 2013): 29–32.

Derks, Annuska. *Khmer Women on the Move: Exploring Work and Life in Urban Cambodia.* Honolulu: University of Hawai'i Press, 2008.

De Walque, Damien. "Selective Mortality during the Khmer Rouge Period in Cambodia." *Population and Development Review* 31, no. 2 (2005): 351–68.

Diepart, Jean-Christophe. *The Fragmentation of Land Tenure Systems in Cambodia: Peasants and the Formalization of Land Rights.* Paris: Technical Committee on Land Tenure and Development, 2015.

Diepart, Jean-Christophe, and Thol Sem. *Cambodian Peasantry and Formalisation of Land Right: Historical Perspectives and Current Issues.* Paris: French Technical Committee on Land Tenure and Development, 2018.

Dillon, Linda D., Bruce Burton, and Walter C. Soderlund. "Who was the Principal Enemy? Shifts in Official Chinese Perceptions of the Two Superpowers, 1968–1969." *Asian Survey* 17, no. 5 (1977): 456–73.

Dinkel, Jürgen. " 'Third World Begins to Flex Its Muscles': The Non-Aligned Movement and the North-South Conflict during the 1970s." In *Neutrality and Neutralism in the Global Cold War,* edited by Sandra Bott, Jussi M. Hanhimaki, Janick Schaufelbuehl, and Marco Wyss, 108–23. New York: Routledge, 2015.

Doğan, Erkan. "Socialism and Nationalism in the Third World in the Age of Third Worldism." *METU Studies in Development* 44, no. 3 (2017): 281–300.

dos Santos, Theotônio. "The Structure of Dependence." *American Economic Review* 60, no. 2 (1970): 231–36.

Draguhn, Werner. "The Indochina Conflict and the Positions of the Countries Involved." *Contemporary Southeast Asia* 5, no. 1 (1983): 95–116.

Duggett, Michael. "Marx on Peasants." *Journal of Peasant Studies* 2, no. 2 (1975): 159–82.

Duiker, William J. *The Communist Road to Power in Vietnam*. New York: Routledge, 2018.

Dy, Kamboly. *A History of Democratic Kampuchea (1975–1979)*. Phnom Penh: Documentation Center of Cambodia, 2007.

Ea, Meng-Try. *The Chain of Terror: The Khmer Rouge Southwest Zone Security System*. Phnom Penh: Documentation Center of Cambodia, 2005.

Eagleton, Terry. *Why Marx Was Right*. New Haven, CT: Yale University Press, 2011.

Eaton, Henry. "Marx and the Russians." *Journal of the History of Ideas* 41, no. 1 (1980): 89–112.

Ebihara, May. "A Cambodian Village under the Khmer Rouge." In *Genocide and Democracy in Cambodia: The Khmer Rouge, the United Nations and the International Community*, edited by Ben Kiernan, 51–63. New Haven, CT: Yale University Southeast Asia Studies, 1993.

———. "Intervillage, Intertown, and Village-City Relations in Cambodia." *Annals of the New York Academy of Sciences* 220, no. 1 (1973): 358–75.

———. "Residence Patterns in a Khmer Peasant Village." *Annals of the New York Academy of Sciences* 293, no. 1 (1977): 51–68.

———. *Svay: A Khmer Village in Cambodia*. Ithaca, NY: Cornell University Press, 2018.

Edelman, Marc. "Late Marx and the Russian Road: Marx and the 'Peripheries of Capitalism.'" *Monthly Review* 36 (1984): 55–59.

Edelman, Marc, Tony Weis, Amita Baviskar, Saturnino M. Borras Jr., Eric Holt-Giménez, Deniz Kandiyoti, and Wendy Wolford. "Introduction: Critical Perspectives on Food Sovereignty." *Journal of Peasant Studies* 41, no. 6 (2014): 911–31.

Edelman, Marc, and Wendy Wolford. "Introduction: Critical Agrarian Studies in Theory and Practice." *Antipode* 49, no. 4 (2017): 959–76.

Edwards, Matthew. "The Rise of the Khmer Rouge in Cambodia: Internal or External Origins?" *Asian Affairs* 35, no. 1 (2004): 56–67.

Elliott, John E. "Karl Marx: Founding Father of Workers' Self-Governance?" *Economic and Industrial Democracy* 8, no. 3 (1987): 293–321.

Engel-Dimauro, Salvatore. "The Enduring Relevance of State-Socialism." *Capitalism Nature Socialism* 27, no. 4 (2016): 1–15.

Engels, Friedrich. *Anti-Dühring: Herr Eugen Dühring's Revolution in Science*. 1878; repr., Moscow: Foreign Languages Publishing House, 1962.

Escobar, Arturo. "Discourse and Power in Development: Michel Foucault and the Relevance of his Work to the Third World." *Alternatives* 10 (1984–85): 377–400.

Etcheson, Craig. *After the Killing Fields: Lessons from the Cambodian Genocide*. Lubbock: Texas Tech University Press, 2005.

———. *The Rise and Demise of Democratic Kampuchea*. Boulder, CO: Westview Press, 1984.

Evenitsky, Alfred. "Preobrazhensky and the Political Economy of Backwardness." *Science & Society* 30, no. 1 (1966): 50–62.

Fairbairn, Madeline, Jonathan Fox, S. Ryan Isakson, Michael Levien, Nancy Peluso, Shahra Razavi, Ian Scoones, and K. Sivaramakrishnan. "Introduction: New Directions in Agrarian Political Economy." *Journal of Peasant Studies* 41, no. 5 (2014): 653–66.

Fanon, Frantz. *The Wretched of the Earth*. Translated by Richard Philcox. 1963; repr., New York: Grove Press, 2004.

Fernandez, Bina. "Dispossession and the Depletion of Social Reproduction." *Antipode* 50 (2018): 142–63.

Figes, Orlanda. "Collective Farming and the 19th-Century Russian Land Commune: A Research Note." *Soviet Studies* 38, no. 1 (1986): 89–97.

Fine, Ben, and Alfredo Saad-Filho. *Marx's "Capital."* 5th ed. New York: Pluto Press, 2010.

Fitzpatrick, Sheila. *Everyday Stalinism: Ordinary Life in Extraordinary Times: Soviet Russia in the 1930s*. Oxford: Oxford University Press, 2000.

Foglesong, David S. *America's Secret War against Bolshevism: US Intervention in the Russian Civil War, 1917–1920*. Chapel Hill: University of North Carolina Press, 2014.

Foster, John Bellamy. "Marx's Theory of Metabolic Rift: Classical Foundations for Environmental Sociology." *American Journal of Sociology* 105, no. 2 (1999): 366–405.

Foucault, Michel. "Governmentality." In *Power: Essential Works of Foucault, 1954–1984, Volume III*, edited by James D. Faubion, 201–22. New York: The New Press, 2000.

———. *Security, Territory, Population: Lectures at the Collége de France, 1977–1978*. Translated by Graham Burchell. New York: Picador, 2007.

———. "The Subject and Power." In *Power: Essential Works of Foucault, 1954–1984, Volume III*, edited by James D. Faubion, 326–48. New York: The New Press, 2000.

Fracchia, Joseph. "The Capitalist Labour-Process and the Body in Pain: The Corporeal Depths of Marx's Concept of Immiseration." *Historical Materialism* 16, no. 4 (2008): 35–66.

Frank, André G. *Capitalism and Underdevelopment in Latin America: Historical Studies of Chile and Brazil*. New York: Monthly Review Press, 1967.

Fraser, Ian, and Lawrence Wilde. *The Marx Dictionary*. New York: Continuum, 2011.

Fregonese, Sara. "The Urbicide of Beirut? Geopolitics and the Built Environment in the Lebanese Civil War (1975–1976)." *Political Geography* 28, no. 5 (2009): 309–18.

Friedmann, Harriet. "Commentary: Food Regime Analysis and Agrarian Questions: Widening the Conversation." *Journal of Peasant Studies* 43, no. 3 (2016): 671–92.

Frieson, Kate. "The Political Nature of Democratic Kampuchea." *Pacific Affairs* 61, no. 3 (1988): 405–27.

Gabriel, Satya, Stephen A. Resnick, and Richard D. Wolff. "State Capitalism versus Communism: What Happened in the USSR and the PRC?" *Critical Sociology* 34, no. 4 (2008): 539–56.

Galtung, Johan. "A Structural Theory of Imperialism." *Journal of Peace Research* 8, no. 2 (1971): 81–94.

Glassman, Jim. "Primitive Accumulation, Accumulation by Dispossession, Accumulation by 'Extra-Economic' Means." *Progress in Human Geography* 30, no. 5 (2006): 608–25.

Gordon, Bernard K. "Cambodia: Where Foreign Policy Counts." *Asian Survey* (1965): 433–48.

Gordon, Bernard K., and Kathryn Young. "The Khmer Republic: That Was the Cambodia That Was." *Asian Survey* 11, no. 1 (1971): 26–40.

Gough, Kathleen. "Roots of the Pol Pot Regime in Kampuchea." *Contemporary Marxism* 12, no. 13 (1986): 14–48.

Guérin, Mathieu. "Khmer Peasants and Land Access in Kompong Thom Province in the 1930s." *Journal of Southeast Asian Studies* 43, no. 3 (2012): 441–62.

Gutierrez, Francisco. "Agrarian Inequality and Civil War Revisited." *Geography Compass* 9, no. 8 (2015): 423–31.

Hall, Derek. "Primitive Accumulation, Accumulation by Dispossession and the Global Land Grab." *Third World Quarterly* 34, no. 9 (2013): 1582–1604.

Hammen, Oscar J. "Marx and the Agrarian Question." *American Historical Review* 77, no. 3 (1972): 679–704.

Harmann, Shannon C. "Scripting Mass Atrocity: Cambodia under the Khmer Rouge." Master's thesis, University of Reno, 2018.

Harrington, Michael. *Socialism: Past and Present*. New York: Arcade Publishing, 1989.

Harrison, Mark. "Primary Accumulation in the Soviet Transition." *Journal of Development Studies* 22, no. 1 (1985): 81–103.

———. "Soviet Primary Accumulation Processes: Some Unresolved Problems." *Science & Society* 45, no. 4 (1981/1982): 387–408.

Harvey, David. *A Companion to Marx's* Capital. New York: Verso, 2010.

———. *The Limits to Capital*. London: Verso, 2006.

———. *The New Imperialism*. Oxford: Oxford University Press, 2005.

Heardon, Patrick J. *The Tragedy of Vietnam: Causes and Consequences.* 2nd ed. New York: Pearson Longman, 2005.

Heder, Steve. *Cambodian Communism and the Vietnamese Model: Imitation and Independence, 1930–1975.* Bangkok: White Lotus Press, 2004.

———. "Racism, Marxism, Labelling, and Genocide in Ben Kiernan's The Pol Pot Regime." *South East Asia Research* 5, no. 2 (1997): 101–53.

Heinrich, Michael. *An Introduction of the Three Volumes of Karl Marx's* Capital. New York: Monthly Review Press, 2004.

Helmers, Kent. "Rice in the Cambodian Economy: Past and Present." In *Rice Production in Cambodia*, edited by Harry J. Nesbitt, 1–14. Manila: International Rice Research Institute, 1997.

Henning, Christoph. *Philosophy after Marx: 100 Years of Misunderstandings and the Normative Turn in Political Philosophy.* Chicago, IL: Haymarket Books, 2015.

Heuveline, Patrick. " 'Between One and Three Million': Towards the Demographic Reconstruction of a Decade of Cambodian History (1979–79)." *Population Studies* 51, no. 1 (1998): 49–65.

Heuveline, Patrick. "The Boundaries of Genocide: Quantifying the Uncertainty of the Death Toll during the Pol Pot Regime in Cambodia (1975–79)." *Population Studies* 69, no. 2 (2015): 201–18.

Heuveline, Patrick, and Bunnak Poch. "Do Marriages Forget Their Past? Marital Stability in Post-Khmer Rouge Cambodia." *Demography* 43 (2006): 99–125.

Hewitt, Kenneth. "Proving Grounds of Urbicide: Civil and Urban Perspectives on the Bombing of Capital Cities." *ACME: An International E-Journal for Critical Geographies* 8, no. 2 (2008): 340–75.

Hiebert, Maureen S. "Genocide, Revolution, and Starvation under the Khmer Rouge." *Genocide Studies International* 11, no. 1 (2017): 68–86.

Hills, Jill. "Dependency Theory and Its Relevance Today: International Institutions in Telecommunications and Structural Power." *Review of International Studies* 20, no. 2 (1994): 169–86.

Hinton, Alexander. *Man or Monster: The Trial of a Khmer Rouge Torturer.* Durham, NC: Duke University Press, 2016.

———. *Why Did They Kill? Cambodia in the Shadow of Genocide.* Berkeley: University of California Press, 2005.

———. "Why Did You Kill? The Cambodian Genocide and the Dark Side of Face and Honor." *Journal of Asian Studies* 57, no. 1 (1998): 93–122.

Hoefinger, Heidi. *Sex, Love and Money in Cambodia: Professional Girlfriends and Transactional Relationships.* New York: Routledge, 2014.

Hope, Kempe R. "Self-Reliance and Participation of the Poor in the Development Profess in the Third World." *Futures* 15, no. 6 (1983): 455–62.

Hornborg, Alf. "Post-Capitalist Ecologies: Energy, 'Value' and Fetishism in the Anthropocene." *Capitalism Nature Socialism* 27, no. 4 (2016): 61–76.

Horowitz, Irving L. *Taking Lives: Genocide and State Power.* New Brunswick, NJ: Transaction Books, 1980.

Howard, Michael C., and John E. King. *A History of Marxian Economics, Volume I: 1883–1929.* London: Palgrave, 1989.

Hunt, Richard N. *The Political Ideas of Marx.* Pittsburgh: University of Pittsburgh Press, 1974.

Huxley, Margo. "Geographies of Governmentality." In *Space, Knowledge and Power: Foucault and Geography*, edited by Jeremy W. Crampton and Stuart Elden, 185–204. Aldershot, UK: Ashgate, 2007.

Huy, Ratana C. "Khmer Rouge Wedding." *Searching for the Truth* 25 (2002): 26–28.

Im, Hyug Baeg. "Collectivization and Socialist Transition in Soviet Union and China." *Pacific Focus* 5, no. 2 (1990): 39–76.

Immerman, Richard. "The United States and the Geneva Conference of 1954: A New Look." *Diplomatic History* 14, no. 1 (1990): 43–66.

Institute of Foreign Affairs. *Summit Declarations of Non-Aligned Movement (1961–2009)*. Kathmandu, Nepal: Institute of Foreign Affairs, 2011.

Isaacs, Arnold. *Without Honor: Defeat in Cambodia*. Baltimore: Johns Hopkins University Press, 1983.

Itoh, Makoto. "Money and Credit in Socialist Economies: A Reconsideration." *Capital & Class* 20, no. 3 (1996): 95–118.

Jackson, Karl D., ed. *Cambodia, 1975–1978: Rendezvous with Death*. Princeton: Princeton University Press, 1989.

Jackson, Karl D. "The Ideology of Total Revolution." In *Cambodia, 1975–1978: Rendezvous with Death*, edited by Karl D. Jackson, 24–250. Princeton, NJ: Princeton University Press, 1989.

Jackson, Stevi. "Why a Materialist Feminism Is (Still) Possible—and Necessary." *Women's Studies International Forum* 24, no. 3–4 (2001): 283–93.

Jain, Neha. "Forced Marriage as a Crime against Humanity." *Journal of International Criminal Justice* 6 (2008): 1013–1032.

Jerome, William, and Adam Buick. "Soviet State Capitalism? The History of an Idea." *Survey: A Journal of Soviet and East European Studies* 26 (1967): 58–71.

Jian, Chen. "China's Involvement in the Vietnam War, 1964–69." *China Quarterly* 142 (1995): 356–87.

Johnston, Monty. "Democratic Centralism." In *A Dictionary of Marxist Thought*, edited by Tom Bottomore, 2nd ed., 134–37. Malden, MA: Blackwell, 1991.

Jossa, Bruno. "The Democratic Road to Socialism." *Revista Internazionale di Scienze Sociali* 3 (2010): 335–54.

Ka-kui, Tse. "Agricultural Collectivization and Socialist Construction: The Soviet Union and China." *Dialectical Anthropology* 2, no. 3 (1977): 199–221.

Kalter, Christoph. "From Global to Local and Back: The 'Third World' Concept and the New Radical Left in France." *Journal of Global History* 12, no. 1 (2017): 115–36.

Kamola, Isaac A. "The Global Coffee Economy and the Production of Genocide in Rwanda." *Third World Quarterly* 28, no. 3 (2007): 571–92.

Karkaria, Zal. *Failure through Neglect: The Women's Policies of the Khmer Rouge*. Master's thesis, Department of History, Concordia University, Montreal.

Kaser, Michael. "The Soviet Ideology of Industrialization: A Review Article." *Journal of Development Studies* 3, no. 1 (1966): 63–75.

Kaufman, Adam. "The Origin of 'the Political Economy of Socialism.'" *Soviet Studies* 4, no. 3 (1953): 243–72.

Kerkvliet, Benedict J. T. "Wobbly Foundations: Building Co-Operatives in Rural Vietnam, 1955–61." *South East Asia Research* 6, no. 3 (1998): 193–251.

Kerkvliet, Benedict J. T., and Mark Selden. "Agrarian Transformations in China and Vietnam." *China Journal* 40 (1998): 37–58.

Keyfitz, Nathan. "Alfred Sauvy." *Population and Development Review* 16, no. 4 (1990): 727–33.

Khoo, Nicholas. "Breaking the Ring of Encirclement: The Sino-Soviet Rift and Chinese Policy toward Vietnam, 1964–1968." *Journal of Cold War Studies* 12, no. 1 (2010): 3–42.

Kiernan, Ben. "The American Bombardment of Kampuchea, 1969–1973." *Vietnam Generation* 1, no. 1 (1989): 4–14.

Kiernan, Ben. *How Pol Pot Came to Power: A History of Communism in Kampuchea, 1930–1975*. London: Verso, 1985.

————. "Introduction." In *Peasants and Politics in Kampuchea, 1942–1981*, edited by Ben Kiernan and Chanthou Boua, 1–33. New York: M. E. Sharpe, 1982.

————. "Kampuchea and Stalinism." In *Marxism in Asia*, edited by Colin Mackerras and Nick Knight, 232–50. London: Croom Helm, 1985.

————. *The Pol Pot Regime: Policies, Race and Genocide in Cambodia under the Khmer Rouge, 1975–1979*. New Haven, CT: Yale University Press, 1996.

————. "Origins of Khmer Communism." *Southeast Asian Affairs* (1981): 161–80.

Kiernan, Ben, and Taylor Owen. "Making More Enemies than We Kill? Calculating U.S. Bomb Tonnages Dropped on Laos and Cambodia, and Weighing their Implications." *Asia-Pacific Journal* 13, no. 16 (2015): 1–9.

Kirk, Donald. "Cambodia's Economic Crisis." *Asian Survey* 11, no. 3 (1971): 238–55.

Kristjanson-Gural, David. "Value, Cooperatives, and Class Justice." *Rethinking Marxism* 23, no. 3 (2011): 352–63.

Landsman, Mark. *Dictatorship and Demand: The Politics of Consumerism in East Germany*. Cambridge, MA: Harvard University Press, 2005.

LeBlanc, Paul. *Marx, Lenin, and the Revolutionary Experience: Studies of Communism and Radicalism in an Age of Globalization*. New York: Routledge, 2014.

Lebowitz, Michael A. *The Socialist Imperative: From Gotha to Now*. New York: Monthly Review Press, 2015.

Ledgerwood, Judy, May M. Ebihara, and Carol A. Mortland. "Introduction." In *Cambodian Culture since 1975: Homeland and Exile*, edited by May M. Ebihara, Carol A. Mortland, and Judy Ledgerwood, 1–26. Ithaca, NY: Cornell University Press, 1994.

Ledgerwood, Judy, and John Vijghen. "Decision-Making in Rural Khmer Villages." In *Cambodia Emerges from the Past: Eight Essays*, edited by Judy Ledgerwood, 109–50. DeKalb, IL: Center for Southeast Asian Studies, Northern Illinois University, 2002.

Lee, Susan H. *Rice Plus: Widows and Economic Survival in Rural Cambodia*. New York: Routledge, 2006.

Liefer, Michael. "Cambodia: In Search of Neutrality." *Asian Survey* (1963): 55–60.

Lenin, Vladimir I. *Essential Works of Lenin: 'What Is to Be Done?' and Other Writings*. New York: Dover Publications, 1987.

————. "The Right of Nations to Self-Determination." In *Lenin: Selected Works, Volume I*. Moscow: Foreign Language Publishing, 1961.

Levene, Mark. "The Chittagong Hill Tracts: A Case Study in the Political Economy of 'Creeping' Genocide." *Third World Quarterly* 20, no. 2 (1999): 339–69.

LeVine, Peg. *Love and Dread in Cambodia: Weddings, Births, and Ritual Harm under the Khmer Rouge*. Singapore: National University of Singapore Press, 2010.

Littlejohn, Gary. "The Agrarian Marxist Research in its Political Context: State Policy and the Development of the Soviet Rural Class Structure in the 1920s." *Journal of Peasant Studies* 11, no. 2 (1984): 61–84.

Locard, Henri. *Pol Pot's Little Red Book: The Sayings of Angkar*. Chiang Mai, Thailand: Silkworm Books, 2004.

Lüthi, Lorenz M. "The Non-Aligned Movement and the Cold War, 1961–1973." *Journal of Cold War Studies* 18, no. 4 (2016): 98–147.

MacKinnon, Danny. "Managerialism, Governmentality and the State: A Neo-Foucauldian Approach to Local Economic Governance." *Political Geography* 19, no. 3 (2000): 293–314.

Malle, Silvana. *The Economic Organization of War Communism, 1918–1921*. Cambridge: Cambridge University Press, 1985.

Mam, Kalyanee E. "An Oral History of Family Life under the Khmer Rouge." Working Paper GS10, Yale Center for International and Area Studies Working Paper Series. New Haven, CT: Yale Center for International and Area Studies, 1999.

Manning, Peter. *Transitional Justice and Memory in Cambodia: Beyond the Extraordinary Chambers*. New York: Routledge, 2017.

Marx, Karl. *Capital: A Critique of Political Economy*. Vol. 1. 1867; repr., New York: Penguin, 1990.

———. *Capital: A Critique of Political Economy*. Vol. 2. 1885; repr., New York: Penguin, 1978.

———. *Capital: A Critique of Political Economy*. Vol. 3. 1894; repr., New York: Penguin, 1991.

———. *A Contribution to the Critique of Political Economy*. 1859; repr., New York: International Publishers, 1970.

———. *Critique of the Gotha Program*. 1875; repr., New York: International Publishers, 2009.

———. "The Eighteenth Brumaire of Louis Bonaparte." In *Karl Marx: Selected Writings*, 2nd edition, edited by David McLellan. Oxford: Oxford University Press, 2000.

———. *Grundrisse: Foundations of the Critique of Political Economy*. Translated by Martin Nicolaus. New York: Penguin Books, 1973.

Marx, Karl, and Friedrich Engels. *The Communist Manifesto*. 1848; repr., New York: Verso, 2012.

———. *The German Ideology*. 1845; repr., Amherst, NY: Prometheus Books, 1988.

Matar, Linda. "Twilight of 'State Capitalism' in Formerly 'Socialist' Arab States." *Journal of North African Studies* 18, no. 3 (2013): 416–30.

Maurer, Bill. "The Anthropology of Money." *Annual Review of Anthropology* 35 (2006): 15–36.

McIntyre, Kevin. "Geography as Destiny: Cities, Villages and Khmer Rouge Orientalism." *Comparative Studies in Society and History* 38, no. 4 (1996): 730–58.

McLaughlin, Paul. "Rethinking the Agrarian Question: The Limits of Essentialism and the Promise of Evolutionism." *Human Ecology Review* 5, no. 2 (1998): 25–39.

Merrington, John. "Theory and Practice in Gramsci's Marxism." *Socialist Register* 5, no. 5 (1968): 145–76.

Mertha, Andrew. *Brothers in Arms: Chinese Aid to the Khmer Rouge, 1975–1979*. Ithaca, NY: Cornell University Press, 2014.

Millar, James R. "Mass Collectivization and the Contribution of Soviet Agriculture to the First Five-Year Plan: A Review Article." *Slavic Review* 33, no. 4 (1974): 750–66.

———. "A Note on Primitive Accumulation in Marx and Preobrazhensky." *Soviet Studies* 30, no. 3 (1978): 384–93.

———. "Soviet Rapid Development and the Agricultural Surplus Hypothesis." *Soviet Studies* 22, no. 1 (1970): 77–93.

Minh, Pham Quang. "In the Crossfire: Vietnam's Relations with China and Soviet Union during the Vietnam War (1965–1972)." *VNU: Journal of Science, Social Sciences and Humanities* 5, no. 5E (2009): 24–36.

Mitchell, Don. "Historical Materialism and Marxism." In *A Companion to Cultural Geography*, edited by James S. Duncan, Nuala C. Johnson, and Richard Schein, 51–65. Malden, MA: Blackwell, 2004.

Molyneux, John. "The Working Class." *Irish Marxist Review* 7, no. 20 (2018): 5–8.

Moyo, Sam, Praveen Jha, and Paris Yeros. "The Classical Agrarian Question: Myth, Reality, and Relevance Today." *Agrarian South: Journal of Political Economy* 2, no. 1 (2013): 93–119.

Musacchio, Aldo, and Sergio G. Lazzarini. *Reinventing State Capitalism: Leviathan in Business, Brazil, and Beyond*. Cambridge, MA: Harvard University Press, 2014.

Nadesan, Majia H. *Governmentality, Biopower, and Everyday Life*. New York: Routledge, 2008.

Naughton, Barry and Kellee S. Tsai, eds. *State Capitalism, Institutional Adaptation, and the Chinese Miracle*. New York: Cambridge University Press, 2015.

Nguyen, Lien-Hang. *Hanoi's War: An International History of the War for Peace in Vietnam.* Chapel Hill: University of North Carolina Press, 2012.

Nhem, Boraden. *The Khmer Rouge: Ideology, Militarism, and the Revolution That Consumed a Generation.* Santa Barbara, CA: Praeger, 2013.

Nim, Hu. "Land Tenure and Social Structure in Kampuchea." In *Peasants and Politics in Kampuchea, 1942–1981*, edited by Ben Kiernan and Chanthou Boua, 69–86. London: Zed Press, 1982.

Nove, Alec. "The Agricultural Surplus Hypothesis: A Comment on James R. Millar's Article." *Soviet Studies* 22, no. 3 (1971): 394–401.

Office of the Co-Prosecutors. Co-Prosecutors' Rule 66 Final Submission. Public redacted version, Case No. 002/19/09/20007-ECCC/OCIJ. http://www.eccc.gov.kh/en.

Office of the Co-Investigating Judges. Closing Order. Case File No. 002/19-09-2007-ECCC-OCIJ. http://www.eccc.gov.kh/en.

Ollman, Bertell. *Alienation: Marx's Conception of Man in Capitalist Society.* 2nd ed. Cambridge: Cambridge University Press, 1976.

Ovesen, J., and I.-B. Trankell. *Cambodians and Their Doctors: A Medical Anthropology of Colonial and Post-Colonial Cambodia.* Copenhagen: Nordic Institute of Asian Studies, 2010.

Owen, Taylor, and Ben Kiernan. "Bombs over Cambodia." *Walrus Magazine* (October 2006): 62–69.

Owens, Peter B. "The Collective Dynamics of Genocidal Violence in Cambodia, 1975–1979." *Social Science History* 38, nos. 3–4 (2014): 411–36.

Paige, Jeffery M. *Agrarian Revolutions: Social Movements and Export Agriculture in the Underdeveloped World.* New York: The Free Press, 1975.

Path, Kosal, and Angeliki Kanavou. "Converts, not Ideologues? The Khmer Rouge Practice of Thought Reform in Cambodia, 1975–1978." *Journal of Political Ideologies* 20, no. 3 (2015): 304–32.

Petras, James, "State Capitalism and the Third World," *Development and Change* 8, no. 1 (1977): 1–17.

Phuong, Chan Pranith. "Forced Marriage to Avoid Death." *Searching for the Truth* (Third Quarter, 2013): 18–19.

Pipes, Richard. "Russian Marxism and Its Populist Background: The Late Nineteenth Century." *Russian Review* 19, no. 4 (1960): 316–37.

Porter, Gareth. "Vietnamese Communist Policy toward Kampuchea, 1930–1970." In *Revolution and Its Aftermath in Kampuchea: Eight Essays*, edited by David Chandler and Ben Kiernan, 57–98. New Haven: Yale University Southeast Asia Studies, 1983.

Postone, Moishe. *Time, Labor, and Social Domination: A Reinterpretation of Marx's Critical Theory.* New York: Cambridge University Press, 1993.

Potter, Robert P., Tony Binns, Jennifer A. Elliott, and David Smith. *Geographies of Development.* 2nd ed. New York: Pearson, 2004.

Prasso, Sheridan T. "The Riel Value of Money: How the World's Only Attempt to Abolish Money Has Hindered Cambodia's Economic Development." *Asia Pacific Issues* 49 (2001): 1–8.

Preobrazhensky, Evgeny. *The New Economics.* Translated by B. Pearce. 1926; repr., Oxford: Oxford University Press, 1965.

Pryor, Frederic L. *The Red and the Green: The Rise and Fall of Collectivized Agriculture in Marxist Regimes.* Princeton, NJ: Princeton University Press, 1992.

Qiang, Zhai. "China and the Geneva Conference of 1954." *China Quarterly* 129 (1992): 103–22.

Quinn, Kenneth M. "Cambodia 1976: Internal Consolidation and External Expansion." *Asian Survey* 17, no. 1 (1977): 43–54.

———. "The Pattern and Scope of Violence." In *Cambodia, 1975–1978: Rendezvous with Death*, edited by Karl D. Jackson, 179–208. Princeton, NJ: Princeton University Press, 1989.

Raco, Mike, and Rob Imrie. "Governmentality and Rights and Responsibilities in Urban Policy." *Environment and Planning A* 32, no. 12 (2000): 2187–2204.

Rakove, Robert B. "The Rise and Fall of Non-Aligned Mediation, 1961–66." *International History Review* 37, no. 5 (2015): 991–1013.

Ramadan, Adam. "Destroying Nahr el-Bared: Sovereignty and Urbicide in the Space of Exception." *Political Geography* 28, no. 3 (2009): 153–63.

Raymond, Chad. " 'No Responsibility and No Rice': The Rise and Fall of Agricultural Collectivization in Vietnam." *Agricultural History* 82, no.1 (2008): 43–61.

Razavi, Shahra. "Engendering the Political Economy of Agrarian Change." *Journal of Peasant Studies* 36, no. 1 (2009): 197–226.

Read, Jason. *The Micro-Politics of Capital: Marx and the Prehistory of the Present*. Albany: State University of New York Press, 2003.

Resnick, Stephen, and Richard Wolff. "Between State and Private Capitalism: What Was Soviet 'Socialism'?" *Rethinking Marxism* 7, no. 1 (1994): 9–30.

———. *Class Theory and History: Capitalism and Communism in the U.S.S.R.* New York: Routledge, 2002.

———. "Communism: Between Class and Classless." *Rethinking Marxism* 1, no. 1 (1988): 14–42.

———. "State Capitalism in the USSR? A High-Stakes Debate." *Rethinking Marxism* 6, no. 2 (1993): 46–68.

———. "State Capitalism versus Communism: What Happened in the USSR and the PRC?" *Critical Sociology* 34, no. 4 (2008): 539–56.

Rice, Stian, and James A. Tyner. "The Rice Cities of the Khmer Rouge: An Urban Political Ecology of Rural Mass Violence." *Transactions of the Institute of British Geographers* 42 (2017): 559–71.

Roberts, Paul C. " 'War Communism': A Re-examination." *Slavic Review* 29, no. 2 (1970): 238–61.

Ross, Scott. " 'The Masters of the Khmer Rouge': Cambodia between China and Vietnam, 1954–1975." PhD diss., University of Missouri, 2008.

Rothenberg, Mel. "Lenin on the State." *Science & Society* 59, no. 3 (1995): 418–36.

Ruane, Kevin. " 'Containing America': Aspects of British Foreign Policy and the Cold War in South-East Asia, 1951–54." *Diplomacy and Statecraft* 7, no. 1 (1996): 141–74.

Ryan, James. " 'Revolution Is War': The Development of the Thought of V.I. Lenin on Violence, 1899–1907." *Slavonic and East European Review* 89, no. 2 (2011): 248–73.

Saith, Ashwani. "Primitive Accumulation, Agrarian Reform and Socialist Transitions: An Argument." *Journal of Development Studies* 22, no. 1 (1985): 1–48.

Sanchez-Sibony, Oscar. *Red Globalization: The Political Economy of the Soviet Cold War from Stalin to Khrushchev*. Cambridge: Cambridge University Press, 2014.

Sayers, Sean. "Alienation as a Critical Concept." *International Critical Thought* 1, no. 3 (2011): 287–304.

Scott, James. "Hegemony and the Peasantry." *Politics & Society* 7, no. 3 (1977): 267–96.

Seekins, Donald M. "Historical Setting." In *Cambodia: A Country Study*, edited by R. R. Ross, 3–71. Washington, DC: US Government Printing Office, 1990.

Selden, Mark. "The Crisis of Collectivization: Socialist Development and the Peasantry." *IDS Bulletin* 13, no 4 (1982): 4–11.

Shaw, Martin. "From Comparative to International Genocide Studies: The International Production of Genocide in 20th-Century Europe." *European Journal of International Relations* 18, no. 4 (2011): 645–68.

———. "New Wars of the City: Relationships of 'Urbicide' and 'Genocide.' " In *Cities, War, and Terrorism: Towards an Urban Geopolitics*, edited by Stephen Graham, 141–53. Malden, MA: Blackwell, 2004.

———. *What Is Genocide?* Malden, MA: Polity Press, 2007.

Shawcross, William. *Sideshow: Kissinger, Nixon, and the Destruction of Cambodia*. Revised ed. New York: Cooper Square Press, 2002.

Short, Philip. *Pol Pot: Anatomy of a Nightmare*. New York: Macmillan, 2005.

Simmonds, Stuart. "Laos and Cambodia: The Search for Unity and Independence." *International Affairs* 49, no. 4 (1973): 574–83.

Slocomb, Margaret. *An Economic History of Cambodia in the Twentieth Century*. Singapore: National University of Singapore Press, 2010.

———. *The People's Republic of Kampuchea, 1979–1989: The Revolution after Pol Pot*. Chiang Mai, Thailand: Silkworm Books, 2003.

Smith, Mary. "Revolution." *Irish Marxist Review* 7, no. 20 (2018): 36–39.

Smith, Neil. "The Satanic Geographies of Globalization: Uneven Development in the 1990s." *Public Culture* 10, no. 1 (1997): 169–89.

Smith, Tony. "The Underdevelopment of Development Literature: The Case of Dependency Theory." *World Politics* 31, no. 2 (1979): 247–88.

Straus, Scott. "Organic Purity and the Role of Anthropology in Cambodia and Rwanda." *Patterns of Prejudice* 35, no. 2 (2001): 47–62.

Summers, Laura. "Cambodia: Model of the Nixon Doctrine." *Current History* 68, no. 388 (1973): 252–56.

Sunkel, Osvaldo. "National Development Policy and External Dependence in Latin America." *Journal of Development Studies* 6, no. 1 (1969): 23–48.

Tabah, Léon. "Alfred Sauvy: Statistician, Economist, Demographer and Iconoclast (1898–1990)." *Population Studies* 45, no. 2 (1991): 353–57.

Taşdemir Yaşin, Zehra. "The Adventure of Capital with Nature: From the Metabolic Rift to the Value Theory of Nature." *Journal of Peasant Studies* 44, no. 2 (2017): 377–401.

Thomson, Ross. "Primitive Capitalist Accumulation." In *Marxian Economics*, edited by John Eatwell, Murray Milgate, and Peter Newman, 313–20. London: Macmillan Press, 1990.

Todaro, Michael P. *Economic Development in the Third World*. 4th ed. New York: Longman, 1989.

Tomlinson, Brian R. "What Was the Third World?" *Journal of Contemporary History* 38, no. 2 (2003): 307–21.

Tully, John. *A Short History of Cambodia: From Empire to Survival*. Crow's Nest, Australia: Allen & Unwin, 2005.

Turok, Ben. "Zambia's System of State Capitalism." *Development and Change* 11, no. 3 (1980): 455–78.

Twining, Charles H. "The Economy." In *Cambodia, 1975–1978: Rendezvous with Death*, edited by Karl D. Jackson, 109–50. Princeton: Princeton University, 1989.

Tyner, James A. *From Rice Fields to Killing Fields: Nature, Life, and Labor under the Khmer Rouge*. Syracuse, NY: Syracuse University Press, 2017.

———. "Gender and Sexual Violence, Forced Marriages, and Primitive Accumulation during the Cambodian Genocide, 1975–1979." *Gender, Place & Culture* 25, no. 9 (2018): 1305–21.

———. *The Killing of Cambodia: Geography, Genocide and the Unmaking of Space*. Aldershot, UK: Ashgate, 2008.

———. *The Nature of Revolution: Art and Politics under the Khmer Rouge*. Athens, GA: University of Georgia Press, 2018.

———. *The Politics of Lists: Bureaucracy and Genocide under the Khmer Rouge*. Morgantown: West Virginia University Press, 2018.

Tyner, James A., Andrew Curtis, Sokvisal Kimsroy, and Chhunly Chhay. "The Evacuation of Phnom Penh during the Cambodian Genocide: Applying Spatial Video Geonarratives to the Study of Genocide." *Genocide Studies and Prevention: An International Journal* 12, no. 3 (2018): 163–76.

Tyner, James A., Samuel Henkin, Savina Sirik, and Sokvisal Kimsroy. "Phnom Penh during the Cambodian Genocide: A Case of Selective Urbicide." *Environment and Planning A* 46, no. 8 (2014): 1873–91.

Tyner, James A., Mandy Munro-Stasiuk, Corrine Coakley, Sokvisal Kimsroy, and Stian Rice. "Khmer Rouge Irrigation Schemes during the Cambodian Genocide." *Genocide Studies International* 12, no. 1 (2018), 103–19.

Tyner, James A., and Stian Rice. "Cambodia's Political Economy of Violence: Space, Time, and Genocide under the Khmer Rouge, 1975–79." *Genocide Studies International* 10, no. 1 (2016): 84–94.

———. "To Live and Let Die: Food, Famine, and Administrative Violence in Democratic Kampuchea, 1975–1979." *Political Geography* 52, no. 1 (2016), 47–56.

Tyner, James A., and Rachel Will. "Nature, Post-Conflict Violence, and Water Management under the Communist Party of Kampuchea, 1975–1979." *Transactions of the Institute of British Geographers* 40, no. 3 (2015): 362–74.

Tyner, James A., Xinyue Ye, Sokvisal Kimsroy, Zheye Wang, and Chenjian Fu. "Emerging Data Sources and the Study of Genocide: A Preliminary Analysis of Prison Data from S-21 Security-Center, Cambodia." *GeoJournal* 81, no. 6 (2016): 907–18.

Uimonen, Paula. "Responses to Revolutionary Change: A Study of Social Memory in a Khmer Village." *FOLK—Journal of the Danish Ethnographic Society* 38 (1996): 31–51.

Uldricks, Teddy J. "Russia and Europe: Diplomacy, Revolution, and Economic Development in the 1920s." *International History Review* 1, no. 1 (1979): 55–83.

Valentino, Benjamin A. *Final Solutions: Mass Killing and Genocide in the 20th Century.* Ithaca, NY: Cornell University Press, 2004.

Van Ree, Erik. "Lenin's Conception of Socialism in One Country, 1915–1917." *Revolutionary Russia* 23, no. 2 (2010): 159–81.

———. "Socialism in One Country: A Reassessment." *Studies in East European Thought* 50 (1998): 77–117.

———. " 'Socialism in One Country' before Stalin: German Origins." *Journal of Political Ideologies* 15, no. 2 (2010): 143–59.

Vannak, Huy. *The Khmer Rouge Division 703: From Victory to Self-Destruction.* Phnom Penh: Documentation Center of Cambodia, 2003.

Verwimp, Philip. "Development Ideology, the Peasantry and Genocide: Rwanda Represented in Habyarimana's Speeches." *Journal of Genocide Research* 2, no. 3 (2000): 325–61.

———. "The Political Economy of Coffee, Dictatorship, and Genocide." *European Journal of Political Economy* 19, no. 2 (2003): 161–81.

Vickery, Michael. *Cambodia, 1975–1982.* Chiang Mai, Thailand: Silkworm Press, 1984.

Vlachou, Andriana. "The Socialist Transformation of China: Debates over Class and Social Development." *Rethinking Marxism* 6, no. 4 (1993): 8–39.

von Beyme, Klaus. "A Comparative View of Democratic Centralism." *Government and Opposition* 10, no. 3 (1975): 259–77.

Wada, Haruki. "Marx, Marxism and the Agrarian Question, II: Marx and Revolutionary Russia." *History Workshop* 12 (1981): 129–50.

Waller, Michael. *Democratic Centralism: An Historical Commentary.* Manchester, UK: Manchester University Press, 1981.

Wang, Tao. "Neutralizing Indochina: The 1954 Geneva Conference and China's Efforts to Isolate the United States." *Journal of Cold War Studies* 19, no. 2 (2017): 3–42.

White, Ben, Saturnino M. Borras Jr., Ruth Hall, Ian Scoones, and Wendy Wolford. "The New

Enclosures: Critical Perspectives on Corporate Land Deals." *Journal of Peasant Studies* 39, no. 3–4 (2012): 619–47.

White, James D. *Marx and Russia: The Fate of a Doctrine*. London: Bloomsbury Publishing, 2018.

White, Stephen. "What Is a Communist System?" *Studies in Comparative Communism* 16, no. 4 (1983): 247–63.

Willett, Robert L. *Russian Sideshow: America's Undeclared War, 1918–1920*. Dulles, VA: Brassey's Inc., 2003.

Williams, Timothy, and Rhiannon Neilson. " 'They Will Rot the Society, Rot the Party, and Rot the Army': Toxification as an Ideology and Motivation for Perpetrating Violence in the Khmer Rouge Genocide." *Terrorism and Political Violence* 31, no. 3 (2019): 494–515.

Willmott, W. E. "Analytical Errors of the Kampuchean Communist Party." *Pacific Affairs* 54, no. 2 (1981): 209–27.

Wu, Friedrich W. Y. "From Self-Reliance to Interdependence? Development Strategy and Foreign Economic Policy in Post-Mao China." *Modern China* 7, no. 4 (1981): 445–82.

Yates, Michael D. "Nothing to Lose but Their Chains." *Monthly Review* 70, no. 5 (2018): 15–29.

Yuon, Hou. "The Peasantry of Kampuchea: Colonialism and Modernization." In *Peasants and Politics in Kampuchea, 1942–1981*, edited by Ben Kiernan and Chanthou Boua, 34–68. London: Zed Press, 1982.

———. "Solving Rural Problems: A Socialist Programme to Safeguard the Nation." In *Peasants and Politics in Kampuchea, 1942–1981*, edited by Ben Kiernan and Chanthou Boua, 136–65. London: Zed Press, 1982.

Zatlin, Jonathan R. *The Currency of Socialism: Money and Political Culture in East Germany*. Cambridge: Cambridge University Press, 2007.

Zhang, Qian Forrest, Carlos Oya, and Jingzhong Ye. "Bringing Agriculture Back In: The Central Place of Agrarian Change in Rural China Studies." *Journal of Agrarian Change* 15, no. 3 (2015): 299–313.

Zhang, Shu Guang. "Constructing 'Peaceful Coexistence': China's Diplomacy toward the Geneva and Bandung Conferences, 1954–55." *Cold War History* 7, no. 4 (2007): 509–28.

Zhang, Xiaoming. "China's Involvement in Laos during the Vietnam War, 1963–1975." *Journal of Military History* 66, no. 4 (2002): 1141–66.

Index